Design and Implementation of Distributed-Processing Systems

Design and Implementation of Distributed-Processing Systems

C. Bradley Tashenberg

amacom

American Management Associations

This book is available at a special discount when ordered in bulk quantities. For information, contact Special Sales Department, American Management Associations, Publications Group, 135 West 50th Street, New York, NY 10020.

Library of Congress Cataloging in Publication Data

Tashenberg, C. Bradley.
Design and implementation of distributed-processing systems.

Includes index.
1. Electronic data processing—Distributed processing.
2. System design. I. Title.
QA76.9.D5T37 1984 001.64 83-45205
ISBN 0-8144-5780-0

Printing number
10 9 8 7 6 5 4 3 2 1

To B.A.T., who encouraged and inspired me to write this book

Preface

Over the last ten years, American business has experienced an acceleration in computer technology and high-tech resources, unmatched by that of any other industry or era. Not only has this steady stream of products confused and concerned management, it has had a devastating effect on seasoned data processors, forcing them into the frustrating position of continuously trying to catch up with this fast-moving field.

Now, with the advent of distributed processing, the problem of hardware and software selection becomes considerably more complicated. Compatibility between systems, communications protocols, networking considerations, security provisions, and many other concerns are all equally important to this new generation of data processing. Previously, managers and data processors had to concern themselves only with the capabilities of mainframe technology. Now they must choose among mainframe computers, minicomputers, and microcomputers. And the choice is not a simple one.

The advantage of having so many options is that the right choice can have a dramatic impact on the capability of the organization to respond flexibly to the demands of business. As John Naisbitt points out in *Megatrends* (New York: Warner Books, 1982), we are in the midst of an information revolution. How they deal with it will separate the progressive companies from the faltering companies. Information is power. And fast, flexible access to information at all levels of the organization is what distributed processing is all about.

The commonly sought goals of cost saving, greater efficiency, improved productivity, and higher throughput have all been realized through the use of distributed-processing techniques. After 30 years, the pendulum has swung from decentralized processing to centralized processing and has finally come to rest at distributed processing. Information is being processed in a more effective manner, providing better control at divisional and corporate levels while, in most cases, achieving substantial reductions in operations costs.

Like any major change, the switch to this new technology has far-reaching implications for nearly every sector of business. The purpose of this book is to help the reader overcome some of the problems that others have experienced in the transition to distributed processing. It addresses the main issues that should be considered in implementing a distributed systems network, from an organizational as well as a technical viewpoint. Although there are of course many possible approaches to the problem, the one described here has worked successfully for many companies and, if properly administered, will work for yours.

I must express my appreciation and thanks to Mark Misercola, who spent many hours assisting me in the preparation of this book, and Daniel Peters, whose firm provided much of the content of Chapter 11 on security provisions.

C. Bradley Tashenberg

Contents

1	A Time for Decision	*1*
2	From Decentralization to Centralization	*9*
3	Distributed Processing: The Logical Alternative	*19*
4	Batch Met Its Match with On-Line	*35*
5	Getting Your Act Together	*49*
6	Selecting the Right Computer	*61*
7	Evaluating Systems Software	*80*
8	Setting Standards for the Network	*87*
9	Building the Network: Intrastructures	*111*
10	Building the Network: Interstructures	*128*
11	Security Issues	*148*
12	On the Horizon	*156*
	Appendix A Comparative Analysis of Two Computer Systems	*167*
	Appendix B Installation and Training Procedure	*219*
	Index	*235*

Design and Implementation of Distributed-Processing Systems

1

A Time for Decision

Since its inception, the computer industry has been rife with turmoil. For nearly two decades, the industry has been in an extended crisis that has had an enormous impact on everyone from the biggest manufacturers to the smallest customers. Giant corporations like IBM, General Electric, Control Data, and RCA vied to become the nation's top computer manufacturer, with an ever-changing arsenal of weapons. At the same time, internal skirmishes broke out within America's corporations. In many instances, data processing professionals were pitted against end-users; internal struggles developed quickly as lower- and middle-management teams took opposing sides on critical issues; and upper-management officials, seeing little reason to take part in the battle, did their best to ignore what was going on in their own data processing areas. This 20-year crisis, detailed in the predecessor of this book (*Distributed Processing Systems: End of the Mainframe Era*?), was brought about by technological revolutions, and it thrived at the expense of the very entity it was supposed to help—Corporate America.

There are still plenty of scars from that turbulent era, but most of the problems are now disappearing. For the first time, companies are working—without all the internal bickering—to develop computer processing to its fullest, cost-efficient capabilities. Still, the industry is surrounded by change. The flames of conflict have been rekindled by another new technology called distributed processing, an economical data processing method that is thrusting the industry into a bright, new era.

From a current vantage point, the evolution of computer processing can be divided into three distinct eras—decentralized, centralized, and distributed. During the first era, small computers were decentralized, and they operated at the most basic levels of the company. In the second period, decentralized systems were replaced by a centralized data processing center servicing the entire organization. Each concept had advantages and disadvantages. When the disadvantages of decentralization became painfully obvious, the industry shifted to centralization. By the same token, when centralization began to lose its appeal, development began on distributed processing. From an organizational standpoint, distributed data processing provides the optimum balance between increased operating efficiency at the local level and effective overall cost and management control.

There are three critical elements in effective data processing: technical capability, cost, and organization. Distributed data processing offers advantages in all three areas. According to a leading data processing research company, distributed data processing is the delegation of data processing to a point as close to the operational level as is cost-effective and technically sound. It allows local management to perform a maximum of its own work, while potentially minimizing operating costs at the local level in terms of computer hardware and expensive personnel.

Figure 1. The costs of data processing.

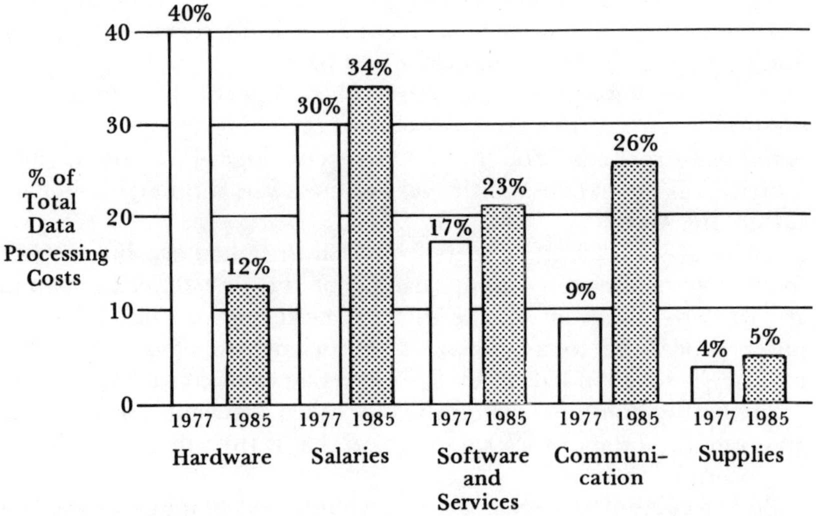

In a distributed-processing environment, existing personnel at the operating level must be able to use computers *without* large and costly technical data processing staffs at each site. Therefore, technical considerations should be initially and centrally resolved for everyone's benefit. The importance of cost can be seen clearly in many authoritative industry studies which predict a dramatic shift of total data processing costs. For example, according to a 1977 study by International Data Corporation, hardware costs, decreasing at an annual rate of 20 percent to 30 percent, will become only 12 percent of the total data processing budget in 1985, while inflation and scarcity of qualified personnel will increase salaries to a point where they represent 34 percent of the total data processing costs. (See Figure 1.)

Distributed processing represents a substantial change in procedures for most firms (including all of the top *Fortune* 1000 companies) that use computers. Many would be forced to dismantle their large central data processing organizations or substantially reduce their workload and responsibilities. In either case, a shift in responsibility results, along with a reduction of centralized control.

Management's Abdication

When data processing first arrived on the corporate scene, management chose not to become involved. Early computers did not really have a major impact on the company as a whole, because they were delegated to mundane roles such as calculating payroll and accounts payable. One of the disadvantages of the early centralized approach stemmed from the fact that little data were generated that could be used for operational decisions. So, unwisely, management abdicated its responsibility to manage.

With the next generation of computers in the late 1960s (the centralized era), management abdicated even further, leaving data processing decisions to "technicians." In retrospect, the consequences were devastating. Managers pleaded ignorance as an excuse for failing to assume responsibility for a valuable asset—information. The computer had become a technological tyrant, playing a critical role as decision-maker and information processor. At the same time, it became increasingly expensive, and it intimidated even top executives.

IBM, during its antitrust fight with the federal government, privately conceded that the management of many companies no longer felt that computers provided a good return on investment.

The reasons, according to an internal memorandum:

- The technical complexity of the computer.
- Management's unwillingness to learn about or become involved in computer operations.
- Increasing awareness of the rapidly escalating costs of data processing.
- The data processing professionals' unwillingness to encourage management involvement, because most DP professionals perceived such involvement as a threat to their status within the field and the company.

Statistics dramatically back these conclusions. During federal antitrust hearings against IBM, it was established that many companies had, in fact, ignored competitive bidding on computers in favor of sole-source procurements. In multimillion-dollar decisions, this is ludicrous. As Table 1 shows, 73 percent to 88 percent of procurement decisions were made without the benefit of competition. In those situations where IBM was involved in competitive bidding, IBM's success rate ranged from 31 percent to 64 percent, showing that competitive computers existed in the market.

Table 1. Computer decisions and competitive bidding involving IBM computers.

Size of System	*Year*	*Competitive Bid*	*Non-competitive Bid*	*Competitive Success Rate (%)*	*Non-competitive Bids (%)*
Very large	1970	N/A	N/A	50	88
Large	1970	N/A	N/A	59	81
Medium	1970	133	1,013	38	88
	1971	N/A	N/A	64	73
Small to medium	1970	302	1,636	37	84
Intermediate	1970	760	915	31	55
	1971	597	2,411	40	80
Small	1970	1,326	4,989	42	79

Source: Judson Breslin and C. Bradley Tashenberg, *Distributed Processing Systems: End of the Mainframe Era?* (New York: AMACOM, 1978).

This is dramatic proof that misguided managers were not doing their job. In fact, many were leaving major decisions to their technical staffs, which at many firms are not in the best position to evaluate overall company requirements and goals. In many instances, managers followed the recommendations of influential outside computer salesmen or consultants, without critical examination, and this resulted in detrimental effects on their company's computer systems.

Every era of computer history is linked by one disturbing trend: management's inability to deal with technology. As the industry enters a new data processing era, management is in a unique position to manage. Therefore, the problems inherent in the previous centralized generation must be dealt with now. More specifically, mainframe vendors must cope with the situation in order to remain competitive. Common information problems stemming directly from large-scale computing and centralized data processing centers exist today. They created the need for technically sound, cost-effective distributed processing. These problems *can* be resolved with current technology—if management will manage.

Some Misguided Arguments Against Distributed Processing

There are many popular excuses against becoming involved in decisions on data processing systems. "I don't understand computers," "Leave that to the technical guys," and "Hardware is hardware, I don't care what they select" are some of them. But management can no longer afford those excuses. It must open its eyes and evaluate a workable concept of data processing—distributed data processing, which has made the critical tools and technologies available.

A memorandum issued by the data processing staff of a major *Fortune* 500 company recently informed management that distributed data processing would not be feasible for ten years. And management, playing the typical abdicator role, accepted this evaluation without hesitation. At a seminar conducted several years ago by *Computer Decisions*, mainframe manufacturers lauded distributed data processing as the wave of the future. But then they added that it was not a viable alternative in the marketplace. Don't laugh, their remarks were published.

In the late 1970s, several arguments surfaced to discredit distributed data processing. Some critics feared losing control over the data processing function under the new system. Most other arguments struck at the same lease-of-control chord. Leading criticisms included (1) the cost to convert systems, (2) the unavailability of adequate technology, and (3) the investment in existing systems. But none of these arguments holds up to critical examination.

The conversion cost issue. As pointed out in my first book, the conversion cost is insignificant compared to the cost of systems that are outmoded and do not provide timely or useful information. In fact, the cost is irrelevant if such conditions prevent a company from being competitive or a government from providing service to its constituency. Prior to the development of on-line minicomputer technology, which allowed immediate access to information, computers operated in the batch mode. That is, computer applications such as manufacturing, payroll, or accounts payable were run one at a time and the information was batched. But neither companies nor governments operate in batch mode, so there is little justification for having data processing in the batch mode. If your systems operate in batch mode, they are not taking advantage of the latest technology and are not as effective as they could be. So they should be changed. And although conversion cost should be kept to a minimum, it must not become the obstacle to undertaking the task.

Actually, conversion costs tend to be lower than might be expected, because it is easier to develop new systems from old systems than it was to develop the original system. The industry learns from the past, including unpleasant experiences. Professionals can look at the existing system and extract and retain those features which were beneficial and have proven their merit. They can rethink and refine those features which have not worked well during the life of the original system, and can improve them. Therefore, new systems that are better than the originals can be developed and used with the latest on-line technology. The results in most cases will justify the effort and conversion costs.

The technology issue. Another argument against distributed processing was the inadequacy or riskiness of existing minicomputer technology. Distributed data processing is feasible because of the low cost of computing—the result of the introduction of minicomputer technology. Today, technology is available to disperse minicomputers to the lowest operating level of the organization, even though some still deny it.

New advances have taken place in data processing. The primary ones are (1) communications capabilities, (2) on-line, time-sharing operating systems, and (3) data base management systems. These technologies are critically important to the architecture and design of minicomputers.

Communications software is available from Hewlett-Packard (DS 3000), Digital Equipment Corporation (DECNET), Data General, and Datapoint, as well as other manufacturers. This communications software allows computers in a network to converse in order to transfer information, query data bases, and update programs.

Time-sharing operating systems that have been tested and designed for on-line information processing are also available. On-line processing is critical for distributed data processing, because a major goal of distributed processing is to return control over the computer to the user so as to provide data when needed, and in the form required, by the ultimate user. Time-sharing accomplishes this by allowing many users to enter or retrieve data simultaneously as the computer "shares" its resources among these users. Time-sharing operating systems are a key architectural feature of the minicomputer.

Finally, powerful and reliable data base management software is available to operate on minicomputers. These data base management systems manage and maintain data with a minimum of redundancy structure for processing by multiple applications. A data base management system is also critical in distributed data processing, because information must be readily available and easily accessible to a user in a remote location of a network. Additionally, it must be available to many users who have been authorized to use the information and who clearly need access to it. The best way to open up data for users is through the file management technique called data base management. It is currently available on the sophisticated minicomputers manufactured by Data General, Prime, and Hewlett-Packard.

Investment in existing systems. Of course, companies still balk at new expenditures because of large investments in existing systems. Executives frequently complain that too much capital has already been spent on existing systems to justify a full-scale change. Such thinking should have followed the dinosaurs into extinction by now. If a user's hardware and systems are designed for batch processing and don't satisfy his needs; if the organization must bend to meet the needs of the computer; and if the system is still in a centralized mode of data processing; then distributed data processing using the latest minicomputer technology must be considered, regardless of the investment in existing systems.

First, development expenditures on early systems have already been made and cannot be recovered. If these systems are obsolete, then corporate growth will suffer. Already, progress has been severely crippled at many large firms which have held on to their old systems, sometimes because of a fear that computer technology will continue to change rapidly, outdating equipment and software purchased today. But on-line technology is most unlikely to change overnight; it should flourish and improve for at least 15 years while mainframe producers play catch-up. The effort in computer manufacturing now is toward miniaturization and cost reduction. This means more power for the dollar, not just new technology for the sake of "innovation."

Second, distributed-processing technology provides real opportunities for cost savings. In fact, minicomputers are inflation fighters, because they are inexpensively priced and provide tremendous computer power. They also drastically reduce clerical effort in such areas as data entry and data control. Inputting data directly through entry terminals eliminates many tedious tasks. In addition, faster processing of data and expedited printing of forms and reports saves money. For example, one manufacturer realized substantial savings by switching from batch technology to a minicomputer. The previous system, a batch IBM 360 computer, produced invoices at night according to schedule. A real-time minicomputer, capable of handling accounting, manufacturing, and customer order-entry functions simultaneously, was installed. Because of the minicomputer's power and versatility, invoices and shipping papers were generated at the time of the customer order and were included with the order, eliminating hundreds of thousands of dollars in mailing costs annually.

The Real Issue

This leads to the real issue in distributed data processing—control. In the early days of data processing, the era of decentralization, control was lost and expenditures for data processing became unmanageable. The resulting change to centralization virtually assured management's control over data processing. But it also created a processing overload and ultimately led to the alienation of users.

The industry is again entering an era when data processing is decentralized or "distributed" back to the user. Hence, the data processing manager wants to know if he will again lose control. Specifically, management wants to know if it will lose the control it gained only a decade ago. At the same time, users must decide whether they want to control the same data processing function which caused them so much trouble before.

Over the years, arguments against distributed data processing have acted only as smoke screens blocking out the problem of control. So this book is directed specifically at the control issue. How will control be maintained? Who will be in charge? Will it work? How will it shape the business climate of tomorrow? For the answers, read on. . . .

2

From Decentralization to Centralization

Distributed data processing is the logical result of the evolution of data processing itself. This evolutionary or historical perspective is important in understanding the basics of distributed data processing and the urgency of control in the new philosophy of information processing.

Data processing evolved through three distinct eras from 1955 to 1980. The first two eras, decentralization and centralization, may have reflected the management philosophies of the times, according to some observers. But more realistically, they represented the status of computers and computer technology. Figure 2 illustrates the eras from decentralization to distributed data processing. To understand the current era and its relationship to past eras, we should begin by looking at decentralization.

The Era of Decentralization

The decentralized era was a period when computers were used as independent units for different functions or in different geographical locations. Under decentralization by geography, a computer might be located in a remote division to process say, payroll, accounts-payable, and general-ledger accounts. Under functional decentralization, on the other hand, a small computer was used for a single function such as manufacturing or, more commonly, accounting.

Figure 2. The three data processing eras.

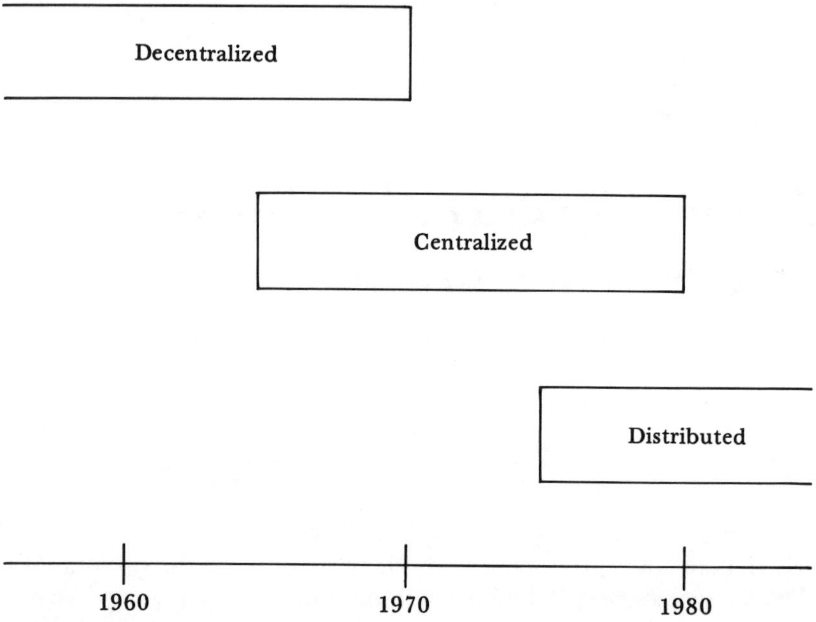

Figure 3. Decentralized processing.

DEFINITION: Each geographical or functional entity has its own *independent* computer.

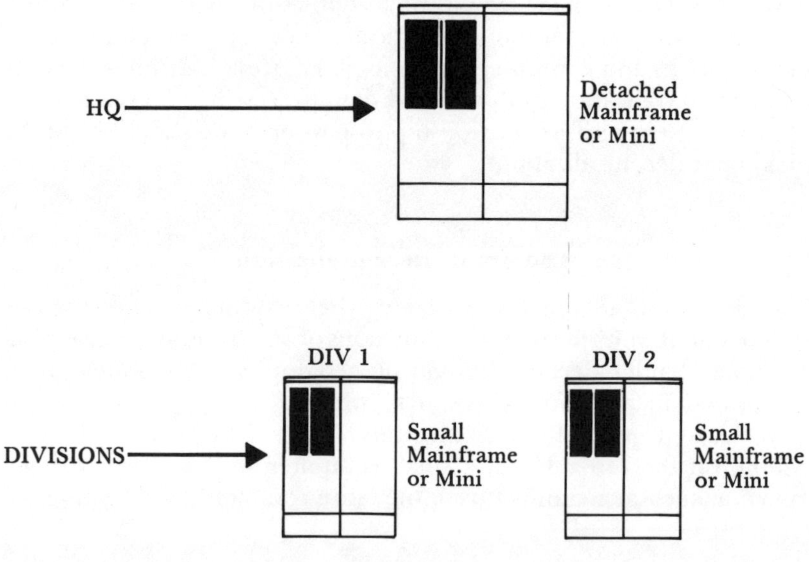

Each computer in this environment operated independently, because intercomputer communications technology did not exist and the management philosophy favored independence. This era was dominated by unit-record equipment—a punched card being processed by mechanical devices such as the accounting machine, sorters, and collators. (It was also the era of the workhorse 1401 computer manufactured by IBM.) Corporate computer setups generally followed the process illustrated in Figure 3.

The decentralization era had no networking or electronic communications capabilities. And therein lies a major difference between this mode of processing and distributed data processing: data communications were normally handled by mail, and information exchange between systems was handled by physically transporting punched cards or magnetic tape from one site to another. Operations were batch-oriented again, meaning only one system operated at one time. This put the computer and computerized information out of phase with the real-time operations of the organization.

Advantages and Disadvantages of Decentralization

Decentralized processing, by its very nature, offered customers some distinct advantages and a few latent disadvantages. It's important to understand both, because distributed data processing was basically conceived to incorporate the advantages of decentralized processing while eliminating its disadvantages.

The advantages of decentralization were threefold. First, end users could design their own systems and select the computer that best fit their needs. Functions to satisfy unique requirements could be built into each system, so decentralization satisfied local users.

A second, related advantage was the relative accessibility of systems and information. Because an end user controlled the computer, he could demand reports in the sequence or priority which he established. There was no competition with other users of the computer, because *there were no other users*. It was this control over computers that made decentralized processing a valid and acceptable mode of processing data.

Third, decentralization resulted in lower incremental costs at operating levels, because smaller computers could be used to process limited local requirements. There was no need to consider requirements for the organization as a whole, because this system (or computer) was dedicated to one geographical unit or one function. Decentralization was also consistent with the management philosophy of accountability, responsibility, or profit-center control. The profit-center manager was responsible for computer and data processing costs and effectiveness, and was pleased to be in control.

On the other hand, there were some latent disadvantages to the decentralization approach. First, *overall* control of data processing was impossible, so advances made in one location were not incorporated into similar efforts in another location within the organization. There were no organizationwide standards, and the quality of information and data processing itself was inconsistent within the company or organization.

This overall lack of control and standardization quite naturally led to duplicate data processing staffs at each individual location or functional area, and to duplicate systems and peripheral equipment. So decentralization actually did not provide any economy-of-scale savings for the organization as a whole.

Finally, decentralized small mainframe computers, as illustrated in Figure 3, could not communicate effectively. As a result, the cost of producing consolidated and meaningful reports for the organization began to increase and cause concern among top managers. Incremental costs at the operating level were within reason, but duplication and communication difficulties resulted in higher total costs than seemed necessary. The issue of control from the top began to appear as an important inducement for change. Control at the top was lacking, and information coming up from the operating levels was slow, inconsistent, and expensive. A change was necessary.

With the introduction of larger computers in the mid-1960s, led by the Model 360 manufactured by IBM, corporate data processing changed from decentralization to centralization.

The Era of Centralization

Centralization is the mode of information processing in which all data processing capability is concentrated in a single, central location. If the volume of transactions and activity exceeds the capacity of one central mainframe computer, the answer in this mode of operation is to add yet another mainframe computer. Basically, there is no computing power at remote locations or for different functional areas, because all computing is handled centrally.

All local processing is accomplished through a technique called remote data entry, or remote job entry (RJE). In this system, small data-capturing devices are located at the remote location. Information, such as customer orders, is collected locally where the transaction occurs, entered by keyboard into a terminal, and recorded on magnetic tape or disk. The local unit has limited or no computer processing capability. It may be able to edit some information, but not much more. At the end of a work day, or at some designated time period, information is transmitted over a leased line to headquarters, where a similar unit gathers the data for subsequent processing on the mainframe computer. The process is illustrated in Figure 4.

Data, on tape or disk at headquarters, are fed to the computer, which performs all calculations and other operations such as price lookup. The results can be returned to the local unit in the same manner the data were originally sent. For customer orders, invoices can be generated and mailed from a central location. In this form of remote job entry, the important element is the central control over data. This differentiates centralized processing from distributed data processing.

It is clear now, in retrospect, that the move to centralized processing was necessitated by the weaknesses of decentralized processing and

Figure 4. Centralized processing.

DEFINITION: A central computer handles all corporate requirements.

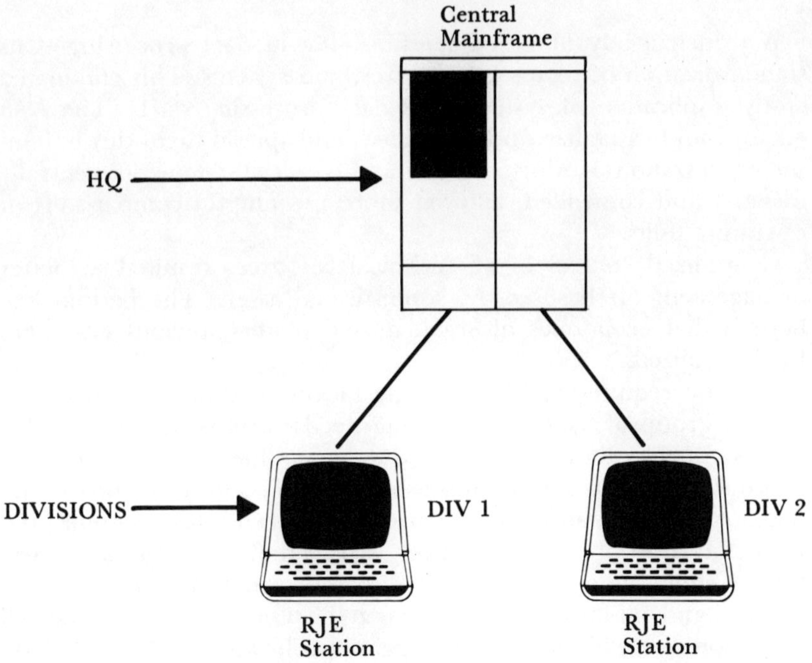

the need to reduce the cost of data processing. It was prompted by the introduction of larger-scale computers which could process more data faster and more consistently than the multitude of independent, decentralized processors. Basically, it was a crusade to cut the cost per transaction by using these large-scale number crunchers.

The centralization of computers had major organizational effects in corporations throughout the country. It was a major force behind the formation of a new organizational entity—the management information systems (MIS) group. This group, centrally located at corporate headquarters, was charged with the awesome task of developing generalized systems to satisfy the diverse requirements of all remote locations or diverse functions. After designing these all-purpose systems, the MIS group was told to implement them on very large, not totally tested mainframe computers. The simplicity of the stand-alone small computers—the IBM 1401s, for example—was gone. The task was great, and there were many failures.

The era of centralization, had some concrete advantages and some very real disadvantages. It is important, as before, to be aware of them, because the advantages were later preserved in distributed data processing while the disadvantages were eliminated.

Advantages and Disadvantages of Centralization

A principal advantage of centralization in data processing is its standardization of forms, procedures, and systems. This eliminated costly duplication of systems and data processing staffs. The MIS group could capitalize on bright ideas and spread them throughout the organization. Uniform reports and financial statements, centrally dictated and controlled, allowed more meaningful comparisons of operating units.

Centralized control of all technical resources resulted in better management of these costly, sophisticated assets. The bottom line here is that economies of scale, missed in the previous era, were finally realized.

Yet, the requirement for a single facility to support a large and diverse group of users with varying needs foretold of future difficulties. As Felix Kaufman observed in a pamphlet called "Distributed Processing," "Despite its enthusiastic response, centralized processing had a spotty reputation. There are effective centralized systems, but many fall short of the service levels expected of them. In some cases, these systems generate frictions between providers and users of data on one hand, and processors of data on the other." Today, centralized operations are still plagued by nagging problems.

Cost of centralized systems. The cost of large-scale mainframe computers is high, and as users tried to put more applications on a saturated computer complex, the cost increased substantially. For example, a large service organization was formed at one time with three large mainframe computers to handle an admittedly large volume of transactions. When these mainframes ran out of capacity, a fourth mainframe was acquired just to continue development for a data processing staff with 250 technical employees. When managers at this installation tried to use the computer for their own functional needs, a fifth mainframe was required. The operating system on these large mainframes was so complex that a staff of 44 technicians was needed to maintain it. After the setup was in place, management realized it would take three to four years, or 440 man-years, to implement a system handling 30 percent of the company's potential revenues and transactions. Still, the system was operated manually, and the company's total data processing budget climbed 22 percent. At the same time, one-third of the company was operating without benefit of computers.

As this case illustrates, the complexity and size of the centralized environment lead to extremely high incremental costs, which can suffocate an organization. Although this example is a bit extreme, the company is representative of firms that experience the escalating and prohibitive costs associated with a central data processing entity while trying to handle all the diverse requirements of a complex organization. Remember: "Big systems often mean big troubles."

Delays in systems implementation. Another big trouble spot often found in the centralized environment is the user priority problem created when many users vie for implementation of their systems or preparation of reports. "Payroll comes first" is a frequent corporate battle cry. In the service organization example, changing systems frequently took several years because of the complexity of the systems and because the data processing staff feared the effects of a systems change. Long lead times were also caused by a lengthy backlog of requests from the various users. Requests were literally backlogged for months with corrections.

Vulnerability of the organization in case of system failure. Another major disadvantage to centralized data processing is the enormous risk involved when the central system fails. Dependence on one central mainframe environment leaves the organization in a vulnerable position. When the central system is large and complex, the availability of adequate backup is questionable. To begin with, it is highly unlikely that a similar configuration of CPU, tapes, disks, printers, and input devices can be found. And even if such a compatible configuration were found, it is improbable that the installation would provide adequate time and capacity to process its own work and that of the organization whose computer has failed.

This inescapable risk has given birth to a new insurance industry offering coverage to companies with large-scale computer installations. These insurance plans provide large-scale computers to companies whose computers have failed. Apparently, the configurations offered are of sufficient size and have enough peripherals to process applications from the very largest data processing installations. Fees are very high, consisting of monthly fees (for example, $4,000 for an IBM 370/168 system) and a large service charge of $4,500 to $6,500 if the facilities are actually used, plus a "disaster initiation" fee of from $25,000 to $50,000, depending on how much advance notice the insurance company is given. This insurance is just one more cost in an already expensive mode of data processing, but it is necessary because of the high risks associated with centralized data processing.

Inaccuracy of data. Prior to centralized data processing, each department was responsible for data gathering and reports. With centralized computing, data gathering remained with department managers, but data preparation—a new requirement—became the responsibility of a new computer department, namely, the "data entry" unit within the data processing department. So responsibility for reports was diffused between the originating department and the data processing department. The results were inaccurate data, conflict, and inevitable finger pointing.

To begin with, an extra clerical step was required to prepare data for the computer. This step, usually keypunching of original data, obviously introduced an additional chance for human error. Furthermore, the data preparation was being performed by the wrong person—someone who was not familiar with the objectives or situation of the user department. Finally, because of the nature of centralized processing, each system was independent of the next, so each system was processed separately on the computer. This meant that the same information had to be input separately in each system, resulting not only in duplication and extra costs but, again, in additional chances for errors.

Inaccessibility of data. To be effective, data must obviously be readily accessible. But in the centralized computer environment, this is not always possible. In fact, it was impossible except in the most expensive computer departments. The reason stems from the sequential or batch-processing mode of the centralized computer. Simply stated, one system runs at a time. The consequences are obvious:

- Information was available to the user when the *computer* was scheduled to produce it, not always when the *user* needed it.
- Because of "one-shot" processing of batch operations, *all* information was reported during the cycle, whether or not it was needed. For example, a complete list of parts inventory was produced even when a customer had ordered just one part.

To deal with this problem, department personnel, from accounting clerks to shop-floor foremen, often maintained their own records separately from those produced by the computer. Inaccessibility of data forced this unproductive and costly practice and created conflicting data between the end user and the data processing center.

Untimeliness of data. Data processing is the transformation of raw data into useful information for decision and control. If, however, the raw data are not transformed in a timely manner, they will be useless. Such was the case with centralized computer centers.

In order to schedule a batch program or system, there must be a cutoff time for coding worksheets and preparing data. But companies are *continuous* rather than batch-oriented. The results are predictable, even with daily processing of data. Reports can be as much as 18 or 24 hours out of phase with real operations. And if errors occur in the data-generation or data-preparation phases, corrected data will be 36 to 48 hours out of phase, because users must wait until the next processing cycle on the following day. Again, those who need current information get it from a "second set of facts" maintained manually and separately from the computer records.

The End of the Mainframe Era

Throughout the 1970s, substantial advances were made in small-computer technology and the development of the minicomputer. Memory technology improved, and new low-cost memory boards and large-scale integrated circuits were introduced to the world of data processing. Improvements in small-system architecture, discussed later in this book, enhanced the price/performance ratio of these minicomputers and made them feasible alternatives for existing small mainframe computers.

Manufacturers such as Data General, Digital Equipment Corporation, Prime, and Hewlett-Packard developed sophisticated systems software that operates on small computers. These systems support high-level languages such as COBOL, SPL, FORTRAN, BASIC, and RPG. These are the very same languages used on the mainframes. Most minicomputers support all of these languages rather than being restricted to one, such as RPG on the original System 3 computer manufactured by IBM.

Sophisticated operating systems were developed by the manufacturers for their minicomputers. These operating systems, unlike a majority of their predecessors, were time-sharing systems that provided instant access to the computer by multiple end users. This offered the potential to move away from batch-processing modes, which plagued earlier eras.

Data base management capabilities were introduced on minicomputers, led by Hewlett-Packard's award-winning IMAGE data base management system. Previously, this sophisticated file-handling technique was available only on the largest and most expensive mainframe computers. Later, we will look at data base management systems as they relate to distributed data processing. It is important here, in this historical perspective, to understand that this software breakthrough simplified programming and systems development and improved users' ability to obtain data from the computer quickly and flexibly.

Finally, data communications were also enhanced to the point where information could easily be transferred between computers. Files could be easily accessed and data shared by multiple users with multiple computers. Computer programs could be accessed and shared by multiple computers and multiple users. Peripherals such as disk drives, printers, and terminals could also be accessed and shared by multiple computers due to the sophisticated software that had been developed.

These advances in systems software (including high-level languages, real-time operating systems, data base management capabilities, and communications) generated an opportunity to move into a new generation of data processing, which came to be called distributed data processing. This mode of processing eliminated the disadvantages and retained the best qualities of previous generations.

In distributed data processing, individual data processing tasks are performed wherever needed and where they can be handled most effectively. Separate computers are electronically interconnected, using new communications software to share and enhance data processing at multiple locations or between multiple functions. Distributed data processing is an approach to processing which provides a wide range of alternatives between total centralization and total decentralization.

Let's take a closer look at this exciting alternative now.

3

Distributed Processing: The Logical Alternative

Flexibility is the major inherent advantage of distributed data processing. In previous eras, computer limitations often forced organizations to change the way they processed data. Under distributed processing, management is in control. The network design, tailored to the unique needs of the organization, dictates the choice of computers, data-capture devices, and systems. The result is a unified, flexible systems network that supports the organization, as opposed to a series of computers spread throughout the organization or a rigid, unresponsive central data processing structure.

Three Dimensions of Distributed Processing

Distributed data processing allows a range of alternatives in three areas: (1) nature or mode of distribution, (2) location of computer resources, and (3) communications. Each of these areas must be analyzed so that a network that best suits the organization can be developed.

Nature or Mode

Nature or mode of distribution refers to the alternatives of *geographical* versus *functional* distribution. In Figure 5, a typical network distributed by function is illustrated. The figure also details the concept of hierarchical design, that is, information flow from the bottom (operating) level to the top.

***Figure 5.* A typical distributed-processing network.**

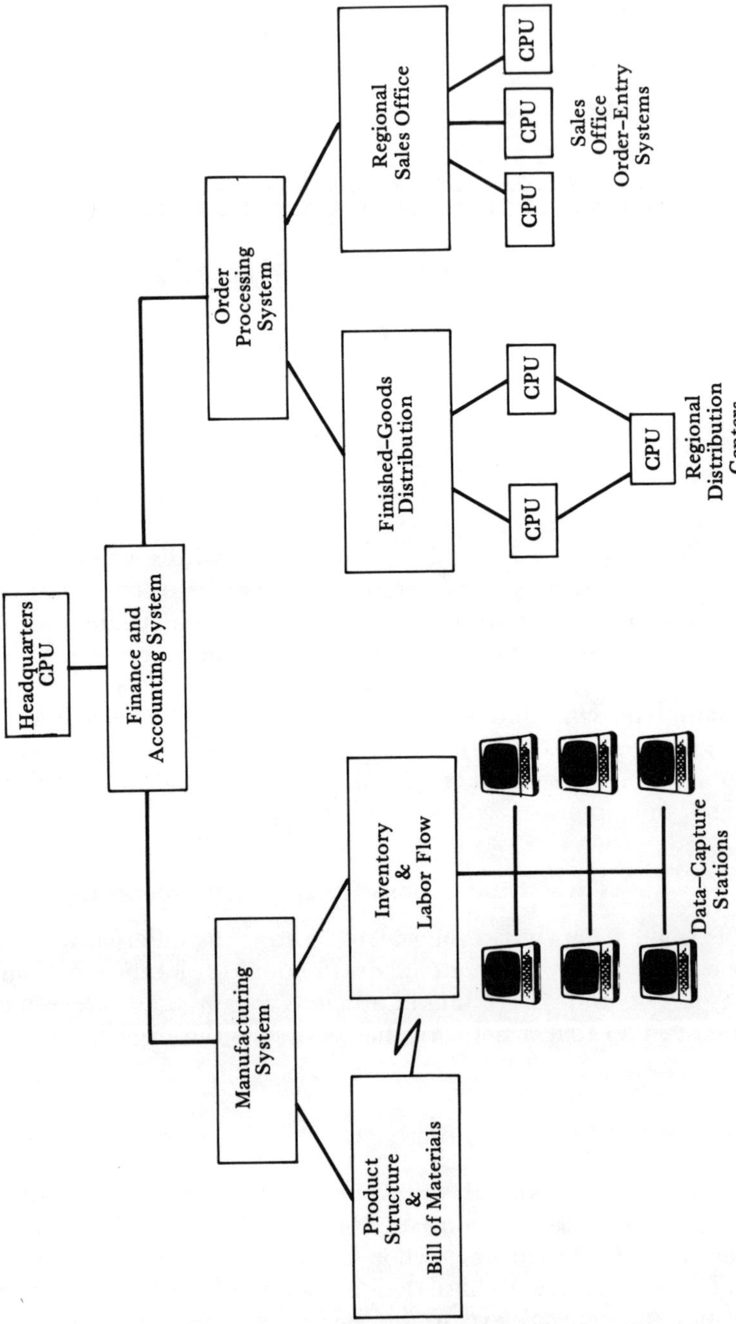

In *functional* distribution, computer processing power is located where the function is being performed. In Figure 5, the three functions are manufacturing, finance and accounting, and order processing. In an insurance application, the functions may be life insurance, home insurance, and automobile insurance. In banking, the functions may be demand-deposit accounting, loan services, and estate planning. Functional distribution could require a computer and processing power for each of these functions.

Again in Figure 5, a minicomputer could be dedicated to manufacturing and linked to a corporate computer for summary data and cost accounting. The manufacturing system of a firm in Cincinnati, Ohio, operates on a minicomputer manufactured by Digital Equipment Corporation. The computer controls all manufacturing processes and inventory. Manufacturing orders are numbered and controlled. The product is exploded into its component parts under reserved-inventory status, and cost figures are transmitted daily for distribution and product-availability reports.

This is an effective way to distribute data processing. Control over production and raw materials, and planning for capacity of different operating departments, are appropriately maintained at the plant. Summary figures are transmitted upward where they are needed.

Referring to Figure 5 again, a computer could also be dedicated to accounting and finance or, as is more frequently the case, to the customer-order-processing function. For example, one of the largest ball bearings distributors in the world is installing minicomputers at corporate headquarters and five regional distribution centers. The logical functional application: order entry. Each distribution center maintains an inventory of 40,000 parts, which will now be accessible to its 28 sales branch offices via terminals. The branch will transmit orders to its regional distribution centers for packing, shipping, and invoicing. The minicomputer at the regional center will reserve the product, create picking lists and invoices, and set up an accounts-receivable record and a sales record. Sales and receivables will be transmitted to the corporate office daily for management and collection and to update the general corporate ledger.

The network is complete, since regions can query each other for the availability of parts in the 40,000-part finished-goods inventory. This type of network configuration is an example of distributing data processing predominantly on a functional basis (an element of geographical distribution is present insofar as there are remote regional distribution centers and remote sales branch offices).

In a typical *geographical* distribution, each location has similar systems operating on the computer and, most often, a complete set of systems and programs. Computers are distributed geographically to handle a majority of functions locally. This would include all manufacturing systems, accounting systems, and customer-order entry systems. The network is connected through communications software to interchange summary financial data. This network grows, without loss of central control, as the organization opens new divisions and subsidiaries.

Location of Computer Resources

If distribution is geographical (which is most often the case), location of computer power becomes a question of centralization versus decentralization. Figure 6 illustrates this point.

In the first, more centralized, alternative, a large and powerful computer does a majority of the processing, with two smaller computers handling the remote divisions. The smaller computers may be processing daily manufacturing orders for the divisions while providing all daily operating functions. They may be small, economical processors that cannot perform large-scale, heavy-duty pro-

Figure 6. Alternatives in distributing computer resources among different locations.

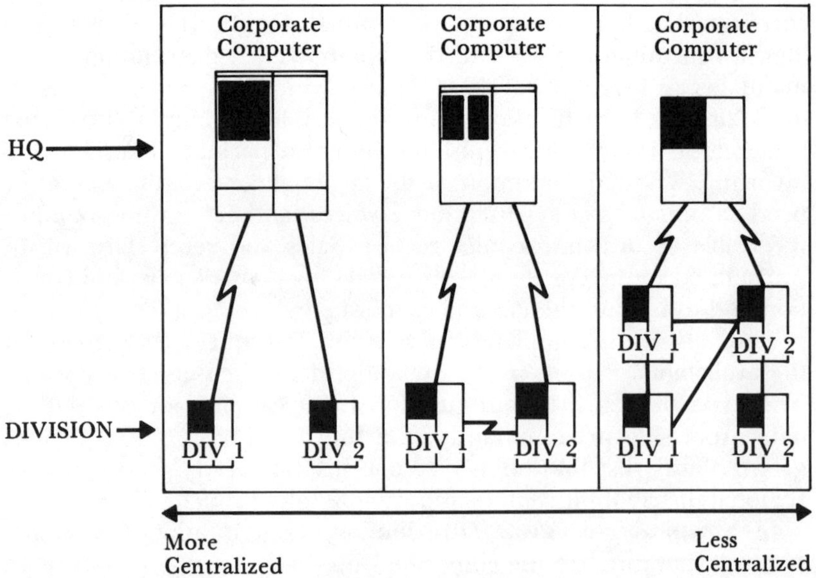

cessing—and that *do not need such power* for the efficient and effective operation of the divisions.

For example, a time-consuming process of determining material requirements (referred to in the industry as material requirements planning, or MRP) may be performed on a larger computer at headquarters. This might involve a large-scale mainframe computer. By allocating this once-a-week batch processing to a mainframe, the division can do all of its processing at home on a less expensive computer. Clearly, this is a very cost-effective alternative.

Another alternative shown in Figure 6 is to use two general-purpose computers that can communicate well with each other in the divisions. This means more processing power at the division level and fewer processing requirements for the corporate computer.

In this alternative, inventory levels or production information may be transferred. Because the information is being provided by a lower organizational level, there is less need to communicate with the corporate computer. In this case the company may prefer a minicomputer at headquarters as the most cost-effective answer for the organization. If, for example, invoicing and collections are handled by the divisions, there is no need for the corporation to maintain massive customer and accounts-receivable files for several divisions. Accordingly, a smaller processor and smaller file storage devices are required.

In the final alternative illustrated in Figure 6, even less computer power is given to the central site, and functional dedication of computers is apparent at the division level. Again, more processing is completed at each operating level, and the need for a large central processor becomes negligible or nonexistent. These, of course, are only a few of a multitude of configurations for distributing data processing. Which leads us quite naturally into the third aspect of information processing—communications.

Communications

Referring again to Figure 6, it is apparent that location and communications are closely related concepts in distributed data processing. Straight communications lines indicate hard-wired links from one computer to another. The broken lines depict long-distance leased or common telephone lines that are linked to each computer through a modem (a device which *mo*dulates and *dem*odulates signals). This will be discussed later.

The degree of distribution will depend on the cost of communications and the need for information at various levels of the organization. There is an obvious trade-off. Desirable but nonessential information may not be justifiable from a pure cost perspective. The decision on the final network configuration will depend on an analysis of the information needs at all levels of the organization, the required speed of data availability, and communications costs.

Making the Decision

As mentioned earlier, the range of distributed data processing alternatives for the end user is virtually limitless and depends solely on what best suits the organization. Determining what is best for an organization can be resolved by an analysis that focuses on "where best to do what." Such an analysis must deal with the three dimensions of distributed data processing:

- Should data processing be distributed geographically, functionally, or both?
- How much computing power should be given to each location?
- What type and degree of communications should be implemented between the different locations?

The first step should be an analysis of the present use of data processing in these terms. That is, the process starts with a thorough systems analysis.

It may seem elementary that such an analysis should be required, and it certainly is not a new concept. However, there are new requirements. The first, often ignored, requirement stipulates that all involved players be included in the analysis. In Figure 7, interested players are those who will potentially benefit from data processing at headquarters, divisions, or remote plants. This encompasses all those individuals who may require information or access to data processing resources.

Another new requirement is to evaluate where a given function can be best performed. This was not an issue in centralized data processing, since all processing under such a setup was centralized on a large mainframe computer. It was not an issue in the era of decentralized data processing either. But now it may be *the* issue, and it can be resolved by analyzing the five functions illustrated in Figure 7: (1) data collection, (2) editing and error correction, (3) file creation and maintenance, (4) inquiry, and (5) processing. Let's take a close look at those five functions.

Figure 7. Analysis must focus on where best to do what.

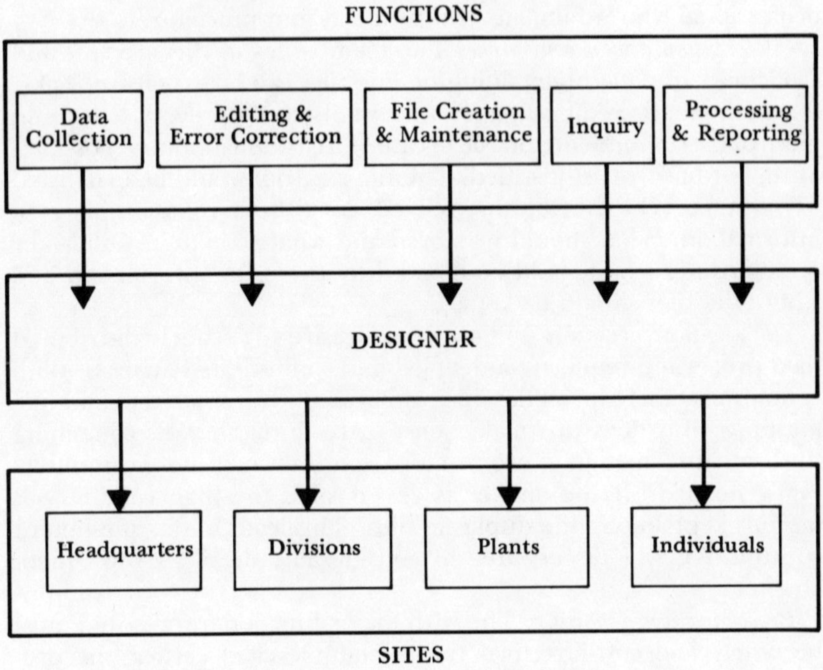

Data collection. If costs justify it, data collection should be located *at the source.* To do otherwise requires unnecessary paperwork, coding, and communications. Additional people are required to accomplish the same goal: getting information to the computer.

An analysis of data collection in a distributed environment includes the means of collection as well as the location. Direct input to the computer may be the best answer, but often is prohibitive from a cost-benefit standpoint. One large eyeglass-frame manufacturer, for example, gathers data on customer orders at five regional offices and transmits them daily in a batch mode for invoicing. While it may be a cost-effective setup, data gathering is not the best available system, because inventory availability at each remote center is unknown. The remote batch edit occurs hours after the customer order. In this case, it would be far more desirable to edit the order while still talking to the customer.

Editing and error correction. Editing of data should always be as close to the source of data collection as possible. In fact, it should be as close as costs justify. This holds true for the same reasons (cost and time) as mentioned earlier. Under this system, a customer can better handle error corrections, because he is dealing directly with a professional who is familiar with products and procedures.

File creation and maintenance. The main issues in this are cost and availability of data. Maintaining on-line files can be expensive. Take, for example, a credit manager who wants to keep every letter and piece of correspondence on file in case of a customer inquiry. Possible? Sure, but hardly cost-justified. The file capacity would be exhausted in no time. Of course, the related issue here is accessibility to information. What should be stored and what shouldn't? Other key questions are who should be allowed to access the information and where the files should be kept.

File location, creation, and maintenance are key issues in distributed data processing requiring a detailed and sophisticated analysis. With communications capabilities, files can be easily transmitted to multiple locations. But does this make sense? Are duplicate files containing the same information at two or more sites on two or more computers really needed? If the answer is yes, despite the high cost, how is *integrity* kept among the duplicate files? This leads to the question of control. We will discuss this in considerable detail in subsequent chapters.

Processing and reporting. The fifth major function, processing, must be timely and cost-effective. In an example cited earlier, the production information at a divisional facility had to be transmitted to the corporate facility for large-scale processing. This was neither cost-effective nor timely, though it did provide a reasonable level of control. But far too often corporate data processors confuse this type of arrangement with distributed data processing. They feel that since the division has the ability to enter and update its own information through a remote job entry (RJE) device, they have access to and control over the information. This is a nearsighted view at best.

Moving Toward Distributed Processing

The evolution from centralized to distributed processing may be seen as one of offloading activities from the central computer and increasing capability at the satellite or remote location, division, or region. Five states logically fit into this evolution, and each data processing center is at one of these stages. In Figure 8, the size of the arrow represents the functional capability at the remote location. The larger the arrow, the greater capability.

Each stage is defined in the following paragraphs so that management, in its analysis, can identify where the organization stands in

Figure 8. The evolution toward distributed processing.

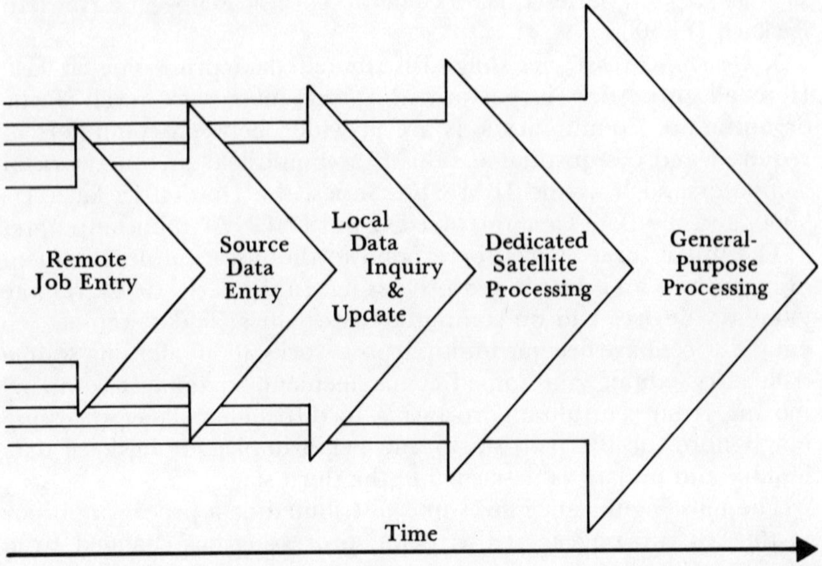

its evolution toward distributed processing. It will make the transition easier and identify the amount of effort involved.

1. *Remote job entry*: The user at a satellite location submits batch jobs to a mainframe computer for processing. The information is returned to the satellite for error correction and final reporting. This is still centralized processing and not distributed data processing. The road ahead is long and winding.

2. *Source data entry*: The user at a satellite location enters information (for example, a customer order) directly into a terminal as the information is received. Data entry, therefore, takes place at the source, and data editing is provided, moving an important function away from the mainframe.

3. *Local data inquiry and update*: The user at the satellite location has limited computing capabilities but extensive data files, which can be accessed and updated without communication with the central host computer. Data editing and some file manipulation are possible, but the main data base remains with the mainframe, as does all extensive processing.

4. *Dedicated satellite processing*: The first real step into distributed processing, where all processing of one particular function (such as accounting or customer-order entry) is done at the satellite organi-

zation. This could be accomplished by a dedicated minicomputer such as an IBM Series I, Data General Nova or Eclipse, or Hewlett-Packard DS 3000.

5. *General-purpose processing*: Distributed data processing at last. Here all processing is performed at the most basic level of the organization. Communications are provided between computers as required and cost-justifiable. This is accomplished by a network of computers, such as the IBM 8100 series, the Hewlett-Packard DS 3000, and the Data General, or DEC and DECNET minicomputers.

The initial three stages correspond to the historical development of computers and distributed processing. In the early 1970s, remote job entry devices had no computing capabilities. Today, remote job entry devices have become multipurpose workstations allowing source data entry, editing, and some file management. So, today, a company moving from centralized processing to distributed data processing may ignore the first two stages and begin implementing local data inquiry and update as described in the third stage.

The most significant moves into distributed data processing occur in the last two stages. At this point, processing has changed from merely offloading a mainframe computer to efficient and cost-effective handling of all the informational needs of the organization. The satellite or remote location has gained greater responsibility for processing data and takes sole responsibility for data accuracy.

A similar evolution has taken place for companies moving from decentralized processing to distributed data processing. In this case, the change involves increasing the networking and data communications between the existing satellite processors, rather than increasing functional capability at the satellite locations.

Moving to distributed data processing from a centralized environment or a decentralized environment requires planning and centralized control. Again, planning starts with a thorough analysis of the existing systems, procedures, and practices and a functional analysis of where best to do what, as described in the preceding section.

The Foundation of Distributed Processing: New and Understandable Technology

New technology makes it possible to distribute computing power to the most basic corporate levels, closer to the point of responsibility. Unlike the technology of centralized processing, the technology of distributed processing is understandable to management. It includes on-line, real-time systems, data base management, minicomputers, and communications. Quite simply, it is a technology that strikes at the heart of the informational problems discussed earlier.

On-Line Real-Time Systems

As previously mentioned, batch processing dominated the early days of electronic data processing. Perceived inefficiencies caused a search, led by MIT, for a means to communicate more directly with mainframe computers. The search led to the design of *on-line systems.* Communicating with a computer through video terminals was accomplished in the early 1970s. A new technology using integrated circuitry and communication linkages made this possible.

The concept of *real-time systems* emerged simultaneously with on-line systems technology. Real-time simply means information can be retrieved instantly from computer files, as required for effective time-sharing. Information interfaces with the computer are controlled electronically without human intervention. Instant access to information by multiple users with terminals is important for management.

As this technology has improved and matured, computers with on-line and real-time capabilities have become increasingly powerful. Airline reservation and banking demand-deposit systems are prominent examples of such systems. In both cases, many users are able to tap into large information banks to check reservation status or bank balances, respectively. Needed information is immediately available on a time-shared basis.

It's easy to see that these technological improvements would have a very positive effect on data accessibility in any business environment. Because data are instantly available and always up to date, there will be no need for a "second set of facts," as under centralized processing. This information processing concept allows convenient access to a valuable tool, the computer. In many ways, it turns the computer into a handy calculator that is used to transform raw data into useful information—only it is much more powerful, because of its ability to store and retrieve a vast quantity of information.

On-line systems have the potential, then, to resolve the problems of accessibility. Real-time architecture, likewise, has the potential to resolve the problems of timeliness. The ability to input, manipulate, and retrieve data in an instant means the elimination of all the delays characteristic of batch processing. In airline reservation systems, reservations are requested and made on a real-time basis; in the same way, in industry, orders are placed and goods are manufactured and shipped, and each of these transactions can be fed to the computer as it occurs. The need to cut off paperwork, prepare data, and schedule a batch process is eliminated, along with the 18-hour to 24-hour delay.

On-line real-time systems have the potential to resolve two problems of centralization, timeliness and accessibility. What about the third problem—accuracy? Here, new technology also has an impact because of the nature of on-line systems and their organizational implications. First, working directly with the information to be processed means that errors will be caught almost immediately. Early detection and correction will improve the accuracy of final reports and data bases. Some computer experts maintain that this direct interaction with the information stored in the computer can improve accuracy by as much as 30 percent. The interactive nature of on-line systems means the computer prompts the end user with questions while the user is editing data. This give-and-take is important in error prevention. A visual data check on video screens prior to data submission to the computer for processing or storage also improves data accuracy.

Second, accuracy is improved with on-line systems because of the organizational structure of distributed processing. On-line systems are flexible enough to tailor the computer to the organization, and return responsibility for data and systems to the end user. This is the very essence of distributed processing. Accuracy is directly improved by the elimination of an artificially imposed "data entry" group introduced under centralized data processing. But even more important, in distributed processing with on-line capability, those who deal with the information are the *most knowledgeable* about that information. Those whose job depends upon the information most—the end users—are responsible for it. Knowledgeable people entering information and reacting to it should certainly make more responsible decisions on data than those who are unfamiliar with the work. History and any experienced profit-center manager will confirm this statement.

Data Base Management

Distributed processing, grounded in advanced technology, can have a major impact on accuracy. Meanwhile another technique exists in the centralized data processing world, and it has been enhanced for the requirements of distributed data processing. This is the concept of data base management.

Without getting into a detailed technological discussion, data base management is the logical ordering and organizing of data within computer files. It is necessary to organize files so that the information is readily available and easily accessible. Proper organization of files ensures that the efficiencies of on-line processing are maintained and maximized. But it is also important to eliminate duplication of information or data redundancy, and data base managment achieves this as well. This feature of data base management has a drastic effect on accuracy.

Under traditional data organization, systems are designed, implemented, and used as separate entities. Consider three common business applications—payroll, pension history, and labor distribution—each with its own independent files. In a batch environment, these systems will be scheduled on the computer autonomously. The problem is that the required information is the same in each applications—namely *name, Social Security number*, and *salary*. Without an organized and integrated bank of information, the same information will be fed into the computer three separate times—once each for payroll, labor-distribution, and pension-history systems. This duplication of effort—with three people independently entering information—will undoubtedly cause errors. Labor costs, of course, triple—all for the sake of redundant data. There will be inconsistencies, too, because no one person in the organization is assigned responsibility for reconciling independent systems.

A proven data base management system, designed for computers by the manufacturer or a software company such as Cullinane or Cincom, can reduce the potential for errors. Management does not have to understand this technique in order to reap the benefits from it. The benefit is that required information is stored in the computer "data base" just once. This means it is input once by a user or department with the assigned responsibility and accountability for accuracy.

The data base management concept, incorporated into distributed data processing, makes it possible to work from *one set of facts*. This is recognized by all data processing professionals and students as another major advantage of distributed processing as practiced today. The data base management concept of information storage, coupled with on-line, real-time capabilities, allows a broad attack on common problems of inaccuracy, inaccessibility, and untimeliness of data. But what strides has distributed processing made in cost-effectiveness?

Minicomputers and Communications

One reason behind the strong movement toward distributed processing has been the declining cost of minicomputers. These small but powerful systems are not produced by the mainframe manufacturers with which large business is familiar: IBM, Honeywell, NCR, Burroughs. Rather, the minicomputer era is represented by companies that have only recently come to prominence, such as Digital Equipment Corporation, Data General, Hewlett-Packard, and Wang Laboratories.

Minicomputers, so-called because of their size and price, are real-time computers with on-line operating systems, as we have discussed. They can replace labor and increase productivity and profits fast. They are mass-produced with chips of integrated miniaturized circuits, which is one reason for their low (and declining) cost.

What this means to management is simple: some very powerful yet economical computers are available in the market with state-of-the-art technology. They can significantly cut costs on a single installation or be employed economically in a distributed-processing network. One southern-based retail chain and a bank in California, for example, replaced large mainframes with minicomputers at substantial savings. Another *Fortune* 500 company saved more than $1 million annually by replacing one dedicated application on a mainframe with a dedicated minicomputer. It is surprising that these computers still retain the designation "minicomputer." A price/performance comparison should be revealing. For instance, the city of Malmö, Sweden, found that a CPU-to-CPU comparison between mainframe and mini yielded a ratio of 10 : 1 in favor of the minicom-

Figure 9. Minicomputer shipments by size class. (Reprinted with permission of International Data Corporation.)

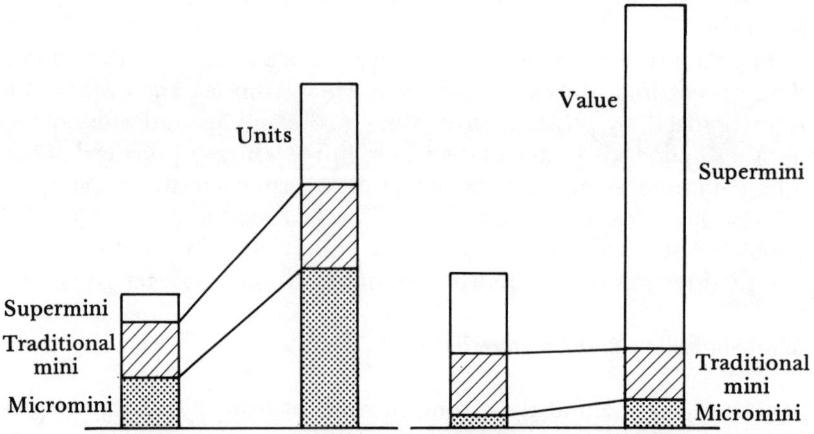

puters. Not surprisingly, the city decided to switch from a centralized mainframe system to a distributed network employing 14 Data General minicomputers and 80 terminals.

Although minicomputers are small in size and price, they have powerful large-scale memories and support the same peripheral equipment (printers, terminals, tape drives) as the mainframe computers. At the same time, these minicomputers can support an almost unlimited amount of data base information on their disks. So only the largest applications (like an airline reservation system) would strain the capabilities of the minicomputer.

As stated in Ulric Weil's book *Information Systems in the 1980s*, and as can be seen in Figure 9, minicomputers are well on their way to doubling in unit sales since 1979; at the same time they have demonstrated an unparalleled price/performance ratio in relation to comparable mainframe configurations.

Advent of Microcomputers

If anything bears witness to the effect of user demand on the advancement to distributed processing, it is the almost uncontrollable influx of microcomputers into big business. As one market analyst put it, they are propagating through organizations like rabbits. This comment should tell us something! Why would people be so eager to go out and buy their own computer when they have an entire data processing department and large in-house system at their disposal?

Unfortunately, the answer is too obvious. Large centralized data organizations and oversized computer systems overwhelm the average user. Instead of representing the service function that they were devised for, they represent a bureaucratic bottleneck that the user just does not want to have to contend with. Microcomputers provide an inexpensive and expedient solution that circumvents the problem. Their great popularity demonstrates how strongly the users feel about having more control over, and access to, the computer resources they need and desperately depend on to do their jobs successfully.

Because of the true user-friendly nature of the microcomputer, and because of the size and portability of the unit, this technology has advanced the cause and functionality of true distributed processing far beyond the range that the minicomputer technology set in place.

Without a doubt, microcomputers are the next wave of expansion in the distributed-processing market.

Conclusion

Today's technology exists to solve informational problems that arose in the era of centralized data processing. Furthermore, the technology is an inexpensive and cost-effective solution to an organization's information processing needs. The question now is twofold: First, why has distributed processing been resisted? Second, how do we overcome the obstacles that appear to be blocking the path toward the third era of data processing.

4

Batch Met Its Match with On-Line

In the late 1960s, which was not that many years ago, data processing primarily meant batch processing. Telecommunications and telecommunications devices were only beginning. Companies like AT&T had set up corporate projects to test the feasibility of this exciting new mode of processing. But only the *Fortune* 500 giants dared to venture into the data processing pond. Most firms held tight and simply waited until the good news overshadowed the bad.

Minicomputers had recently arrived on the scene. DEC had its PDP-8 processor on the market for several years, and companies such as Data General and General Automation were just getting off the ground. Although the only true commercial environment was a mainframe environment, it was hard to discount the new entrants which were being introduced almost weekly through such well-read journals as *Computerworld* and *Datamation*. These computers were so new and versatile that they were perceived as "mini" computers without committed purpose. They were modern-day rebels without a cause.

Another popular newcomer was the video display terminal, or cathode-ray tube (CRT), as IBM referred to it. IBM promoted two models at the time. One was a pure character terminal, supporting 60 columns and 12 rows. It was impressive and expensive. The other was designed specifically for graphic use, requiring strict mathematical programming. While this model was clever, it did not lend itself to normal commercial programming applications. It was designed more for architects, electrical engineers, or automotive designers.

Both of these devices were very expensive, and in light of their limited capabilities, they could not easily be cost-justified. Some aerospace companies purchased these units for simulator studies, because they could justify the procurement as part of project expenses required for their large defense contracts. But the average company could not justify them for commercial use. Remember, this was a period of heavy batch processing. Most systems were designed to process large sequential files. And in many cases, the files weren't even supported on disk. They still resided on tape. Disks were new at the time. So what would a company with batch processing do with a video terminal?

It was impractical to display an entire file of information on such a unit, because it could only handle 12 lines of information at a time. To use it as an inquiry device would require on-demand access, which was unrealistic in a scheduled batch environment. So until the advent of indexed-sequential file management and data base management, companies that were locked into batch processing had no practical way of using these devices. A great idea was born, but it required a substantial change in processing approach before it could become useful.

In retrospect, it's interesting how these three major technologies evolved together and how much impact they have had on the data processing community. Think about it! Has any other technology advanced so far so fast? In just ten years, the industry evolved from a world of large keypunch staffs and voluminous daily reports to an era of instantaneous access to information supported through complex communication networks and distributed computer systems. Why it took so long for the data processing community to accept distributed processing is understandable: distributed processing represented a radically new way of thinking, not only from a management standpoint but, more important, from a technical standpoint.

A Well-Established Tradition

Between 1950 and 1970, several generations of hardware appeared and disappeared. Wire-board circuitry gave way to vacuum-tube logic, which in turn relinquished its reign to the transistor. Now transistors are obsolete, having been replaced by integrated circuits and microprocessor "chip" technology. Today, complete technological functions can be placed on a single silicon chip.

Ironically, during the same period, there was essentially *no* change in the concepts and procedures used in applications design. During the days of unit-record equipment, all processing was handled through cards. The input consisted of card decks; files were retained in card decks; and reports were generated directly from card decks. Mechanical sorters were used to sequence the decks and organize them into the order required for processing and reporting. This, without doubt, was grass-roots batch processing.

When vacuum-tube technology came along, it had a dramatic impact on the data processing community from a hardware and programming standpoint, but not from a systems standpoint. Although the equipment was more functional then the older systems and programs could now be loaded into the computer for execution, the advance in systems design was still basically lateral.

Techniques changed. Equipment changed. But the basic concepts didn't change. The same concepts that became well established during unit-record days were practiced even more fervently during this period. Card files were converted to tape; wire-board procedures were converted to memory-based programs; internal program sorts replaced the function of the older sorting equipment. Essentially, the game was faster, but otherwise the same.

If we could call record processing "introductory batch processing," then this period can be called "intermediate batch processing." Input was still being keypunched, probably in the same format used on the unit-record equipment. Reports were still being generated in the same form as on the unit-record printers. So what had really changed?

For the most part, the change was cosmetic: expanded programming flexibility. Faster processing. More compact data storage. These were the major benefits derived from the second generation. And as we moved into the third generation of computers, these were still the fundamental areas being addressed.

The third generation was characterized by compact transistor technology. Smaller circuitry augmented processing capabilities offered by third-generation systems. Memory limits expanded from 16 kilobytes to one megabyte; tapes increased in density and speed; card readers and printers were replaced by faster card readers and faster printers. And new mass-storage devices appeared on the horizon.

The third generation brought the age of "advanced batch processing," and with it a variety of new programming tools. Languages such as COBOL, PL/I, FORTRAN IV, and RPG IV brought tremendous programming advances to the industry. In the world of IBM, Autocoder was replaced by Basic Assembler, and the primitive operating system of the 1440 gave way to the advanced operating systems of the 360. TOS, DOS, and OS became the buzzwords of this generation.

Companies with substantial investments in second-generation software couldn't afford to move rapidly into this new environment. As a result, emulators were developed to bridge the gap between equipment generations and allow systems coded on older equipment to operate on the new. The idea seemed a good one, and companies took advantage of this approach. However, it turned out to be shortsighted. Though it enabled quick conversions, users paid through poor systems performance and limited flexibility. Programs that functioned under emulation operated only in object form. The source program could not be converted or maintained on third-generation equipment. By the end of the 1960s, software companies had discovered a lucrative business converting second-generation programs operating under emulation into third-generation languages such as COBOL.

What really changed after 20 years of computer evolution, as far as the approach to application systems was concerned? Instead of wiring up boards, the same logic was being programmed in COBOL. And instead of running card sorters to sequence the information, parameters to the sort utilities were issued. Lengthy batch procedures were still being scheduled, and gigantic reports were still being printed. The innovations of the 1950s had become the established traditions of the 1970s. The status quo reigned supreme.

The Coming of Change

Everything considered, change could not be expected overnight. Forces were needed to overcome the inertia of tradition and set the industry on the road toward a new objective.

Still, the time was ripe for new ideas. Batch processing had evolved a long way from its inception, and the pace of business was quickening. Requests surfaced faster than they could be serviced, and as management imposed more pressures on data processing, data processing, in turn, demanded more resources. The "batch syndrome" had taken over. More resources required more equipment; more keypunchers, computer operators, programmers, and systems designers; and above all, more money. An unbelievable amount of time was being wasted. Forms had to be meticulously completed, cards keypunched and verified, jobs scheduled and executed, reports collated, and the final results distributed back to the user—all before the next work day began.

But inefficient use of time and labor were not the only problems. Inherent to the operation was the risk of failure. Every good batch system required an editing program to verify and, if necessary, reject transactions that could not be processed. Therefore, there was never a guarantee that all transactions submitted to data processing would be processed. Consequently, there was a strong possibility that information appearing in the reports was incomplete and inaccurate.

The accountant, who had the time to correct errors, would eventually receive a report. But consider the plight of a production manager who didn't have the time to weed out all errors. Would he rely solely on the results of a semi up-to-date inventory report that was produced by an organization over which he had no control? Highly unlikely. He would most probably devise his own system to get total control and information accuracy. Understandably, this is why many who faced these problems resorted to a second set of records.

Batch processing was designed for applications such as payroll, accounts payable, or general ledger, where large amounts of data can normally be processed together in batches. But batch processing is not suited for applications such as manufacturing control, order processing, or customer service, where responsiveness is important and information must be available on demand.

Change was inevitable. Batch systems devised for accountants were not necessarily practical for others. An accountant could be asked for the result of an income statement all day, and he'd give you the same answer. But if a production manager were asked every half hour how much raw materials he had on hand, he'd have to send an expediter to count it, because it changes continuously. So although batch worked well for static information, it was impractical as a data processing mechanism for dynamic information.

The Catalyst—A Random Alternative

Up to the third generation, data processors had no alternative but to stick with traditional batch processing. First- and second-generation equipment encouraged sequential processing, and under such circumstances batch processing was undoubtedly the most efficient manner of processing. But with the third generation, a new invention appeared—the random-access device.

When originally announced, it was offered in three different mass-storage forms: film, drum, and disk. Of these original forms, the disk quickly surpassed the others in popularity. The disk used magnetic encoding techniques, like tape, but offered a powerful processing alternative not found on traditional sequential devices. Because of its unique design, it was able to access information directly.

Now specific information could be pinpointed, eliminating sequential reading of data. Information could also be accessed in the usual sequential manner, but this new method was intriguing.

Unfortunately, it took time for the total benefits of disks to be understood. Luckily, vendors anticipated as much. Disk devices were frequently sold as high-speed replacements for tape. Twenty-five years of sequential processing couldn't be uprooted overnight.

By the early 1970s, random processing techniques were quickly taking hold. From Assembler-generated systems using physical input/output control to the large-scale COBOL systems using the indexed sequential-access method (ISAM), new systems were being designed and developed to take advantage of this powerful tool. Terms such as relative random, direct random, and indexed sequential became the new buzzwords of this generation. Every data processor in the industry, whether he was using them or not, knew what they meant. Acceptance had been achieved.

The disk became a catalyst for a new way of thinking. It was no longer necessary to wade through volumes of data to find information. Access was immediate. Also, there was no need to schedule lengthy jobs to acquire the information. The capability implied that the information was available at any time. But was it?

Conceiving a New Idea

Just as the evolution of card systems can be attributed to the innovation of batch processing, the evolution of disk systems can be traced to the innovation of on-line processing. But the disk by itself was insufficient to do the job.

On-line meant real-time, on-demand, always available. It did not mean keypunching data cards, configuring job streams, queuing schedules, and waiting for printouts. In the late 1960s, as we previously discussed, another device called the video display terminal (or cathode-ray tube—CRT for short) appeared on the computer scene. As far as batch processing was concerned, it offered little. However, to an on-line designer, it was an exciting development.

Keypunched cards, job streams, scheduled queues, and printouts all became obsolete. Requests could be made directly through the input device, with information retrieved immediately from the disk and the result displayed instantaneously on the screen. If the device was then placed in the user's area, there was no need for the user to fill out time-consuming forms, pass information between departments, and wait for a job to run. The entire operation was totally under the user's control. Within seconds of issuing a request, the user had results.

To accomplish all this using third-generation equipment required sophisticated software and strong technical expertise. The majority of operating systems available in the late 1960s supported only single-task batch processing, meaning only one program could be run in the computer at a time. So if an on-line operation was set up in this kind of environment, an entire computer would have to be dedicated to one on-line program. And since there was no communications software, the program would only be able to address one or two terminals at a time. Therefore, to make on-line processing practical, it was necessary to wait until more than one program could be executed in the computer at a given time.

The Need for Multiprocessing

Third-generation machines offered tremendous processing capabilities, but when time delays in servicing the various input/output requests were analyzed, it was discovered that the computer was idle more than 50 percent of the time. This was primarily because commercial applications require very heavy utilization of I/O devices. These applications fundamentally consist of creating files, updating files, and printing reports. So during the processing of these applications, the computer wasted more than 50 percent of its processing ability waiting for information to be passed between it and another device. In simple applications, such as a card-to-print utility, this could create a situation where only 5 percent of the computer's *total* capabilities was exploited. This translates into an extravagant waste of resources.

If single-phase processing had persisted, there would have been no justification to retain such high-powered central processors. A simpler, less expensive processor would have been more than adequate. It wouldn't have processed as fast, but it would not have been idle so much. In short, a simpler processor could have performed the same operation more cost-effectively.

Such inefficiencies could not continue. First, vendors addressed the problem of speeding up unit-record operations. Time consumed in reading input cards, punching output cards, or writing report lines to the printer represented a large portion of daily processing requirements. Improving these devices, which were the slowest devices on this system, would have a significant impact on the system as a whole.

Around 1968, companies like IBM announced a new feature called "spooling," a software enhancement that was designed to improve overall performance of the system. The concept was simple: instead of feeding application programs directly from the card reader or writing the output directly to the line printer as in the past, information could be queued up by placing it on a disk file in an intermediate step. Card input was placed in a disk file by the operating system, while an unrelated program might be executing. When control was passed to the application program using the card input, the program could then read the content directly from the disk file. Correspondingly, in a report program, print lines were first written to a disk file, which was subsequently transferred to the printer by the operating system. These disk files were referred to as "spoolers." By using the spooling technique, the operating system transferred information from the card reader to the input spooler or from the output spooler to the line printer while the system was allowed to perform other operations.

Two goals were accomplished by this approach. One, since the disk was so much faster than the unit-record equipment, program throughput and computer efficiency improved substantially. Two, by removing the unit-record function from the application program and replacing it with spooling, a major step toward multiprocessing was made.

Within a year after the concept was introduced, the industry advanced from spooling to true multiprocessing. By 1969, IBM offered fixed-partition multiprocessing to its 360/OS shops. This enabled the IBM 360/OS user to run as many programs concurrently within this system as there were partitions configured and available. Later that same year, IBM announced variable-partitioning multiprocessing (MVP), and the age of multiprocessing had arrived. Other computer companies offered advanced operating systems functions, but IBM, without a doubt, had taken the lead in the commercial marketplace. Independently of IBM, packages such as POWER appeared on the IBM 360 market. POWER offered spooling to DOS users who had not advanced to the OS stage. A later release of the same product offered dual processing through fixed partitioning. Since DOS was even more widely used as an operating system than OS, the POWER package had a great impact on the IBM community.

The Birth of On-Line Processing

By 1970, most of the ingredients required to support a true on-line operation were available. Terminals, random-access storage and retrieval, multiprocessing, and communications software were available. But above all, users were anxiously waiting.

On-line processing, like batch processing, evolved in stages. Bell Telephone, one of many progressive companies involved in on-line, was using video terminals on its shop floor in several Western Electric manufacturing operations, so that production people could inquire about the status of production orders and inventory levels. Information was not yet updated through these units. Updating was still being done through scheduled batch job streams. But the production controller was closer to his information than ever before. And for the first time, he didn't have to rely on anyone else for it.

In conjunction with the development of on-line processing, new methods for real-time transaction processing and data capture were also being employed. Although information was still processed in batch, for example, through remote job entry (RJE) terminals, data could be collected from remote locations on a real-time basis. Companies such as Western Electric used these units as shop-floor data collection stations. Since they were independent from the main processor, they were always ready to transmit shop floor production information back to a central receiving station. From there, the information was processed in a late-afternoon or early-evening batch stream.

It may seem unusual that a company already using video terminals in an on-line manner would not opt for on-line updating, but the rationale is simple: it's much easier to progress one step at a time than to achieve everything at once. Implementing the display of on-line information is relatively risk-free. If the program functions, the information appears; if the program does not function, no information appears and there is no harm to the data. This is not the case in an update environment. Once an update program is executed, information is altered and the original content is gone forever. IBM used to refer to this in its computer training programs as a "destructive write." The phase describes the consequence aptly, especially if the update fails.

So it's not surprising that during the early stages of on-line processing, the method was restricted to inquiry and updating was reserved for batch.

Emergence of the Mini

While on-line processing was developing for larger mainframe users, the minicomputer quietly arrived on the scene. Minicomputers first appeared in the scientific market as instructional, lab analysts' and process-control equipment. Basically, they were single-unit systems supporting relatively slow peripheral devices.

Unlike the mainframe market, the minicomputer market evolved in a "piecemeal" fashion. One company manufactured computers, another manufactured printers, others manufactured video terminals, cassette units, card readers, paper-tape readers, and, eventually, disk units. Because of this fragmentation, products were generally produced by a third party called the original equipment manufacturer (OEM). OEMs capitalized on specialized systems in vertical markets. Some OEMs specialized in legal systems, others in medical systems. Telephone systems, process control monitors, multiplexers, data concentrators, and dozens of other specialized systems emerged from this technology and OEMs. Companies such as Basic Four and Quantel developed systems resembling vendor systems, and competed against other vendor systems, when they were no more than an assembly OEM.

The approach was unique: no mainframe company had ever attempted to enter the computer market in such a fashion. Companies such as Digital Equipment, Data General, Diablo, Data Products, Hazeltine, and Honeywell became multimillion-dollar firms practically overnight. Most of these minicomputer companies were run by technicians with little or no background in business.

At this point, the minicomputer industry was riding on the tail of a comet. Some fell off and were left behind with no hope of catching up. Others barely held on. The growth rate was astounding. Facilities were occupied and put to use as fast as they were completed. One top official hiring 200 technicians in 1975 was forced to hire another 200 just to retain a sufficient level of support.

What causes a situation like this? Inexpensive technology. Reliability is an important factor. But because users could get computer power at a fraction of the cost of larger mainframe systems, the mini became an inviting alternative.

IBM saw the potential of the medium-size business-computer market early in the game and answered it with the IBM System 3. This system, though highly successful, was only a token gesture to the computer market and offered no innovative technology. It was a brilliant repackaging of obsolete technology, which drove the small-computer industry back to the unit-record days. Ironically, most of its success was linked to the simplicity of the system.

However, as minicomputers advanced through the 1970s, they increasingly threatened IBM's base of System 3s. Most of the minicomputer systems were on-line-oriented. The card reader was replaced by the video terminal. Early cassettes were replaced by medium- to large-scale disks. Output had been upgraded to support a multitude of different printers.

By 1975, most major minicomputer companies were offering their own peripherals. Companies such as DEC, Data General, Varian Associates, Hewlett-Packard, and others decided to expand from their OEM base and directly enter the end-user market. Their single-task operating systems had been replaced by sophisticated on-line multitask operating systems. Their file management system offered data base management as an optional replacement. The systems supported all the necessary elements to compete on a one-to-one basis against small to medium-size mainframes.

As the 1970s progressed, the law of diminishing returns became gospel in the mainframe industry and economies of scale became a buzzword for minicomputers. Companies that were on the treadmill of batch processing and the financial drain of uneconomical centralized systems slowly recognized the inherent cost-savings benefits of redistributing the processing load into multiple on-line minicomputer systems.

By 1975, when mainframe users were paying $1,000 a month or more for on-line and data base capabilities, similar capabilities were available as part of the standard operating software on several large-scale minis. Initially, this may appear incongruous, but a closer look shows why that's not so. Minicomputer vendors are out to sell systems. In order to sell systems, they must supply impressive credentials. What would be more impressive than offering the same capabilities found on a large mainframe?

The minicomputer vendor has no interest in attempting a one-to-one replacement of any mainframe system, so he doesn't have to consider the factors required in such a move. His only interest is attracting business by supplying software features comparable to those of mainframe systems.

By 1982, signs of the demise of the mainframe era began appearing more frequently. The strongest report came from *Business Week* magazine, which referred to the industry as: "Moving Away from Mainframes" (February 15, 1982). The article simply confirmed what many insiders had been saying for years—the mainframe business was dying. Of course, *Business Week* put it a little more diplomatically, claiming the industry was merely "maturing." Nevertheless, as the article graphically pointed out, mainframe sales are expected to plunge from a high point of 83 percent of the market in 1975 to an estimated 36 percent share in 1985.

Many analysts support this opinion, envisioning a vibrant minicomputer world of the future, dominated by IBM but strong enough to support dozens of smaller competitors. Indeed, companies such as Digital Equipment, Data General, Hewlett-Packard, Tandem Computers, and Wang Laboratories have made major inroads into the minicomputer market. The growth of minis will relegate mainframes to roles of electronic librarians that will manage mammoth centralized data banks. Market growth for mainframes is expected to slow, and competition will heat up for whatever remains of the mainframe business.

Of the major mainframe manufacturers, only IBM foresaw the unfolding trend toward minicomputer and microcomputer technology and took an aggressive stance in the changing computer market. Other mainframe manufacturers were left scrambling in the sales competition derby. As a result, many competitors are being forced to narrow their sales focus to specific computer arenas. Others are teaming up with small companies to offer competing lines. Many are retooling at considerable financial loss to compete effectively in a distributed-processing world.

Many observers believe that not all of IBM's traditional competitors in the mainframe business will survive in the long run. Some may have to merge with other companies or may be acquired, perhaps even by Japanese competitors trying to establish a market position in the United States.

How will the major combatants fare in this distributed-processing war of the minis? This is how the fight shapes up for non-IBM producers in the eyes of *many experts*:

Sperry Corporation. Of all the major mainframe producers, Sperry Corporation entered the "maturing" computer market in the most vulnerable position. More than half of the company's revenues stemmed directly from mainframe sales, so that Sperry was forced to spread quickly into new areas. The company is focusing on three new markets—office automation, personal computers, and software services—with the aim of changing into a full-line information-handling company. There are also plans for a product that will turn a standard terminal linked to one of Sperry-Univac's mainframe systems into an essentially personal computer.

The restructuring has forced the company to overlook some areas, such as defense work, and sell off some of its interests. Nevertheless, Sperry officials claim their moves will set the company on an "aggressive path toward the future.

Honeywell, Inc. For 25 years, Honeywell struggled to establish itself in the mainframe market. When it finally did in 1980, the market began to fall apart. Fortunately, the company began developing minicomputers in the mid-1970s, and by the time the mainframe market began slipping, minicomputer sales accounted for 30 percent of Honeywell's revenues. By 1985, Honeywell anticipates, 40 percent of its revenues will come from the mini market.

Honeywell's "compatible minis," designed to work with software that will also run on its large mainframe computers, have put the company in an advantageous market position. This compatibility factor—which allows existing systems to be expanded without risking software investments—is helping the company attract new customers.

But the diversification effort has hampered Honeywell in its ability to compete with IBM in the mainframe area. Honeywell's products, which have generally failed to match the power of IBM's lines, have cost the company sole-supplier status with some customers. Still, analysts believe Honeywell is following a prudent course by moving quickly into familiar territories.

Burroughs Corporation. This Detroit-based computer giant was the first to suffer the impact of the changing mainframe market. The company was plagued with manufacturing problems and unsatisfactory customer service, according to *Business Week.* At the same time, poor product planning caused the firm to lose a substantial share of its market position, and earnings subsequently plunged.

Burroughs officials, however, called the problems a blessing, because they forced the company to shift its production and planning gears long before any of its competitors. Today, the company is beginning to benefit from those early plans, mostly in the area of small computer and equipment lines. The firm is also producing plenty of equipment that can work in unison with its large mainframes. A number of acquisitions, ranging from processing companies in California to disk memory operations from Memorex Corp., have improved Burrough's competitive posture on several fronts. But despite its progress, Burroughs still has more than its share of management problems to contend with.

NCR Corporation. A relative latecomer to the mainframe crowd, NCR is still the third largest mainframe maker in the country and the leading producer of retail and financial terminal systems. But the company faces problems on two fronts: demand for its mainframes is dwindling, and there is increasing competition from IBM in the terminal business. Some analysts think the company is just plain confused over its role—computer maker or terminals company.

NCR is fighting what amounts to two wars at the same time, and many are wondering how long it will continue spinning in opposite directions. Already, some say NCR is spreading itself too thin, as evidenced by heavy financial losses in the late 1970s.

The company is very secretive about its future plans. However, it is known that NCR is branching out to sell small and medium-size computers to manufacturing, distribution, and health-care areas. In fact, *Business Week* reports these are now the company's strongest markets. Its most ambitious goal, however, is to achieve a dominant position as supplier of equipment and services for electronic funds transfer, a market that is growing rapidly. Accordingly, NCR has about doubled its manufacturing capacity for automated teller machines. Even so, most analysts say the firm faces a stiff uphill battle because of its broad-based production and marketing plans.

5

Getting Your Act Together

When data processing professionals talk about computer hardware and software, they often discuss these subjects as if they were unrelated. Actually, they are very close and extremely dependent on each other. Hardware determines what software can be used, and the efficiency of the software is linked directly to the hardware's capabilities. Therefore, it's important to keep this reciprocal relationship in mind when any computer evaluation is undertaken.

The two most common mistakes made by professionals when evaluating computer equipment are (1) selection of computer hardware solely on the basis of the software options available, and (2) inefficient use of equipment (forcing equipment to conform to programming languages and practices it wasn't designed to handle). These kinds of mistakes occur when too much consideration is given to the software and not enough attention is directed at determining what *real* capabilities exist within that black box containing the software.

Asking someone who is not familiar with the technology to perform a computer evaluation is like asking a jazz musician to evaluate a classical music manuscript. Why do so many assume that DP professionals with experience solely in mainframe processing are qualified to evaluate minicomputers for distributed processing? Unfortunately, this occurs more often than it should today. The result, as expected, reflects a slanted perspective favoring accepted procedures and techniques. Such evaluations often give no serious consideration to new techniques that could benefit the company and advance current processing levels.

The programming languages and programming techniques used on older machines worked well because the equipment was designed especially for that purpose. And without question, there's a large investment in programs that nobody looks forward to redeveloping. But, having decided to convert to a new system, is it smart to continue these old habits and not take advantage of the new technology? Burdening a new computer with programming languages and techniques it is not suited for can seriously hinder its performance.

Years ago, when the conversion from the 1400 series to the 360 occurred, Autocoder programs were run under emulation, simulating the new system on the old. As always, speed was critically important. The faster programs could be converted to run on the new system, the sooner the old computer could be released and production transferred. For the most part, unit-record-oriented batch systems were simply transferred to new equipment, with little regard for improved efficiency.

Systems were converted either by emulation or by reprogramming. At the time, computer vendors even encouraged emulation as a viable approach, in order to simplify conversion efforts. Many systems were converted in the same manner. This seemed to be a sensible approach then—logic and economics favored it. However, processing under emulation was sluggish and tedious, and the only effective solution for improving efficiency and performance of those programs was to redevelop them. However, companies which had just finished one conversion were not eager to undertake a second, so redevelopment dragged on forever. Even in the early 1970s, many companies were still laboring to rid themselves of the last vestiges of the 1400 conversion they had begun years before. Surprisingly, many companies that did choose to reprogram their systems took a very conservative position and advanced with caution into their third-generation equipment.

Consider the case of disk technology. The random-access methods that are so widely used and accepted today were slow to be accepted because many of these techniques required professionals to break "old habits." Old habits die slowly. So it was a long time before such computers as the IBM 360 were used as originally intended. Long after the transition from the 1400 to the 360, disks were still being used as alternative tape drives, and the sequential processing techniques of the second generation continued on into the next generation.

In many respects, the industry today faces problems similar to those confronted when the transition from the 1400 series to the 360 took place. The transition from "unit record" to "random access" thinking took a long time. So it's no surprise that the transition from "mainframe" thinking to "minicomputer" and "DDP" thinking hasn't occurred more rapidly. Sooner or later, though, it will happen.

Step 1: Defining the Objectives

Before advancing into distributed processing, it is necessary to define exactly what needs to be accomplished in a transition. Are equipment cost savings the only interest? Or are the long-term benefits of decentralized and distributed processing of paramount concern?

Either way, it's not difficult to achieve substantial cost savings in the process. Minicomputers are far less expensive than mainframes, and in many cases there is little difference between the processing capabilities of the two. Minicomputers are also cheaper to operate, and maintain. It's not unusual to find a mainframe with limited features replaced by a powerful large-scale minicomputer on a one-for-one basis. Besides offering substantial cost savings in a heavily loaded on-line environment, the minicomputer has an excellent chance of outperforming some of the older, classic mainframes. Of course, minicomputers were designed for on-line processing, and the mainframe was not. Though a considerable amount of software has been added to the mainframe to allow it to support on-line processing, it is essentially a "batch" machine.

For example, one medium-size East Coast corporation with an IBM 360/M40 computer supporting a 4-terminal on-line environment decided to convert all of its operations onto a large-scale minicomputer. In the process, not only were all operations upgraded, but at the end of the conversion, the system was actually expanded to a 20-terminal level. Even after the expansion, the company still experienced substantial cost savings compared to the original system.

Similar experiences have also occurred at companies that have pursued a multiple replacement approach. Citicorp, Bank America, Ford, Union Carbide, John Deere, the Brown Group, and other companies have all experienced tremendous savings by using minicomputer technology. One vice president at a large eastern bank was so impressed with this approach that, when asked at an American Management Associations seminar how his bank used minicomputers, he responded: "If one of our user departments has an application they want to have programmed, we give them a minicomputer and the programming support they need to get them on their feet." This attitude may seem a little startling and even a bit nearsighted, but compared to the traditional alternative of continuously adding new peripheral equipment to a single central mainframe computer, the DDP solution is cheaper and more effective. It also satisfies the user.

However, as with all new ventures, there is a degree of risk involved in the transition to distributed processing. Minicomputers are not mainframes and should not be treated like mainframes. Their architecture is quite different, so practices and techniques that worked well on the mainframe may not be right for the new computers. Think twice before repeating the mistakes of the transition from the IBM 1400 to the 360 series. These risks can be easily minimized or avoided by learning from the experiences of users and experts in this area. Today, there are more minicomputers in use than mainframes. So be wary of delegating implementation responsibilities to data processing technicians who are not versed in this technology. The tendency to perpetuate old habits is too great. Educate first, then the danger of misuse will be minimized and the benefits derived will be substantial.

Step 2: Refining the Objectives

When you're looking for effective ways to cut overhead costs without cutting back on valuable managerial services, distributed processing using minicomputers and microprocessors may well be the answer. With proper planning and implementation, the cost savings generated by minicomputers could have a dramatic impact on the bottom line.

However, equipment cost savings are only the tip of the iceberg in benefits. Plenty of additional benefits can be realized by going to DDP. Take service, for example. Cost savings programs rarely improve service, but in this instance, there's an excellent opportunity to do just that. Putting computer resources in the hands of users provides better control and improves accuracy and timeliness of the information processed.

Communications are another example. Many multinational corporations require their subsidiaries to submit financial information to headquarters on a regular basis. This information is then consolidated and reformatted into other reports to enable top management to review and analyze operations and determine their status. The information is necessary to allow the corporation to quickly respond to business changes. Without DDP techniques, this effort is a major headache, both for the people who prepare the information and those who consolidate it at headquarters. A well-organized DDP network could make the work practically trivial.

To appreciate what is needed to achieve the many benefits of distributed processing, consider the situation of a vice president in charge of data processing who is interested in developing a *fully integrated* DDP network within a large, multidivisional corporation. The first question confronting the official is where to start. It's not simply a matter of selecting one or two giant computers to centrally handle all the processing for the entire corporation. Nor is it even a case of devising a chain of identically configured computers, strategically located throughout the world, to handle the processing on a regional basis. What's needed is a vast network of versatile (yet conceivably different) computers, each selected separately to service local needs, but all working together in an *interactive, homogeneous* manner to service the needs of the entire corporation.

The terms "fully integrated," "interactive," and "homogeneous" all have tremendous implications in planning the network design. It's not enough to place minicomputers into the user departments without considering anything other than each department's needs. Such issues as compatibility of equipment and software, strength of local maintenance support, cross-departmental and cross-divisional access to data, and transportability of systems and programs must all be carefully studied and weighed so fundamental characteristics and requirements are not violated. Any potential problems that might jeopardize the network during this phase of its development should also be addressed and solved up front, before the project begins.

The most important consideration should be the obsolescence factor. Don't end up with an obsolete system tomorrow because it looks good today. Think and plan for the future. The same extensive forecasting and long-range planning used by corporations in other vital areas should apply to the data processing function. Regular planning and forecasting will provide the best possible insurance against obsolescence.

Step 3: Stating the Objectives

Let's consider the following objectives for establishing a DDP network:

Objective 1: Document and analyze various business procedures practiced throughout the corporation and identify those that should be standardized.

Objective 2: Get top management's commitment to a policy of corporatewide standardization.

Objective 3: Establish an integrated set of systems and programs to support the processing of these basic common business functions within each area of the corporation.

Objective 4: Place these standard application systems and programs, and all future programs, into a network library, so they will be readily accessible to all operating units within the corporation.

Objective 5: Develop a strong corporate function for planning, coordinating, monitoring, and controlling the development of the network. This also applies to the application systems within the network library.

Objective 6: Depending on the size and complexity of the network, retain a technical staff that is highly proficient and knowledgeable in computer hardware, software, and commercial applications. The sole function of this staff should be to provide the in-house expertise needed to handle the computer-selection and systems-support problems that must be faced during the development phase and life span of the network.

Objective 7: Finally, develop a long-range corporate EDP plan that is compatible with the company's long-range business plan and that provides the necessary direction and guidelines to adequately service the organization and advance the network.

The overall objective is to improve communication of information throughout the organization. The work involved may seem tremendous, but establishing these objectives provides a solid foundation for the network. "Network" implies structure and homogeneity, so the central theme here is standardization. Today, nobody supports the philosophy of reinventing the wheel. So why allow it to be promoted internally within an organization? Differences can be handled, but the basic framework should remain the same. Companies should seek maximum compatibility, and a new computer system using a DDP approach offers the best opportunity for achieving that goal.

An effective way to accomplish standardization is through a thorough systems study that identifies the best practices as well as all the poor ones throughout the company. Next, a network library consisting of the best systems and programs should be created. All divisions will benefit from this, and corporate performance levels will rise. A related benefit is the high level of compatibility of standardized systems, which will give the company plenty of room and flexibility to grow.

All too often, reported information reflects past conditions and is not pertinent to current trends or circumstances. The ultimate goal, of course, is to reach a position where information is readily available and current. In the past, only the largest corporations could afford the necessary tools to achieve such a position. However, technology has opened opportunities in this field to nearly everyone.

Establishing new programs to support standardized systems for a network is not as difficult as it appears. The development effort provides corporations with the opportunity to take advantage of the latest and best techniques in the EDP industry. For example, the concept of modularity has had a dramatic effect on the minicomputer industry. Not only does modularity make sense, it also simplifies the development and maintenance efforts, creating a potential average savings of 30 percent in development and 50 percent in maintenance time compared to conventional EDP techniques. Also, with more emphasis being placed on the development and availability of good application software packages, new users can consider reducing their redevelopment efforts. However, developing a network library will generate immediate benefits when the second system is installed. After the first system is in place, subsequent systems can be installed as quickly as operators can be trained to use them.

For large organizations it may be more practical to have programming support staffs at a local level. However, it is senseless for these staffs to develop the same application software when each could be performing an essential development activity for the corporation. Their completed work can then be provided to other network members. Sharing resources makes the network approach very desirable. It is an excellent method for controlling the high expense associated with software development. Another advantage of a standardized network is that there are always resources in reserve. For example, if an essential member of a division's EDP staff is absent, there will be a backup team of trained professionals throughout the organization who can give temporary support until the situation returns to normal. This would not be possible if the systems were all developed independently, without regard to compatibility or functional design.

Finally, intracompany communications will benefit from this approach. If systems and supporting software are compatible throughout the network, then developing a communications link so that information can be readily transmitted between divisions will be relatively easy. In rare instances where a computer fails within a particular division, systems can be loaded downline to other network computers, which can run the application until the problem is solved.

Network development and the compatibility of application systems across departments and divisions should be the most important goal of the corporation. The success of the network, however, depends on the cooperation of everyone involved in the effort.

Step 4: Fulfilling the Objectives

Formulating rigorous systems development guidelines is as essential to the technical success of distributed processing as establishing standardized management practices and administrative procedures. Ultimately, one set of programs can be used thoughout the organization. It is crucial that the quality of the programs be monitored, and the most effective way of achieving this is through the software itself, as we will discuss shortly. This approach is far more practical than the conventional method of ordering programming staffs to strictly follow 200-page manuals on policies, procedures, and standards. Embedding desired features directly into the system's software greatly reduces the possibility of using improper practices. However, not all programming standards can be internally policed. Some standards will be violated; determined people can always violate standards. But enforcing the standards through systems software functions makes it more difficult for potential rule-breakers to succeed.

The Language Issue

One great obstacle to fulfilling the objective of systems compatibility is the language issue. Currently, there are very few universal packages on the market. Those that exist tend to be marketed by third-party organizations and not by the actual computer vendors. An example is the TOTAL data base management package, which functions on a wide range of computers. However, "standard" computer languages such as COBOL and FORTRAN, which might be expected to adhere to a universal standard, in fact don't. Almost no two computers have identical compiler versions. Computer manufacturers provide their own versions of COBOL and/or FORTRAN, and understandably, those versions are tailored to work best with the manufacturer's computer architecture. Ever hear of a COBOL compiler that didn't support packed decimal arithmetic? It does exist.

Faced with the problem of developing compatible application software for a DDP environment on multiple-vendor equipment, how can you avoid incompatibility? The issue is further complicated because there are *good* computer systems on the market that don't offer all compilers. Although COBOL is a commonly accepted language of the mainframes, it isn't necessarily common to all minis. There are even cases where the COBOL compilers on two computer models of the same manufacturer aren't compatible. This is rare, but it can happen. Remember, it is the *user's* responsibility, not the manufacturer's, to ensure the compatibility of his DDP network.

There are a number of ways to overcome the problem. Of course, one way is for a user to develop his own compiler. Some companies have done that, but it is impractical in that it requires developing a separate version of the language in "machine lingo" for each different type of computer in a DDP network. Another solution might be to define a strict set of programming standards and use a commonly accepted language, such as COBOL. This could work, but it would require all programs to be written in that language, and would limit hardware choice to those computers which support that particular language. This is often inefficient, to say the least.

The ideal solution, of course, would be to develop a universal language with a code that can be reduced to the most efficient language for each network computer. Under this setup, the user would have complete control over any corporate computer system, with minimal restrictions. With slight modifications, the code could be reduced to FORTRAN for Hewlett-Packard and Data General minicomputers; to COBOL on an IBM mainframe; and to BASIC on DEC and BASIC IV computers. All this could be done without a single modification to the original application program. Such a universal computer language is commonly called a *translator language*. Translator languages appeared on the computer scene over ten years ago as tools to augment the capabilities of other languages. Since then, they have been steadily gaining popularity. Because of the minicomputer's diversity, translator languages could eventually become an excellent means of bridging the gap and developing compatibility between minicomputer languages and systems. Until then, the best course is to build network systems that are not limited by the number of standard languages they support. Then select *one* as the language in which all application programs will be developed.

Selecting multilanguage systems allows flexibility to use packaged software. But in-house development should be restricted to one computer language to help enforce good programming standards. So, perform a thorough review of all languages to ensure the best selection for a particular environment. If COBOL is selected, remember that minicomputers are not decimal machines and should not be used as such. Therefore, be sure to perform numerical operations and retain numerical binary information in COMPUTATIONAL form. If the information is longer than ten digits, use COMPUTATIONAL-2. You will be amazed at the difference in performance between COMPUTATIONAL (or COMPUTATIONAL-2) and COMPUTATIONAL-3. Generally, it's a differences of 3 to 1.

The Data Base Issue

Another key to user-oriented systems is the ability to be on-line. In a multi-user environment, this means information within the computer must be stored in such a way that it is readily available to any authorized users. This is the basic function of data base management. And as the term implies, the purpose is to provide a tool that will allow users to *manage* this information.

Today, many computer systems offer little more than an ability to perform on-line data entry, because they do not have file-accessing capability to allow on-line updating. Other systems provide basic file processing capability, but rely heavily on the programmer to perform such vital functions as:

User security filtering.
Chain maintenance of detail files.
Data integration of shared files.
File control over the multi-user environment.
Transaction logging for data base recovery.
Buffer filtering of unauthorized information.
Overall file maintenance.

In a true data base environment, all these functions are handled by the data base management software. This simplifies the processing task and provides a more efficient and secure method of managing and accessing information within the system.

Efficiency is a big reason data base management systems are so popular today. Most mainframe computers and minicomputers offer an optional data base management package, but most of these packages have been developed by third-party software houses and are not directly integrated into the vendor's operating software.

IBM offers a package called IMS as add-on software to its 3300 and 4300 product lines. However, this package is not integrated into the operating system. Hewlett-Packard has taken the lead in this area by offering a data base management package (IMAGE) as standard software on its HP-3000 line of computers. The company also says it plans to integrate the package into the operating software. Hopefully, other manufacturers will follow suit, since data base processing is becoming the standard method of file management in the industry. Through data base processing, the advent of nonprogrammer-oriented query languages will soon follow.

The On-Line Issue

In considering the movement to DDP, another major issue is to define the kind and degree of on-line processing desired. In the mainframe environment, a function is considered on-line if it is supported by terminal-communications software packages like CICS or TOS. But in a minicomputer environment, almost everything qualifies as on-line, because the operating systems of most minicomputers directly support terminal communications. Anything dealing with communications between the computer and an input/output terminal is considered on-line in this new technology. What differs from computer line to computer line, or system to system, is the degree of flexibility and versatility of on-line processing.

Three general modes of on-line processing in the minicomputer and microprocessor technologies are (1) the *interrogative* method, (2) the *text-editor* method, and (3) the *transaction-processing* method.

Interrogative processing is the simplest way to perform on-line processing on a minicomputer. It involves devising a program that displays questions on the face of the terminal and waits until answers are entered before it responds. Interrogative on-line processing is common to all the minicomputers and microprocessor-based systems. Very little sophistication is required by the operating system to support this mode of communication. No intelligence is required on the part of the terminal device, and usually the transmission rates are quite low—30 to 120 characters per second. This form of on-line processing works very well in single-terminal environments and in computer modeling applications.

Text editors were devised as an alternative to data entry or text entry by card readers. They operate on video or hard-copy terminals. Most on-line text editors allow on-line udpating or modification of information entered into the system, as well as primary data or text entry. This processing method resembles mainframe packages like TOS and is very easy to learn and use. Like interrogative processing, text editors are offered on most minicomputers and microprocessors today. Their primary function is to assist in on-line programming development. Programmers, like users, can now sit at a terminal and directly enter their programs into the system without being delayed by routine operations or computer schedules. The result is, of course, improved turnaround time and substantial saving in development costs.

Transaction processing (TP), the last mode of on-line processing, is the one most familiar to mainframe users. With increased use of minicomputers and microprocessors, this mode is receiving more and more attention. Unlike the first two modes of on-line processing, it is supported only by the most sophisticated minis. It requires intelligent video terminals and is performed totally on a page-mode basis (that is, information is transmitted to the computer not one field or one line at a time but only after a full page has been entered).

Transaction processing is done through the guidance of transaction menus which appear as background information on the video screen.

Transaction processing is very much in demand today, and it has become a critical piece of software for managing and controlling large multiterminal environments. Surprisingly, although the large mainframe systems usually support transaction processing, they don't normally support the interrogative form of on-line processing—and they definitely won't support them on the same terminal. This lack of flexibility in on-line processing is not found in the minicomputers. Most minis now support all three modes of on-line processing discussed, and you can find other systems that are capable of doing the same. So in designing your new DDP network, make sure sufficient flexibility is built in to perform all three on-line functions.

Conclusion

When considering a network structure, you must do your homework before moving ahead. Before making any changes to current systems:

1. Make sure hardware, software, and design are all compatible. Networks must have a unified design in order to function properly. Lack of compatibility will make it virtually impossible to share resources in a network environment.
2. Perform hardware studies. This will be fully explained in Chapter 6.
3. Conduct software studies to find a software system that can adequately support the network. This procedure is detailed in Chapter 7.
4. Set high level of standards to uphold all the activities in the network. This will be discussed in Chapter 8.

6

Selecting the Right Computer

Advances in hardware technology have taken place at such an astonishing rate over the past ten years that it is hard to believe such a pace can be sustained much longer. Well, as the cliché goes: "You ain't seen nothin' yet!" It looks like we're at the frontier of another major wave in technology, which will evidence itself very shortly in a host of new products, more sophisticated and powerful than anything we've seen to date. And consistent with the trend, prices will become more and more attractive.

Where does it stop? Or perhaps more aptly, where do we stop in order to decide which product best serves our needs, knowing that three to six months down the line a cheaper and better one will be available? This undoubtedly poses a major problem, especially with new product announcements proliferating daily.

For example, when I talked with a minicomputer salesman recently, he informed me that a new product had just been announced that perfectly fit the requirements of a small subsidiary that we were about to computerize. But in the very next statement, he went on to say that if we could wait six months longer, a refined version of the same product would be available with twice the CPU speed and four times the memory capacity (at the same basic price, of course).

So there you are! Back in the same perplexing dilemma you started with. Where do you draw the line? It becomes painfully obvious that there is no clearcut answer to this problem. Usually, circumstances make the decision for you. In most cases you just can't wait another six months. A decision has to be made on the basis of what's available now, and how well it can do the job.

Although top management usually decides these issues, evaluation and recommendations are often up to others—users, the manager of data processing, or an outside consulting firm retained by top management. DP professionals and consultants can no longer afford to make recommendations on the basis of software features, as has been the practice in the past. Performance and cost-effectiveness must be given equal weight in the evaluation. The explosion in computer products, coupled with the diverse styles and types available, make this evaluation process more than just a simple comparison of software options.

Sometimes compromises are necessary. If a computer demonstrates excellent performance under benchmark, provides superb on-line capability, and offers the company considerable cost savings, perhaps there is justification in considering it even though it might not support all the features you're looking for. The fact is that the software performance of the system must be placed in perspective with the hardware on which it operates. There are some excellent systems that have been overlooked only because the individual responsible for the evaluation was biased by his own software interests. Trying to put a Cadillac engine into a Mercedes might not produce the best results. On the other hand, to disqualify the Mercedes because it could not meet Cadillac specifications is just as absurd. There are a lot of very good products available on the market. It's your responsibility not to sell them short.

There is no doubt that commercial data processors or DP consultants must become more knowledgeable about what makes those "black boxes" they're evaluating work. The growth of new technologies, with their spin-offs and steady flow of products, has placed new demands on the DP professional, forcing him to become more conscious of the underlying hardware architecture. This is evidenced by recent advertisements in *The Wall Street Journal*, where Big 8 accounting firms are openly recruiting candidates with such qualifications. There will always be those who say, "Hardware is hardware—it's all the same." But the members of this fraternity are diminishing in number.

IBM dominates the commercial computer market today. But who knows what the future will bring. Digital Equipment, Hewlett-Packard, and Wang Laboratories are all prime contenders. What is certain is that the world is becoming more technically astute. Whereas there were essentially a handful of companies marketing computers 15 years ago, there are dozens today. So the task of selecting the right one for you, from a standpoint of performance and cost, is not easy. If the selection is to be handled responsibly, an in-depth hardware evaluation is essential.

Previous Methods of Selection

Computer selections in the past were based primarily on the number of features each system supported, such as how many peripherals were available (tapes, card readers, disks, optical scanners) and what languages and functions the system supported (COBOL, RPG, DOS, OS, SORT/MERGE). Very little attention was given to hardware details, such as CPU speeds, memory speeds, data-path widths, the number of true hardware registers, the number of software-coded instructions, the channel speeds, the channel capacities, and so on. These kinds of questions were formerly left to the experts—that is, those smooth, intelligent-looking people who represented the computer manufacturer.

It's unfortunate that many companies that have already computerized still rely heavily on their computer vendor for advice, even though they employ a sizable staff of data processing experts who are responsible for keeping in-house operations afloat. This probably is rooted in the fact that, from a technical standpoint, it was the manufacturer's responsibility to make sure the computer ran successfully. Therefore, when peformance problems arose, the manufacturer, not the data processing staff, was responsible for resolving them.

This may appear to be a natural and logical division of functional responsibilities, but the result is that companies have put themselves totally at the mercy of the computer vendors. When problems in systems performance occur, who is held responsible for assessing the problem and determining the solution? Not someone from the company—an outsider, the vendor himself. Therefore, when recommendations call for an upgrade of the operation, perhaps in the form of more memory, or maybe even an upgrade to a more powerful model, who within the company can contest the recommendation? Certainly not the average data processor. His expertise is in application programming and computer operations. He is in the same uncomfortable position as management and must either go along with the recommendation the expert makes or live with the problem.

Obviously, management is not in a position to oppose the expert's recommendation. What does it know about computers? Therefore, who within the organization is going to protect the company's interest? Unfortunately, the answer is equally obvious: nobody! This can be bad for both the vendor and the user. No doubt many of these kinds of recommendations are well founded. But without being able to personally evaluate the problem, many corporate treasurers and presidents must be skeptical as they sign the approval for new computer equipment.

Today, it's irresponsible for management to continue to blindly place its trust in the recommendation of outside vendors, without retaining qualified in-house experts who can appraise the validity of these recommendations. In many cases, hundreds of thousands of dollars are at stake in the selection of suitable computers for corporate use. There is much to be saved if you are careful not to relinquish control of the technical evaluation process.

Companies can no longer afford the type of vendor–customer relationship that existed in the past and resulted in a loss of control over computer operations and (sometimes unnecessary) upgrades. These kinds of problems can be avoided, or at least minimized, by better planning. Many organizations could learn a great deal from companies like Eastman Kodak, which has made a policy of self-sufficiency in its data processing and computer operations. Kodak retains both hardware and software experts on staff. They diagnose and maintain most of the company's computer equipment themselves. They require each vendor to turn over a full set of schematics to enable them to understand the internals of the system and perform proper servicing of the equipment. Because of their high degree of knowledge and extreme expertise in the field, the likelihood of being taken advantage of by a vendor is extremely low.

If you elect not to take the Kodak route, a good rule of thumb to follow is never to make major hardware decisions on a "sole source" basis. Sole source only encourages escalating cost. No matter how good a rapport you have with your vendor, request competitive bids. This will protect you from making an expensive mistake and, on the other hand, reassure you that you've made the right decision. In either event, you control the situation, and the decision is really yours.

So the first question that comes up is: What do you really need to know in order to do a proper hardware evaluation? To answer this, let's review some of the more important aspects of computer systems.

A Simplified View of Computer Architecture

In Figure 10 you see a simplified structure of a typical computer. The system consists of a group of independent elements that are linked through a central control bus structure. The elements are a central processor, a set of memory modules, general input/output channels, and a bus system that allows communication between the various elements.

Although this is an extremely simplified structure, it does reveal the important components of any computer system. The heart of the system, of course, is the central processing unit (CPU), or central processor. This unit executes the various instructions that are dictated to it by the program residing in the memory unit.

Each instruction the computer is capable of executing is either designed into the CPU through circuitry or implemented through micro-coded firmware. Some systems have even incorporated a combination of both. Then again, systems such as the Varian V-76 (which became a Univac product) offered an interesting concept referred to as "writable control storage," whereby the user could create his own instructions and incorporate them into the basic systems instruction set.

A CPU is limited in storage capability, since it functions specifically for instruction execution. Its storage capabilities are restricted to the number of registers it possesses. By contrast, the memory unit has been designed specifically for the purpose of program and data storage during the execution cycle. Therefore, although the operating program actually resides in memory, a continuous transfer of information takes place between the central processor and memory in order for the programs to function.

This transfer is controlled through a counter retained within the CPU (referred to as the program counter) which identifies the location in memory of the next instruction to be transferred to the CPU for execution. As each instruction is transferred to the CPU, the program counter is updated to the location of the next instruction and the current instruction is executed. Execution takes place by

Figure 10. Schematic structure of a typical computer.

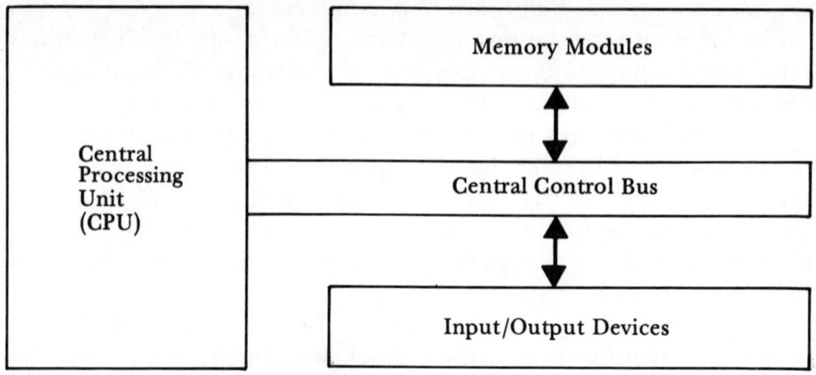

decoding the instruction and branching to that area of circuitry of firmware that is prepared to fulfill the processing task.

The strength of a CPU is in its instruction set, the speeds at which it can process its instructions, and the variety of instructions it can handle. The speed at which information can be transferred between memory and the CPU is an equally important factor. Together they decide the throughput capacity of the system.

However, memory and processing capabilities are only two of the three critical functions. The system must also be able to accept information from peripheral devices and transmit information to them. In modern systems, this means the computer must be able to interface with such units as video display terminals, line printers, and auxiliary storage devices. The more devices the system can support, the more powerful it is—and, generally, the more sophisticated its architecture becomes.

In more primitive systems, I/O is performed through the same central processing unit that controls the program operations. However, since I/O functions require higher-priority servicing, the CPU must stop normal processing in order to satisfy an I/O command. In single, dedicated systems that control sensors and switches, the demand on the CPU is relatively low. But in commercial data processing environments that support a large number of peripherals, the interruption is significant. Therefore, in most commercially oriented systems, interrupt servicing has been buffered by the development of intelligent peripheral controllers, which handle many of the I/O interrupt requirements of the various peripheral devices. In the more advanced systems, there is even a dedicated input/output processor whose sole function is to service all input/output operations, thereby totally freeing the actual processor of this function.

The HP 3000 Series III, illustrated in Figure 11, is a good example of this type of computer architecture. Observe that this system is a large-scale minicomputer and not a mainframe.

The basic unit can be purchased for under $100,000. It includes a dedicated input/output processor (IOP) to support a large peripheral on-line environment. It can expand to 2 million bytes of main memory. For auxiliary memory it can support up to 1 billion bytes of disk storage, either through the input/output processor or through a high-speed selector channel. It can also handle up to 14 additional device controllers for tape units, card readers, other disk devices, and line printers, and support up to 32 interactive terminals used in an on-line manner.

Compare this configuration, or that of the Prime 400 or the Wang, to average mainframe systems of the past and present. You'll be

Figure 11. The Hewlett-Packard HP 3000 Series III minicomputer.

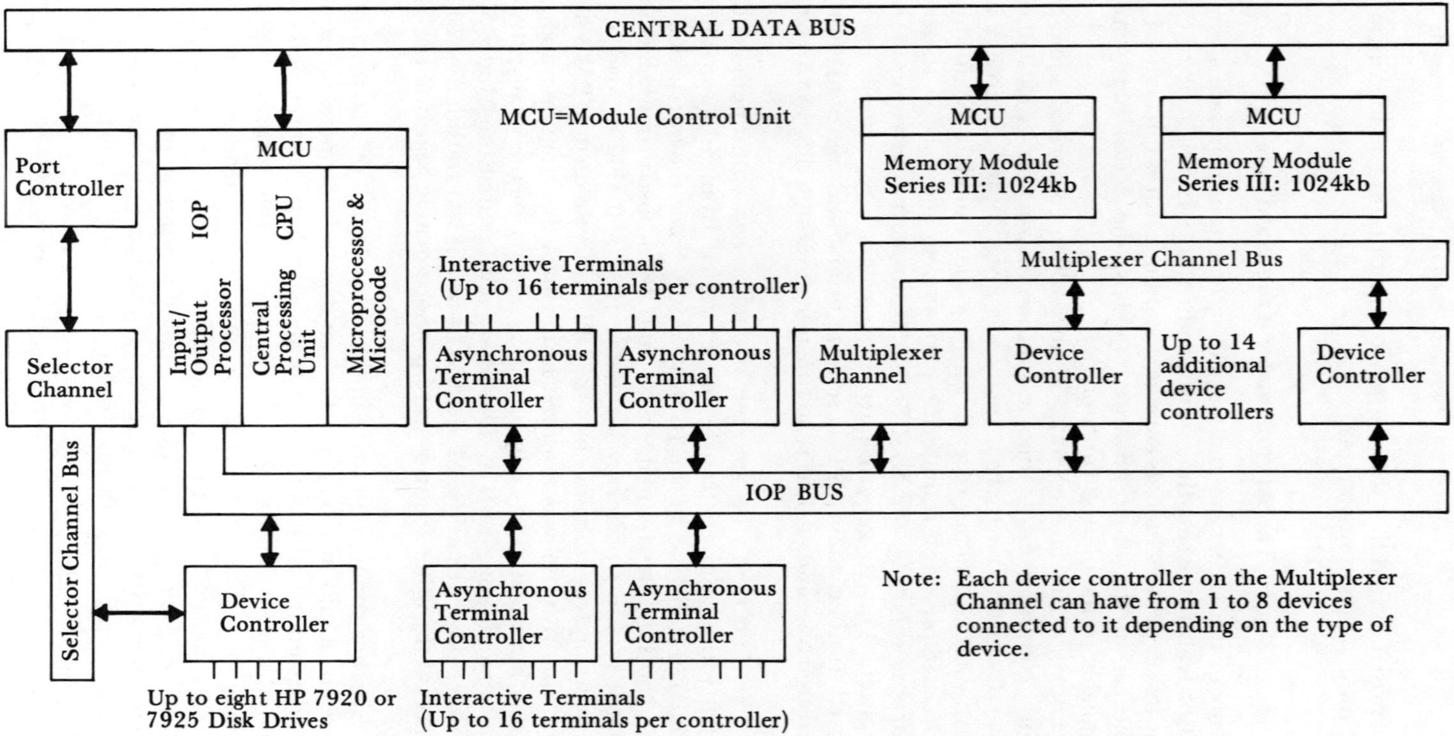

surprised to find that the cost/performance ratio falls heavily in favor of these mega-mini systems.

The Argument for True Hardware

Many of the earlier systems were designed to incorporate a common set of features across the entire product line. In this style of design, the less expensive models emulated system features through software, whereas in the more advanced models, the actual hardware was available to handle the function.

Looking back at the IBM 360 line, which comprised some of the finest computers of its time, a common instruction set existed in the overall design, but there actually was a significant difference in the hardware capabilities of each of the various models within the line. For example, even though the basic system allowed for 16 general-purpose registers, the IBM 360/M30 supported only one hardware register. The 16 general-purpose registers were actually memory-based (rather than CPU-based) registers and were manipulated through operating software to function as though they were hardware registers.

The data path (the amount of data passed from memory to the CPU within a given transfer cycle) varied from 8 bits in the IBM 360/M30 to 64 bits in the IBM 360/M65. Since the instruction set in the 360 supported 16-bit, 32-bit, and 48-bit instructions, this meant that it took 6 transfer cycles in the IBM 363/M30 to load a 48-bit instruction from memory into the CPU, whereas on the IBM 360/M65 only one transfer was required to perform the same operation, and after the transfer was completed, a portion of the next instruction was loaded along with it. This alone implies that the Model 30 ran 5 times slower than the Model 65. In fact, it was considerably slower, since all the other features were proportionately better on the Model 65.

Another common practice in the development of systems architectures in minicomputers was for vendors to implement infrequently used extended arithmetic instructions, such as triple-precision integer and double-precision floating point, through software-supported techniques. The early Data General Novas handled their 32-bit integer and 64-bit floating point arithmetic in just this manner, using 16-bit register. Today, floating-point arithmetic on the Apple II computers operates the same way. If you don't purchase the floating-point board, your floating-point arithmetic is performed not in hardware but in software.

You might say, "What does it matter, as long as it can do the job?" But doing the job in two seconds as opposed to two hours is quite significant. What matters is processing time. And in a multiprocessing environment in which there are between 20 and 30 users on the system at any given moment, hardware processing over software processing is the difference between acceptable response time and systems degradation.

Don't let anybody fool you. Hardware *is* important. And remember, you're the one who's paying the bill. So get your money's worth and make sure that you've got every feature that you negotiated for. Ascertain how many *real* hardware registers are available to you. Also, determine the scope of the instruction set, the size and type of arithmetic accumulators, the character-processing capabilities, the size of the data path, the speed of the data path, whether the system is error-correcting or just error-detecting. Ask a lot of "techy" questions. It's all in your best interest—and what's more, the vendor will respect you for it.

The Impact of Semiconductors on Computer Design

Prior to 1970, the standard method of building a computer was to integrate the instruction set into circuitry within the central processor and join a group of nonvolatile "core" memory modules to the computer through a high-speed data path. Today, core memory has been replaced by semiconductors, and hard-wired instruction circuitry has been replaced by high-speed semiconductors in the form of read-only memory (ROM) or programmable read-only memory (PROM). There are very few core-based systems still in existence. Semiconductor logic has almost totally replaced them.

The advantages of semiconductors are enormous. They operate in millivolts. They take up minimum space. They're faster in execution than their core predecessors. They are more reliable and last longer. Defective components are relatively easy to isolate, and they're inexpensive.

But because of the modularity, flexibility, and speed of these semiconductors, it became a matter of evolution to replace software-coded instructions with micro-coded read-only memories and use these memories as part of the instruction set. This technique first appeared on a major computer line back in the early 1970s when IBM announced its 370 series. The major shift in architecture between the IBM 360 line and the IBM 370 line was the incorporation of semiconductors in read-only memories (ROM) and the CPU, and the introduction of semiconductor random-access memory (RAM) as a replacement for core memory. ROMs, which were used as an extension of the instruction set, were programmed through a convention called micro-code. The micro-coded program or routine was actually burned into the semiconductor. Since the semiconductor was programmed and was not actually wired circuitry, the term *firmware* was developed.

Unfortunately, the term "firmware" is often used interchangeably with hardware when data processors get together and discuss machine instruction sets. But let's not confuse the two. Hard-wired circuitry will always outperform firmware in processing speed. However, firmware offers advantages in the areas of modularity and flexibility of design, and these advantages have overruled the processing advantages of hard-wired circuitry. Many of the newer systems support only firmware instruction sets. Other systems, like the Data General Eclipse, offer a combination of both hardware and firmware instructions.

Although many of the minicomputers (being binary-oriented machines) do not have packed-decimal and zoned-decimal arithmetic features incorporated directly into their hardware design, through firmware they can be adapted to operate in such environments. Also, as new versions of operating systems are developed, older firmware modules can be replaced by newer, more efficient ones without modification to the architecture of the system. This can be done simply by popping out the old firmware chip and replacing it with a new chip. Presto! You just upgraded your computer.

Architectural Considerations for On-line Systems

On-line systems are, in essence, multiprocessing environments designed to serve as many concurrent users as possible. Just as batch processing has its efficiencies of design, on-line processing has its own efficiencies of design. In modern systems, this on-line structure is carried right into the hardware architecture. In older systems, such features have not actually been incorporated into the hardware, but to support the functions, the vendors have incorporated them into the operating software as optional features.

Stack Management

One major on-line feature that has distinguished itself in recent years is the concept of stack management. In conventional computers, when programs are reduced to machine entry format, the data and the instruction code are intermixed into a single module, basically in the order in which they occur in the source program. In stack-oriented computers, the data and the instruction code are compiled into separate segments: a code segment and a data segment. By this technique the dynamic portion of the program, which represents the data areas, is separated from the static portion of the program, that is, the instruction code.

For single-user environments or batch operations, there is no advantage in using stack management. However, in multi-user environments where redundance should be held to a minimum, there is a tremendous advantage in using the stack management approach rather than the conventional approach. The principal reason is that it's more memory-efficient.

Assume, as in Figure 12, that you're supporting an on-line environment where three users are all performing the same operation concurrently, as would be the case in a typical order-entry situation. Using the conventional structure, three copies of the same program would have to be loaded into memory to allow the three users concurrent access. This would have to be done only because of the inability of the conventional structure to separate code from data, or, in other terms, to separate the static portion of the program from that portion which is unique to each user. In the stack-oriented structure, only one copy of the program needs to be loaded into the computer, while each of the three users is provided his own area in which to manage his data.

Consider what happens if you use each approach in multiprocessing environments where there are as many as 20 or 30 users on the system at any given time. Not only would the stack-oriented system be more memory-efficient, it would be more processing-efficient, since the computer would have less of a program-management task.

Another processing advantage of stack-oriented systems is that each segment in the "stack" is a reusable memory area. As the program executes from one segment to the next, the stack area is released as a data area for another program module.

Therefore, like semiconductors in memories, stack-oriented structures and stack management techniques are becoming more popular among computer vendors and data processors alike.

Virtual Memory vs. Real Memory

Another frequently used (and abused) term in systems architecture is that of *virtual memory*. Virtual-memory management is the concept of modularly breaking up a program into small component segments

Figure 12. Computer-memory usage in traditional vs. stack-oriented processing.

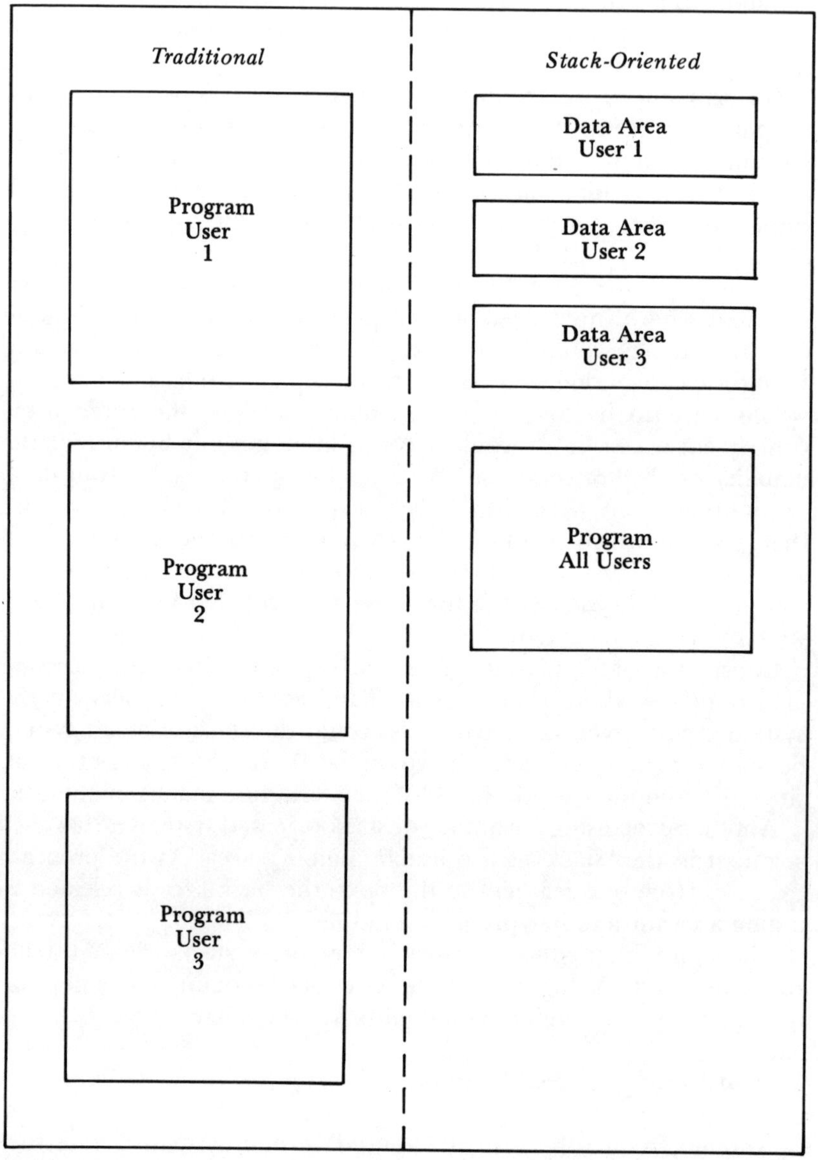

such that each segment individually can be executed in memory. Through this technique a very large program that doesn't fit within the available memory of the system can be segmented so that it can be executed in a limited memory space.

When somebody stresses the need for efficiency in programming, excuses are often made why it's not important. The two favorites are (1) memory is cheap and (2) if you run out of memory, virtual memory is available. Unfortunately, memory isn't cheap. Wasting memory adds processing time onto program execution. So, although you can always go out and buy more memory, eventually there will be a limit that you must cope with. Once that limit is reached, virtual memory will come to the rescue—but ever so slowly.

Realize that virtual-memory usage means real memory is not available. Therefore, in a multi-user environment where each user is given equal priority, program segments must be continuously swapped in and out of memory, in order to accommodate the user demands placed on the system.

In stack-oriented systems, only the data segments need to be swapped out. Program segments are static and undergo no change, so they only require swapping in. However, in conventional structures, the entire program module has to be swapped out when control is passed to another user, and swapped back in when control is returned.

Though the stack-oriented concept makes more efficient use of memory, neither approach works well in environments requiring extensive virtual-memory management. These environments are characterized by sluggishness, poor response time, and system overloads. The system virtually thrashes itself to death trying to keep up with the processing demands. Real memory is the key to peak systems performance.

Terminal Capabilities

Equipment and software required to support on-line environments have been available for well over a decade, and all major mainframe vendors offer them. Terms such as 3270 (IBM's most widely used video terminal) and CICS and TSO (IBM's most popularly licensed on-line communication software packages) are representative of an on-line mainframe environment.

However, minicomputers offer a less expensive and more versatile alternative. They were designed for on-line processing. Terminal communications is their natural mode of processing. In fact, some models don't even support a card reader. Also, the leading minicomputer manufacturers generally offer a wider range of communications equipment and communications software than their mainframe counterparts.

Most minicomputer systems offer a range of terminal processing capabilities, from unintelligent terminals that operate at speeds of 30 characters per second (300 baud) to very sophisticated terminals that operate at speeds of up to 960 characters per second (9,600 baud). Some of the more sophisticated terminals offer a variety of special display enhancements and can even handle multiple character sets, such as line-drawing sets, math-symbol sets, Greek and Scandinavian alphabets, and others.

The more intelligent units can support up to 16,000 bytes of memory, and operate on a page as well as line basis. They can scroll forward and backward through the memory line by line or page by page, to assist the user in recalling information. What's more, models are available that can perform synchronous as well as asynchronous communications. So you can see that there is a great variety of on-line capabilities in the minicomputer environment.

Then again, if you have kept abreast of current developments in the microcomputer markets, you probably are aware that local area networks (LANs), which are one of the most widely talked about concepts in industry today, are just another term for microcomputer-based terminal networks. In essence, they are intelligent terminals sharing common peripherals, such as a mass-storage disk or a medium-speed printer. This LAN concept, which is discussed further in Chapter 12, has not only stirred up a fever in the data processing community but also generated tremendous interest in all levels of management.

However, out of the three possible technologies, minicomputer terminal structures are at present the most cost-effective and usually offer an easier method of implementation. The trend is definitely in this direction, as evidenced by the 30 percent to 40 percent annual growth rates of such minicomputer companies as Digital Equipment, Wang Laboratories, Tandem, Prime, and Hewlett-Packard, and the declining sales of traditional mainframe companies over the same period of time.

Terminal Limitations

The most common on-line method is the "direct link" approach, in which video display terminals wired directly into the CPU reach out like the arms of an octopus into the various user departments of the organization. There are two limitations to this type of approach:

(1) no terminal can be more than 500 to 1,000 feet from the central processing unit and (2) the number of terminals the system can simultaneously support is restricted to the number of physical ports available in the processor itself.

The footage limitation is purely a physical limitation. After a designated number of feet, signal strength simply diminishes and noise interferes with the transmission. In configurations where direct wiring is essential but the distance between the processor and the terminal is greater than 1,000 feet, boosters can be placed at strategic locations along the line (say, every 500 feet) to strengthen the signal during transit. This will ensure that the transmission between the terminal and the computer is at satisfactory levels to retain data integrity.

The second limitation, the number of terminals that can be directly supported by the computer, is dictated by the architecture of the computer system itself. Most systems support their terminal configuration through terminal controllers. Terminal ports are directly configured into the controller. Some controllers can handle as many as 32 ports; others can handle only one or two ports. The number of ports is purely a function of design. But, as an example, in systems that are designed to handle 4 ports, this means that every time the capacity of the controller is reached, another controller is required to service the next group of terminals. Eventually, the incremental expansion of terminals will reach the system's limit.

The cost of terminals and controllers varies from system to system and model to model, but, in general, they are not expensive. However, if your experiences are anything like mine, it always happens that every time a new terminal is needed, the controller limit has been reached and another controller is required. This tends to double the cost of the order and from a budgeting standpoint becomes difficult to justify. In practice, it's better to amortize the cost of controllers within the system and justify only the terminal cost.

Intelligent vs. Unintelligent Terminals

Terminals communicate with the computer in one of two basic modes: asynchronously or synchronously. The mode that is used is usually determined by the type of features the terminal has available. Terminals with limited capabilities are frequently referred to as *dumb* terminals, whereas those that provide powerful processing capabilities are referred to as *smart* terminals. The more features the terminal has, the smarter it is and the more useful it becomes to the system as well as the user.

Dumb terminals offer very little processing capability. They have no memory to speak of and therefore have to operate on a character-by-character basis. With all terminals of this type, as each character is typed on the keyboard, it is immediately transmitted to the computer and held in the computer's terminal buffer until the entire message is transmitted. Generally, the computer in turn retransmits each character back to the terminal as it receives it, so it can be printed on the face of the terminal to verify the success or failure of each transmission. This is asynchronous processing.

Smart terminals tend to economize the transmission of information to the CPU by buffering it up in the terminal's memory before transferring it to the computer. Then, when the user has finished inputting the message, the terminal transmits the entire message in one operation. This is referred to as synchronous processing, and it is less taxing on the computer because it limits the number of interrupts that are required in order to transmit the message.

One of the original benefits of asynchronous terminals was that they were inexpensive. Though applications are demanding more sophisticated terminals, there still is a place for these devices in systems development. Many organizations can economize by using such terminals to perform programming and console-operations functions and reserving the intelligent terminals for the user environment. Since program development is handled on a line-by-line basis, there is no reason to devote a more sophisticated device to such tasks.

The Computer Selection Process

The days of making computer selections on the basis of elaborate programming languages and overhead-burdened system software are over. The name of the game today is performance and cost-effectiveness. Because of the recessionary climate in the late 1970s and early 1980s, cost is becoming increasingly important.

The excuse that minicomputers and microprocessors are still too limited in capacity to do the job won't hold up anymore. No matter what size job you have, there probably is a system on the market that can be configured to handle your needs—and handle them in a *cost-effective* way. So don't underestimate the capabilities of these new computers. Do a detailed comparative evaluation, like the one illustrated in Appendix A, and find out exactly what's available to you.

There are other fringe benefits to be gained from a comparative analysis, besides greater objectivity in your computer selection. The fact that you're making such a study will let the vendors know that

Table 2. Suggested form for computer hardware comparison.

Hardware Capability	*Computer 1*	*Computer 2*
1. *Main Storage (Memory)*		
Storage type, semiconductor		
Quoted capacity, bytes		
Incremental memory size, bytes		
Maximum capacity		
Speed of memory, nanoseconds (10^{-9} seconds)		
Bits reserved for error check and correction		
Error checking		
Error identification or logging		
Error correction		
Multiprocess hardware protection		
Battery backup		
Storage protection		
2. *Central Processing Unit*		
Type of system		
Firmware instruction capability		
No. of instructions in processor		
Data path, bits		
Instruction size, bits:		
stack instructions		
register—register instructions		
register—immediate instructions		
memory—register instructions		
memory—immediate instructions		
memory—memory instructions		
Instruction overlap capability		
Hardware registers		
no. of accumulators		
no. of index registers		
Add time, microseconds		
Hardware multiply/divide		
Hardware floating point		
Hardware byte manipulation		
Real-time clock		

Table 2. (Continued)

Hardware Capability	*Computer 1*	*Computer 2*
3. Input/Output Control		
Direct memory access channel (DMA)		
Maximum I/O rate, bytes/sec.		
No. of external interrupts		
No. of I/O ports		
Separate I/O processor (IOP)		
4. *Peripherals*		
Terminal display units		
alphanumeric keyboard		
10-key numeric keypad		
screen size, characters		
memory capability		
roll-up option		
asynchronous (character) capability		
page or screen capability		
character & page capability		
cursor addressability		
dual intensity		
synchronous terminal speed		
special features		
—inverse video		
—blinking		
—half-bright		
—line drawing		
—optional character sets		
special-function keys		
peripheral support (tape, printer)		
Low-speed printer terminal		
Disk storage		
capacity, megabytes		
seek time, milliseconds		
transfer rate		
overlap capability		
Tape storage		
within basic system		
transfer rate, bytes/inch		
density, inches/second		
Line printer, lines/minute		
Synchronous line printer		

Table 2. (Continued)

Hardware Capability	*Computer 1*	*Computer 2*
5. *Communications*		
Maximum number of lines		
Synchronous		
Asynchronous		
2780 emulator		

you are serious about understanding their products, and that any statements or promises made during the evaluation process will become part of the study and possibly placed in the hands of their competitors for comment. Therefore, vendors will be leary of making false statements, knowing that they will be committed to them at a later date. So, by taking this approach, you have an excellent chance of acquiring the kind of information you need in order to make a responsible decision.

The following areas are generally the most critical in the selection of the right computer to service your company's particular need:

The computer's hardware capabilities.
The computer's software features.
The amount and availability of *local* hardware and software support.
The ease of conversion from your present situation.
Ultimately, *cost*.

A good evaluation should address each of these vital issues, and gauge the strengths and weaknesses of each of the computer systems with respect to these issues. As in the sample report provided in Appendix A, the scope and primary objectives of the evaluation must be defined. If outside reports and research organizations were used in the preparation of the document, this should be stated. Each of the functional areas cited in the report should be analyzed in sufficient detail to allow a rating of each product in that area, and ultimately allow a total rating at the end of the report.

Table 2 is a suggested guideline for your hardware evaluation. It may seem a simple fill-in-the-blanks form, but the information you will acquire in the process of completing the form should prove valuable to you. Although no form can provide a fail-safe quantitative method for selecting your next system, it will at least let the vendor know that you mean business and that you are going to do as objective a study as you can in the quest for a suitable computer.

7

Evaluating Systems Software

The movement to distributed processing can be directly attributed to the widespread acceptance and versatility of the minicomputer. Minicomputer technology has had a tremendous impact on the entire computer industry since the early 1970s. It appeared first in the scientific community, then in the process control area, and subsequently matured to a competitive level in the commercial computer marketplace. Now it has taken the final step by plunging into the new distributed-processing market. This last move has taken a variety of forms, but the most effective was systems that were planned and implemented as homogeneous networks.

There are three primary reasons behind this wave in popularity of minicomputers and distributed processing:

- The low cost of minicomputers compared to the cost of their predecessors.
- The modularity of minicomputers and their ability to adapt well to dynamic changes in configuration of distributed computer networks.
- Versatile and reliable minicomputer operating and communications software (computer programs), which are unquestionably just as sophisticated as those found on mainframes.

Although price and flexibility have persuaded corporations to consider minicomputers in commercial data processing, it is the operating software's completeness and ease of use that should be actually credited to the sale.

Most minicomputers come complete will all the features a commercial data processor expects from his computer system. Features like input/output spooling, multiprogramming, multitasking, on-line transaction processing, virtual-memory management, high-level languages, word processing, and data base management are all offered on minis. Even more astonishing is that many of these features are available on the smaller-size minis, thereby permitting even the smallest members in the distributed-processing network to operate at the same level of sophistication as the largest.

Companies no longer need to retain highly qualified systems programmers to support their operating systems, file-management functions, and communications software supplied from minicomputer vendors. Of course, complex distributed-processing networks will require in-house expertise, but for straightforward networks, you just won't need to retain a large staff of experts. To the contrary, many minicomputer systems have been sold as total turnkey systems, requiring *no* supporting staff, since they were designed to perform specific application functions. They also require little or no on-site support after installation. With the advent of query language and program generators, it is feasible to build, monitor, and support distributed-processing networks in the same manner.

The Shift Toward User-Friendly Systems Software

A shift in attitude toward small support staffs is subtly taking place in the computer industry today. It is no longer fashionable for computer companies to develop systems software that is difficult for the average person to understand and even more difficult to use. The emphasis now is on the development of "friendly" software. Many operating systems today are very sophisticated on the inside, but externally they are models of simplicity. The user simply signs on to the system and works. While he may feel the system is dedicated solely to his use, in reality it is probably executing a variety of tasks simultaneously. Without his knowledge or awareness, the operating software allocates sufficient memory for programs, prepares the data and code segments for memory allocations, establishes the processing priority, and schedules input/output service. It initiates spooling, monitors the time slice during execution, and above all ensures maximum utilization of CPU and input/output resources through the careful supervision of system and program interrupts. This is all done without the need for tedious JCL (job control language) or the continuous intervention of a console operator.

The emphasis is on what is being done, not how it is being done. Most distributed on-line systems function in this way and require little or no console-operator intervention. Actually, many of the systems don't even require a console operator. The end users are the operators, and it makes sense that they should have control over their own operations.

Word processing, for example, requires no systems programmers. There are no systems analysts, application programmers, or computer-console operators. The need does not justify this kind of support. Electronic mail, which is a distributed-processing enhancement of word processing, can be implemented and supported in the same way.

Today, many systems are installed and managed in this manner. Systems are placed into office environments like just another piece of office equipment. Video terminals, keyboard pointers, and computer-driven typewriters are distributed throughout the organization, to improve turnaround time and increase performance while handing control back to those who need it.

The Packaged Solution

End users are now looking at their computer systems as a "packaged solution" to specific problems, not as glorified general-purpose machines that can be programmed to do a number of grand things. This attitude is by no means unique. Businesses in general are leaning toward packaged solutions as an answer to the spiraling costs and time-consuming nature of systems development.

Corporations are cost- and results-oriented—they have to be to survive. They don't want to "reinvent the wheel" or undertake costly development projects if packaged solutions are readily available for purchase. This is especially true in the systems software development area. Companies are not interested in supporting expensive systems software development projects that could result in nonstandard (or, even worse, nonsupported) processing software.

Every organization likes to demonstrate "pride of authorship," but this is the riskiest area to do it in. To begin with, the vendor could easily modify his operating software and render a user's *unique* software inoperative. And if it is not vendor-supported, the vendor has no responsibility to ensure this won't happen. It has happened before to companies that have opted for that route, and they have been left in the unfortunate position of not being able to take advantage of enhanced versions of operating software. In some instances, companies were even pressured into accepting new operating software in order to retain their maintenance contract, even though it meant abandoning their own. So where is the benefit?

Another serious problem with individual software development is that the vendor could someday develop a similar product. So what happens? Does a user continue to use his system or conform to the vendor's version? In any event, this is an embarrassing position for a firm to be in. So, in essence, systems software development is a "no-win" situation and should be left to the vendor or a reputable systems house. A vendor can guarantee its continued performance, and will alleviate the need for users to assume that responsibility.

Choosing Software for Distributed-Processing Networks

So far, little has been said about choosing minicomputer software specifically to support distributed-processing networks. How does a user select the right software for his network, to ensure compatibility and homogeneity?

The best way is to establish suitable criteria for qualifying each vendor as a candidate for entrance into the distributed-processing network. The following capabilities should definitely be included as standard prerequisites:

Systems modularity.
Systems expandability.
Multiterminal communications support.
On-line transaction-processing (TP) support.
Multiprogramming.
Data base management (or the functional equivalent).
Industry-standard languages.
Intercomputer communications.

Intercomputer communications are essential if proper networking is to be supported. They mean the difference between a decentralized system and a true distributed network. All other features in the list are necessary for individual computer systems to adequately handle interactive on-line processing.

Though it seems like a straightforward list, a simple review using these criteria would show that many systems currently do not qualify as acceptable candidates for distributed processing. They lack modularity, cannot handle on-line processing, are not expandable, process in a batch manner, do not support data base management, or simply have no facilities to perform interprocessor communications.

One problem stems from the term "data base," which is becoming very popular within the industry and is frequently used out of context. Vendors and data processors often use the term data base when they are actually referring to conventional file management techniques. Therefore, be careful to find out what type of DBMS is actually on the system.

Another problem is determining the extent of the interprocessor communications offered on the various computer systems Most systems these days support 2780/3780 emulation. But that alone is not sufficient to service the telecommunication needs of a vital information systems network. Limited provisions exist in 3780 to do on-line, interactive interprocessor communications. More powerful communications features are required within the network to allow information to be dynamically retrieved or updated. This communication function is essential in distributed processing.

Network Communications Software

Companies like Digital Equipment and Hewlett-Packard, through DECNET and DS/3000, respectively, have led the way in supplying network communications software in anticipation of this new distributed-processing market. DECNET and DS/3000 have met the need for strong, reliable interprocessor communications software. These packages go well beyond the limitations of 2780/3780 emulation and provide true interactive processing capability. Again, this has been done in a manner which is virtually invisible to the user. The user simply signs on to his local system and identifies which computer in the network he wishes to communicate with. Likewise, programs can be written to perform the same basic function. For example, a user could sign on to a system in Cincinnati and execute a program residing on a system in Dallas. The Dallas system is programmed to access marketing information from systems in New York, California, and Europe, and manufacturing information from systems in Chicago and Cleveland, to determine the demand and production on a particular part. The result is displayed on-line in Cincinnati.

Though this example is exaggerated, the processing route is totally possible. To fulfill this task:

1. The user signs on to any of the remote systems in the normal manner.
2. He indicates through a simple identification code the system on which the program he wishes to execute is resident.
3. The program itself specifies the systems in which the marketing and manufacturing information is located.

The simplicity of communications software makes the transition from stand-alone to distributed processing so easy. In the case of the

DS/3000 package, users can sign on to their own local system or any other system in the network through a simple system qualification technique. They can execute programs residing on their own computer or on other computers in the network, as well as access local or remote data bases for information. Hewlett-Packard uses this very DS/3000 package to support its own worldwide sales network in over 130 localities. You know that if these packages have been operating under field conditions of this magnitude, they must be reasonably reliable; otherwise the vendor would have used an alternative method.

Remote Diagnostic Support

A final area that is attracting industry attention is *remote* field-service support. When problems occur within a user's system and it can't be determined whether they involve the hardware or the software, a field-service engineer phones up the system from a remote diagnostic center and uses a series of tests to identify the problem. To allow these tests to take place, special features are incorporated into the hardware and the operating software of these systems. Today, only a handful of systems on the market have this capability, but most systems will provide it in the future.

Remote testing has tremendous advantages over conventional field-service maintenance. For one thing, it's faster to get to a customer site by phone than by car. For another, by providing diagnostic testing from remote field-service centers, better diagnostic equipment can be made available to the customer and a more exhaustive testing procedure can be used. This method of software maintenance has had such a strong influence on software houses supplying application packages that most are offering comparable remote diagnostic services to help customers isolate problems. As a result, customers can be back on-line in a fraction of the time that was necessary with earlier methods.

In an on-line environment, time is critical. Problems have to be diagnosed and solved quickly, so that faith and confidence in the system are maintained. Distributed processing localizes problems and shelters remote members in the network from problems, but each of the local nodes needs adequate support. On-site field service is far too time-consuming and inefficient. Waiting for a systems engineer to appear on the site means costly and unnecessary downtime. In the future, demand for more efficient service will necessitate the standardization of remote field maintenance.

Summary

It should be quite clear that minicomputer systems software for distributed processing is not nearly as complicated to use and support as the operating software of previous generations. This is due partly to improvements in hardware design and integrated circuiting, and partly to a more thorough understanding of the technology we are working with. Earlier stages in product design are always more primitive and complicated than later stages, and the computer industry is no exception. Systems software design has matured immensely since the mid-1960s, when such ideas as multitasking and on-line processing were first conceived. Everyone has gained from mistakes, and many of the hardware features incorporated into recent systems were added to resolve the difficulties of earlier systems.

Although systems software has reached a high level of sophistication to meet the needs of distributed processing, advances in hardware technology and software design have added much to the operational reliability and simplicity of systems. And now, with the advent of remote diagnostic capabilities, systems can be adequately supported, even in the most remote areas of the country.

8

Setting Standards for the Network

The data processing department is often accused of building an empire within the organization. The fact that businesses invest a substantial portion of their budget annually into computer resources tends to foster this sense of mistrust and apprehension. Whether such feelings are warranted is sometimes difficult to determine.

Computers and data processing are often regarded by laymen as a "black box." Their internal workings remain somewhat of a mystery. Although management has developed an appreciation of the computer's ability to provide useful information, it does not understand the technical details or even principles of the process. Typically, the selection of computer hardware, operating systems, data base structures, and other aspects of the computer has been left to the discretion of the data processor. In many cases, this has resulted in the organization's limited ability to share valuable resources.

All organizational units tend to want to function autonomously, and data processing is no exception. Although many of the data processing functions within the various subsidiary organizations serve the same purpose, there usually is a "pride of authorship" that makes each operation distinctive. From one division to another, financial statements, production reports, payroll vouchers, and payroll registers, all of which are common processing functions, often are generated through different hardware, operating systems, computer languages, and programming techniques. This, of course, is the result of autonomous management in the absence of a corporate network structure.

Without corporate control mechanisms or standard guidelines, divisional data processing people are encouraged to act in their own interests, whether or not those interests are beneficial to the division or the organization as a whole. Divisional data processing organizations can easily fall prey to the dreaded "empire building" disease. It is not difficult to justify the need for more and more resources in order to meet the pressures of developmental and operational responsibilities. But statements like "We operate differently from other divisions," or "We've got a more sophisticated operation here," are not only dangerous to an organization, they're very costly.

Divisional organizations that have allowed this to happen have locked themselves in and are at the mercy of their own folly. When people leave, who will understand how to run the operation? And, be assured, people will leave. In situations like this I've witnessed companies practically being blackmailed, and paying the blackmail, just to keep their operation afloat. Considering the dynamic nature of most data processing environments and the substantial resources needed to sustain them, a certain degree of apprehension toward data processing uniqueness is indeed healthy and perhaps warranted.

From a corporate standpoint, it's irresponsible to allow this trend to continue. Incompatibilities in hardware and redundant development of software should never have been allowed to begin with. The corporation wouldn't encourage the squandering of its other assets. Then why does it encourage the squandering of its information resources?

How Not To Do It—A Case Study

A particularly notable example of a poorly planned transition to distributed processing involved a large New York City bank (which will not be identified). During the 1970s, this highly revered financial institution chose to become a pioneer in the development of distributed processing. The bank allowed each of its internal operating departments to select and install its own minicomputer system. The justification behind this approach seemed simple enough: it was far cheaper to install minicomputers in each major operating department than to place expensive add-on equipment to an already overloaded central computer. Why practice the rule of diminishing returns? It would only impose additional burdens on the system.

Without question, the minicomputer route was the most cost-effective as well as the most practical answer. Bank officials expected drastically improved responsiveness of data processing, accessibility of the computer, and control over information resources by the user.

Long waits for information would disappear. In the early stages, bank officials, from the vice president of data processing on down, thought it was a great idea. Articles appeared periodically, in every data processing magazine and journal in the United States, on the bank's progress. Because of all the favorable publicity, many hardware vendors felt compelled to donate beta testing systems to the bank, in the hope of receiving sizable future orders. Through the use of these beta test systems as well as through more conventional purchases, the bank weaved its way into the era of distributed processing.

At the beginning of the project, applications that handled local departmental needs were the only ones considered for distributed processing. The larger applications still remained on the main processor. But even with such constraining conditions, there were many applications that qualified. Soon, each department lined up for its own computer. Systems analysts and programmers from the bank's data processing department were assigned the task of working with the department head of each requesting department. A preliminary study was performed to determine the processing requirements and storage needs of the new computer. The actual computer selection was left to the discretion of the department head and the assigned systems analyst. Unfortunately, both officials had little or no prior experience in minicomputers or computer selection. The department head was interested in quickly getting his system operational, while the systems analyst was experienced only in mainframe computers.

Regardless of these minor stumbling blocks, the direction was quite clear, and the movement was on. Each departmental request became a project, and each project was handled autonomously. Decisions were made only with regard to the department's needs. Systems analysts and programmers who were assigned to the support functions were familar only with the requirements of the department for which they were working.

Under these circumstances, it is understandable that programmers working in different departments ended up developing similar if not identical systems. Unfortunately, even if they were aware that they were doing similar programming projects, by that stage the two departmental systems may have been incompatible. One project group was programming in RPG while another chose BASIC, FORTRAN, or even COBOL as its programming language. COBOL (the most widely used commercial programming language of the mainframe computer) was quite new at that time, and few minicomputer manufacturers supported the COBOL language during the mid-1970s. Therefore, not only were projects developed in a language that was not common to the programmers within the programming department, but they were developed in several languages, many of which were not standard to a traditional data processing department.

With so many different kinds of computer systems, in operation, it must have been a nightmare to differentiate machine problems from program problems. Also, under such conditions, the programmers may well have been only a step or so ahead of the actual department users when it came to knowledge of and familiarity with the system. Both were learning about the system at the same time. And with so many different manufacturers on hand, the first year of operation must have been like attending a perpetual international computer conference.

Of course, management's objectives in this case were really quite admirable. Surely, bank management felt that by sampling all the available systems, it would gain valuable knowledge and experience. Unfortunately, in many instances this can be accomplished only through a benchmark test. According to the promises and opinions of vendors, each system is able to do the job. And each system is marketed on its unique strengths. So if there is no one knowledgeable in an organization to separate truth from fiction, the only true test is to place the system in an environment where it must perform, and then weigh the results. This obviously was the strategy the bank employed. However, the departments didn't consider themselves test sites, and the resulting pressures and problems they faced far outweighed the benefits.

Another major problem was unrealistic implementation schedules. It is difficult enough to coordinate development and implementation of a new application system, but to compound this task by bringing unfamiliar hardware into the picture will have a tremendous impact on the implementation schedule. It's not unusual to underestimate the time and effort required to install a new computer system. Top managers normally realize this and emphasize the kind of difficulties that can develop in setting firm time schedules for a new computer installation. Trying to rush a new installation is sheer disaster. Adding new hardware, no matter what the size or capability, entails total retraining. Of course, this can be minimized when purchasing a canned package and dedicating the system exclusively to its use, as in a word processing application. But if the system is for general use, time must be budgeted for operational training, systems training, programmer training, user training, and a raft of other tasks.

Besides offering a new operating environment, some minicomputer systems offer multiple operating systems as a part of their optional repertoire of processing capabilities. Therefore, even more time should be reserved in order to properly evaluate which of the various operating systems is best suited for individual needs. This is a complex job, and responsibility for it belongs to a specialist within the organization.

An inspection of the bank's immense data processing facilities would have shown that the DP department was organized to provide better service than it did in the transition to distributed processing. Presumably the department included a systems and programming staff responsible for designing, programming, and maintaining various application functions; and it certainly included a systems programming staff responsible for understanding the architecture and operating software of systems and giving internal support to either the operations staff or systems and programming staff. Though there is little need to provide an operations staff for the departmental minicomputer systems (the department employees themselves will assume this function), there is no excuse for not supplying systems programming services. It's possible that data processing management considered the minicomputer systems less sophisticated or less important than the bank's large mainframe systems and therefore assumed that they didn't warrant systems programming support (or at least not at the level of the central mainframe unit). But even if this were true, the responsibility usually absorbed by the systems programmers should not have been left in the hands of programmers who were unfamiliar dealing with such functions. This mistake surely placed too much responsibility at too low a level in the organization.

In sum, the bank exercised too little control over the whole conversion effort. Just about every vendor was allowed to benchmark his systems on the premises. Besides occasional failures, there were vendor software and application program bugs, design inefficiencies, programming oversights, and a raft of other conditions normal in any new system. Multiply each of these problems by the number of vendors that were represented within the pool, and you can imagine the extent of the problems. If there was unexpected staff turnover, who was left to deal with that particular vendor line? If no one was available, then a new delegate had to be retrained. Retraining is time-consuming and may even prompt additional staff turnover. Even after participating in the training program, a new individual may not be comfortable with the system and ask to be removed from the project assignment.

Even for those units offering the same language, the variations between the compilers made uniformity difficult. So the bank was left with the perplexing problem of nonstandardization. Therefore, what was really being accomplished by this approach? If a system did not function to vendor specification, there was little chance of preserving or salvaging any of the programming effort and transferring it onto another system, because the different systems were so incompatible. Since many of the systems used the same computer language, there was at least a small possibility that the programs could be converted (with some changes) to another minicomputer. But was this the way to set up a reliable distributed-processing operation?

In retrospect, there is no way that this approach could have worked. It would only have created frustrated users, demoralized programmers, continuously broken deadlines, and, in the last refrain, a noncompatible clog of equipment and programs, which could not qualify as a distributed-processing network. Therefore, considering all the adverse effects of this approach, it might have been better had the bank selected the centralized add-on approach.

Establishing Strong Systems Standards

Standards are the heart of a well-planned distributed-processing system. They are more than just guidelines for systems development. They are critical in the development and control of the corporations most valuable data processing asset—its information systems. It should be the organization's goal to achieve as high a level of standardization within data processing as is practical.

In establishing information networks, corporations cannot succumb to divisional partialities; they are simply too expensive. Standard systems must be set up to handle standard divisional operating needs. Standard applications such as accounts payable, accounts receivable, general ledger, and payroll should all be processed through standard systems. Having unique accounts-payable or general-ledger systems for each division does not make good computer sense.

By implementing standard systems, the organization can develop a library of common application programs that are accessible to and sharable with any division within the corporation. This network library can provide a strong incentive for divisions to join into a networking structure. By simply adhering to certain application practices, divisional users can have fully tested systems available to them without redevelopment or major modification. Significant savings can be realized by eliminating or at least minimizing the development and implementation time. On the average, software development and implementation represent 30 percent to 40 percent of the cost of a new system. Network systems will drastically lower these costs.

So as the costs of software maintenance and new development continue to soar, this network approach could provide management with an excellent method for increasing data processing productivity and improving operations while keeping costs to a minimum.

But the library is only one of the sharable resources through which savings can be achieved. A far greater advantage to the divisional user is in the possibility of sharing and exchanging personnel and equipment resources. Since the network is built around compatible equipment, why shouldn't personnel and equipment be made available, just as the library is? It should, and in many networked organizations today, it is. It works like a pyramiding scheme. As more equipment enters the network and more divisional staffs become familiar with the network system, the availability of shareable equipment and trained personnel increases. This can only strengthen the organization as the network expands.

Also, personnel from divisions that are part of the network and familiar with the network systems can assist other divisions that are in a start-up phase in training, support, and systems implementation. This is an easy and effective way to provide an adequate level of support in the early stages of implementation, when it is needed most. At the same time, it gives divisional people an opportunity to participate in corporate projects, which can greatly enhance internal communications and the relationships between corporate headquarters and the divisions.

Another consideration that weighs heavily in favor of the network approach is the migratory nature of professional programmers. This is a problem with which data processing managers have had to cope for years. Each time a new programmer is hired, three to six months of training usually is invested before the individual is familiar enough with the operation to make any kind of contribution. The propensity of programmers to migrate from one organization to another poses a real problem to management and often makes it impossible to find an immediate replacement. Many companies retain large DP staffs just to be sure they're not caught short. This is not only an expensive practice, it's also unproductive.

In a distributed-processing network, the organization is clearly not as susceptible to this problem. The ability of divisions to share programming personnel alleviates the worry that the operation could be left unattended. There is no need to overhire in order to assure adequate support. The sharing of personnel is without a doubt one of the most valuable benefits of a network structure. What a powerful tool this could be for the corporation that thrives on mergers, acquisitions, and new divisional start-ups. Controlled expansion is significantly eased by the availability of systems, equipment, and personnel.

The Manager of Distributed-Processing Systems

One answer to standardization problems that is becoming more and more noticeable in large corporations across the country and throughout the world is the emergence of a new individual on the data processing scene, called a Distributed-Processing Systems Manager. In some organizations, his role has been absorbed by the corporate management information systems (MIS) group. In other organizations, he has been placed on a par with the manager of systems and programming and the manager of operations (see Figure 13).

His responsibility is to act as an overseer of the distributed-processing function. It is through this office that such issues as computer selection, hardware interfacing, communications interfacing, programming-language selection, systems design, systems modification requests, data base design, and data base modification are decided.

Figure 13. Typical organizational position of the manager of distributed-processing systems.

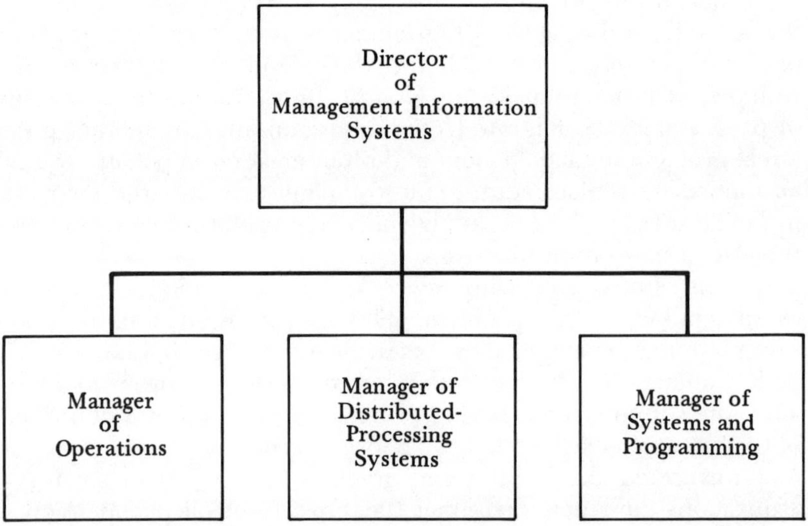

The new distributed computer systems represent a sizeable investment to the organization, not only in terms of capital expenditures but also in terms of the greater effectiveness and efficiency of the organization as a whole. Local support to the operating unit is only one facet of the benefits derived through unification. Improved communications between departments, divisions, and corporate bodies, and resource sharing of equipment, application programs, and even staffs are the greater benefits to be achieved. But they can only be achieved through a homogeneous structure, and many companies are at last ensuring that homogeneity by establishing a strong distributed-processing department headed by a manager of distributed-processing systems.

Exploring Common Needs: The Role of the Steering Committee

The purpose of a distributed-processing network is to provide a reasonable degree of commonality without preventing users from meeting their unique needs.

The first step in the development and design of a network structure is to explore and identify commonality. The most effective vehicle to accomplish this is a *steering committee*. Establishing a good steering committee is a critical undertaking.

In the past, systems design and development took place in a piecemeal fashion. A systems analyst would be the primary agent responsible for development. Typically, he or she would interview end-users of the system individually, determine their specific needs, and go back to "the shop" to hammer out a solution. This approach was laden with pitfalls. First, the needs of the end-users were identified only initially; little or no interaction took place until the system was near completion. Far too often, what the end-user requested and what was eventually provided turned out to be completely different. The user wound up adapting to the system rather than the system to the user. Second, because users were interviewed separately and in isolation, common needs and applications were often overlooked.

In light of these problems, the need for a more global approach to systems development becomes evident. It's important to capture commonalities and standardize policies and procedures where possible. A steering committee that is truly representative of the organization should be established. This committee must be user-oriented and ensure continued input from the users throughout the whole development process, not merely at the start. Each functional area affected by the system should be represented on the committee. In particular, data processing management must make sure that it acts as a single representative and does not dominate the committee.

Standards for On-Line Systems

One of the major functions of the committee is to set standards for applications systems. Applications systems within most distributed-processing networks fall into two major categories: on-line and batch.

On-line functions, as we discussed, are those applications which allow the user to communicate interactively with the computer systems through video terminals (CRTs). Looking up the accounts-receivable balance of a particular customer's account by entering the customer's name or account number is a typical example of this type of processing. Batch functions are those applications which process groups of information at one time before advancing to another operation. Payroll is a good example of a batch operation. Obviously, it is more efficient to prepare payroll checks for all employees at one time than to prepare the checks individually upon demand. Many summary reports are also handled in a batch manner.

Organizations must set standards for both types of applications. First, let's look at some of the features required for effective development of on-line systems in a distributed-processing network. One essential area for which standards must be set is systems software.

Generally, the system software in an on-line environment should not only support communications between video terminals and the computer but also provide a rigorous systems development framework that unifies the programming of all on-line application systems. In effect, the development of a strong on-line structure establishes the design standard for all present and future on-line application programs. This is a major step toward the ultimate goal of integrating all application systems in the network.

On-Line Monitors

Certain universal concepts and standards must be upheld if on-line application systems in a network are to be compatible regardless of hardware. A "monitor" function analogous to a package like CICS, Environment I, or VIEW/3000 is extremely helpful in achieving these objectives. The features underlying a good monitor should not be constrained to any particular piece of equipment or computer system but should be applicable to any computer system the network elects to use.

Most computers today offer monitor capability. All computers support basic program languages such as ASSEMBLER, FORTRAN, and COBOL (though not adhering to a particular standard). Most computers can handle multiprocessing, though in different ways, and all computers handle an on-line video-terminal environment, again each in its own way. So the necessary functions and features to support an on-line environment are available and common throughout the industry. However, there is little compatibility or standardization among different manufacturers' product lines. It's up to the organization to build such universal compatibility or standards into the network. An on-line monitor provides a good base for that effort. The monitor should handle the following functions:

Transaction screen maintenance.
System security.
Data base security.
Terminal communications.
Detailed transaction editing.
Error identification and message display.
Internal data conversion.
Application-programs initiation.
On-line multiprocessing.

Monitors have been developed in various manners. One approach has been the development of a set of on-line functional modules that can be called to execution by any of the on-line application programs. A more sophisticated approach, represented in Figure 14, incorporates the essential on-line program as a central controller, with the application programs handled by the monitor. In this approach, the monitor could easily be viewed as a direct extension of the operating system. In the eyes of the user, all requests and directives are handled by the monitor, and the monitor is the user's only exposure to the operating system. The monitor consists of:

A terminal communications and dispatcher function.
A security function.
An applications editor function.
An applications driver function.

The essential tasks of each of these important elements are discussed below.

Figure 14. Modular structure of an on-line monitor.

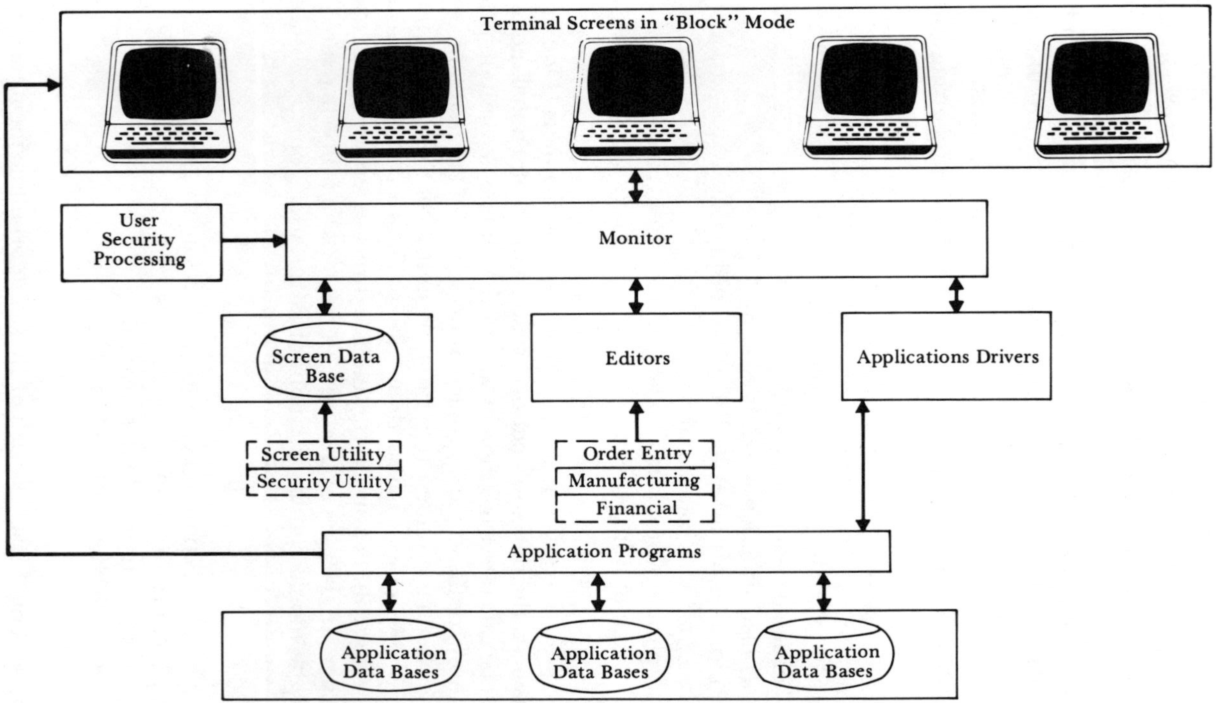

Terminal communications and dispatcher functions. In our sample on-line environment, the terminal communications and dispatcher function is the control module linking all other programs, such as the editors, applications drivers, and applications programs, as subroutines. The terminal-communications portion of the monitor acts as the principal interface between the video terminal environment and the on-line application programs. All communications are handled on a block transmission basis through the use of transaction screens, retained in the screen data base library. One of the purposes of transaction screens and block transmission is to minimize the number of interrupts to the central processor. Asynchronous (that is, character-by-character) transmission often degrades the system, causing unnecessary response delay and reduced throughput.

Accompanying this software should be a *forms utility program,* which allows the programmer to maintain screens within the screen data base, and a *security control program* to control access to the application data bases.

The dispatcher function directs the execution of the various system editors and, upon satisfactory verification, initiates the processing of the particular on-line applications program requesting servicing. These two functions together control the interactions between the user and the application-programs library. They should require no special reconfiguring to support terminal environments of different sizes or types.

Security function. A user security function should exist that ensures that all terminal users are authorized users within the system. Each user is provided password protection and has suitable internal identification specifying the allowed level of access to the on-line data bases. This module interrogates the user's authority before allowing entrance into the on-line environment. After entering the system, the user should still be restricted to perform only those functions that are within his level of security. The accounts-receivable clerk, for example, is allowed access into the on-line environment only to post cash receipts, but not to make inquiries into payroll, unless specifically authorized.

Applications editor function. An applications-editing module within the on-line monitor is made available to allow editing of all on-line transactions. Incorporating this function into the monitor eliminates the need for the programmer to perform extensive transaction editing and field conversion within each of the application programs. This has two advantages: it shortens program development time, and it reduces program size.

Each transaction screen within the screen data base is accompanied by a list of the detailed edits performed on each of the associated input fields within the transaction. If an edit fails, a callable error message routine is issued to indicate the type of error and field in error. Upon satisfactory editing, a conversion routine is invoked to convert the information entered into internal format, thereby allowing the application program to receive the information in the form it needs in order to process it properly.

Applications driver function. The third module of the illustrated monitor is the applications program driver. In effect, this module becomes the directory of currently active application programs. The applications driver acts as the direct interface between the dispatcher and the application programs. It keeps track not only of which application programs are available but which have been added or deleted.

A unique driver exists for each major on-line system. The linkage to these routines, much as in the case of systems editors, is the screen transaction number. All applications drivers conform to a common format. They are small, yet control all on-line application functions.

By incorporating an approach such as an on-line monitor, you can completely eliminate the need for application programs to perform the terminal-communications processing, multitask processing, data base opening, front-end editing, and internal data conversion. From a design standpoint, the programmer still has to define screen layouts and edit requirements. However, this is done through monitor utility routines rather than through creation of new application programs. As a result, program design is reduced to two general functions of on-line processing: *maintenance* and *inquiry*. This simplifies programming and ensures not only modularity of programs but also the operating efficiency of the program modules.

This approach further ensures that no application programs are allowed to be suspended in memory, awaiting a user response. User-response functions are handled only by the monitor, which is small compared with the application modules and therefore more memory-efficient. Each time an application module is requested for service, it must run to completion and then immediately return control to the monitor for subsequent processing.

Design of On-line Inquiry Functions

The strength of an on-line system lies in its ability to retrieve existing data from the data bases and display critical information for the user upon demand. Therefore, it is extremely important that those responsible for the design of on-line functions be sensitive to the needs of the user and provide sufficient inquiry capabilities to allow the user to perform daily job functions.

Program functions designed for on-line displays involve single-pass, single-page processing. A background screen is set up to correspond with the inquiry request, while the responses are received through the entry areas designated in the screen's format. With this technique, the application program need only synchronize to the format of the input information. For display functions requiring several pages of display, the monitor provides a facility to allow the programmer to temporarily store information from the display program into a "common" communications area that can be used in subsequent executions of the module to identify what was accomplished in previous executions.

Design of On-Line Update or Maintenance Functions

As a supplement to the data inquiry function, most systems require the ability to alter or update information residing in the application data base. This can be accomplished through three basic types of procedures: (1) record add, (2) record update, and (3) record delete. Program functions for these three procedures are normally required for all major data sets (files) within the data base. A unique screen is usually devised for performing each of these functions—for example, customer add, customer update, and customer delete. As in on-line inquiry, each program module is designed in such a way that it can be executed in one linear pass, with no suspension for user intervention.

If it becomes necessary to maintain interactive communications with the user during processing, a "common" communications area is made available between the monitor and the application program. This has the advantage that the program need not be kept in memory over the entire duration of the interactive process, which frees memory for other on-line tasks.

Features are also available to provide the programmer with the ability to use additional screens in order to chain related functional processing steps together for ease of user entry. At least one screen should be associated with each of the three maintenance procedures. However, additional screens could be used, at the discretion of the programmer, in order to guide the user through a complicated record add or update process. An example of this is the processing of order entry, where a main screen might be devised for the entry of order information, and additional screens could be devised to capture the individual line-item information.

Each of these screens should be directly associated with a unique application program. For modularity, common application functions should be designed to perform those functions that are common to one or more of the unique programs. This will optimize development and localize program maintenance to a single module.

Standards for Batch-Processing Systems

Though batch operations assume a secondary role in an on-line environment, they still have a very meaningful function in the processing of reports and multiple record operations. The design of batch functions is not as rigorous as that of on-line functions. In the batch environment, efficiency is served best through serial processing. The more the operation is tailored to processing in a sequential manner, the faster it will be executed.

As in the on-line environment, functions should be designed modularly. Each module should represent one program function. It is better to break up a program into several distinct and homogeneous routines than to make it one large self-contained unit. This technique will optimize memory management at execution time.

One major difference between on-line processing and batch processing is that "sequential" as well as data base files can be used in the design of the systems. Sequential files can be used as *temporary* files or *historical* files. Temporary files should be used for sorting and reporting purposes, while historical files should be used for long-term retention of data. For historical files that are long and are used only for weekly or monthly processing, application systems should be designed to allow the files to reside off-line during noncritical processing periods.

The Batch Monitor Concept

To gain further efficiency and control of the batch operations it is worthwhile to consider designing them to be executed through a central monitor routine. In the future, batch operations associated with major application systems will use such a batch monitor to allow the on-line users to schedule their own reports and other batch results. The essential functions that batch monitors serve are to:

- Allow the user to directly request batch operations from the system.

- Provide a program that centrally controls all related batch operations.
- Control the access to data base information and temporary files used by the batch operations.
- Prioritize and order the processing of scheduled batch functions.

To use the batch monitor technique, a request file must be established which acts as the principal interface between the user and the monitor. Each request is placed sequentially into this file by the user. The file is then read by the batch monitor to determine the processing requests desired for the evening. Upon completion of a request, that request is deleted from the request queue. For those functions that have to be performed every night, the batch monitor should be designed to automatically invoke those tasks and not require that they be included in the request queue.

Establishing Programming Standards

To ensure that the network library doesn't turn out to be just an organized refuse tank, certain guidelines must be established to which all programs must conform. Many applications perform similar processing functions, so it is only logical to take advantage of common coding techniques. Strong programming standards will facilitate a "component" or "software factory" approach to program development. Common data definitions and standard record descriptions are a must. Source statement libraries and copy functions should also be heavily used to ensure that each program written has a reuse value.

Allowing programmers to become exotic or unique in their programming practices only results in weaker systems. Insist on a standard approach. Then, as more and more programs are developed, you will have a stock of reusable and versatile programs that make future systems development much more efficient and economical.

Some Reasons for the Low Productivity of Programmers

Most programming assignments involve the maintenance of existing applications. New systems are developed once. But from the time they are developed, a never-ending maintenance cycle begins. This is confirmed by current studies which have revealed that the average productivity ratio of an application programmer in industry today is in the range of 10–15 lines of program code per day. These statistics unquestionably demonstrate that professional programmers spend the majority of their time performing maintenance functions on existing systems rather than developing new programs.

But even at that, this ratio is appalling. One reason for it is that structured programming and modular coding techniques, which are in vogue now, were not practiced in the development of the older systems. The result is that the logic of the older programs is very hard to follow. Unfortunately, many of these programs are still in production.

It's not unusual for a programmer to spend hours reviewing a poorly coded program before he dares to take corrective action. And he can't be faulted for the time he takes. He's only acting responsibly. The blame should fall on those who placed the program in production even though it didn't adhere to suitable programming standards. Far too often the prevailing policy is "If it works, put it into production." This could be one of the major factors for such a low productivity rate.

Another contributing factor could be the way work is assigned in data processing departments. In many data processing organizations, due to the differences between application systems, programmers tend to be dedicated to particular applications, such as payroll, manufacturing, general ledger, or order entry. The reason for such assignments is usually that one programmer in the organization is more proficient than another in the language in which the original system was programmed—ASSEMBLER, RPG, COBOL, FORTRAN, or whatever. Or it could be that certain programmers are more knowledgeable in on-line processing, while others are more familiar with batch-oriented systems. No matter what the reason, this leads to increasingly narrow specializations and unfair distribution of responsibilities across the data processing department.

Here again, the user doesn't understand the problem. In those situations where his request is not properly serviced, if he were to walk down to the DP department, he might be shocked to find that the programmer assigned to service his request is backlogged in work while three other programmers are reading magazines or drinking coffee. This kind of inequitable distribution of data processing resources is a direct result of nonstandardized systems. For if the systems followed a common design and programs adhered to a strict standard, this kind of workload distribution would be unnecessary.

Finally, a major reason for the low productivity rate of programmers is lack of proper documentation. Every programmer knows how to document a program, but somehow it never gets done. Or the documentation is so old that it can't be trusted. The reason behind this problem is simple: the programming load is usually so high that as each program is completed and placed into production, the pressure to get the next program working is much higher than that of documenting the recently completed one. And, of course, as time goes on, the original programmer doesn't even remember exactly how the program worked. So when the time comes for program maintenance, we are back in the pressure cooker of getting it fixed and back into production. Had the documentation been available, perhaps hours of effort could have been avoided.

Programming for the Sake of Programming

Why is it that many professional programmers have such a hard time understanding the concept of simplicity? Every program needn't be an epic. "Bigger is better" hasn't worked in the auto industry. People aren't impressed by size anymore. They're impressed by efficiency. Hopefully this trend will take hold in the computer industry as well.

Some of you will recall the clever programming techniques that were used to overcome the many limitations of the IBM 1400 era. Simplicity had to be the byword during this era. There was no room for anything else. But the mere fact that systems aren't 16K anymore is no reason to abandon these kinds of practices. No matter how large the systems are today, efficient programming results in faster processing. People like Edward Yourdon have made a career out of teaching professional programmers this concept and instructing them in efficient modular techniques.

So why do programmers have the tendency to complicate matters? Complicated programs don't even run well. They require continuous maintenance. And, above all, they're almost impossible to understand. This kind of programming is awkward enough in batch systems; in on-line systems it's disastrous. So let's get back to basics.

No doubt there is a tremendous feeling of self-gratification on the part of the programmer every time a new program is completed. But let's not forget that the purpose of data processing is to serve the needs of the organization, not vice versa. The technical aspects of the job must be kept in perspective and not be allowed to outweigh the importance of getting the job done.

The fact is that almost all application systems consist of a combination of five basic program types: (1) edit programs, (2) posting programs, (3) maintenance programs, (4) sort programs, and (5) report programs. This is well understood by most software firms and evidenced by the myriad generic software products that are appearing on the market every year. Procedure languages, program generators, system generators, and boiler-plate application packages are all based on the fact that systems are derived from the standard functions.

If this is the case, why do so many organizations want to reinvent the wheel every time a new program has to be developed? Isn't it time to take advantage of this fundamental fact? Even on-line systems, which are the heart of most distributed-processing networks, conform to these principles. Strip away the terminal-communications software and the sophisticated data base software, and you're left with the same fundamental functions: editing, posting, maintenance, sorting, and reporting. Although the maintenance function is often handled through the creation of new add, change, and delete prototype programs, it still performs the same function that it did in the batch environment.

Even the unique feature of on-line inquiry fits into this scheme. From a programming standpoint, its just another report program, except that the reporting is done on a video display screen rather than a hard-copy printer.

There is very little difference in the way these functional programs are used in either batch systems or on-line systems. However, there is, or should be, a significant difference in the way they are coded. Few people are concerned about how many milliseconds are consumed in processing a batch operation. But the same is not true for on-line processing. System responsiveness requires on-line programs that are time-efficient. And efficiency can best be served through a simple, straightforward processing technique. Therefore, because of the special response-time requirements, a separate set of program prototypes should be developed to model the batch and on-line environments, respectively.

Selecting a Common Programming Language

It may seem ludicrous to recommend that all systems be developed in one common programming language, especially when the majority of data processing organizations are COBOL-oriented. But if COBOL is not available on the computer selected, what then?

Regardless of circumstances, it's essential that one and only one programming language be used. Every technician will be conversant in it, but if other languages are introduced, immediately the possibility arises that not everybody will be proficient in all languages. As a result, responsibilities will have to be delegated on the basis of specialization, and isn't this what we are trying to avoid?

Selecting a single language will ensure compatibility throughout the development effort, and universality within a network structure. Remember, the organization's goal is to develop a library of applications programs that can be shared throughout the organization. Therefore, let's not create a mongrel before the project starts. The higher the degree of standardization, the more valuable the resource.

Since the language will provide the basis of the entire environment, do a careful analysis and take into consideration all aspects of processing before making the decision.

Although languages such as FORTRAN and BASIC have been selected in the past, these languages generally are not good choices for commercial applications. FORTRAN is extremely efficient in object-code generation, but it is not a structured language, and the manner in which it handles record descriptions is very awkward. Although BASIC offers more programming features than FORTRAN, it is not a self-documenting language and tends to be slow in execution.

COBOL and PL/I are excellent commercial languages. Unfortunately, they are slower in execution and are not offered on all computer systems. PASCAL, a relatively new language, has spurred a considerable amount of interest in the data processing community, but, again, it is not available on all systems.

After a careful evaluation, you should be able to find a suitable language. The important points are: (1) the language must be easy to code in; (2) it should be a structured language; (3) it should offer a reasonable degree of self-documentation; and (4) it should be efficient in code generation. If these conditions are met, then you're on your way.

Data Base—The Unifying Ingredient

From a programming point of view, data base management not only is useful in solving the problems of file integration and data security, it also provides an effective method for ensuring systemwide adherence to common input/output standards. Just by conforming to the standards of the data base system, the individual application programs assume a unified character.

The old practice of individual file management was too loose to provide adequate I/O standards in programming. Structured programming attempted to resolve some of the weaknesses by requiring that the programmer set up general file management routines that could be invoked by all sections of the program whenever I/O servicing was required. This modular approach has been extremely effective in conventional program development. However, the programmer must be willing to conform to the coding standards representative of this technique. There is nothing to *force* him to do it. If he does, great. If he doesn't, you end up with another badly coded program.

This is not to suggest that there haven't been badly coded data base programs. But due to the rigid file management standards required to satisfy the data base interface, they are far from the norm.

An equally impressive feature of data base is that it provides the programmer with global systems visibility. When the programmer codes in data base, he thinks in data base. He doesn't think in terms

Figure 15. Order-entry data base.

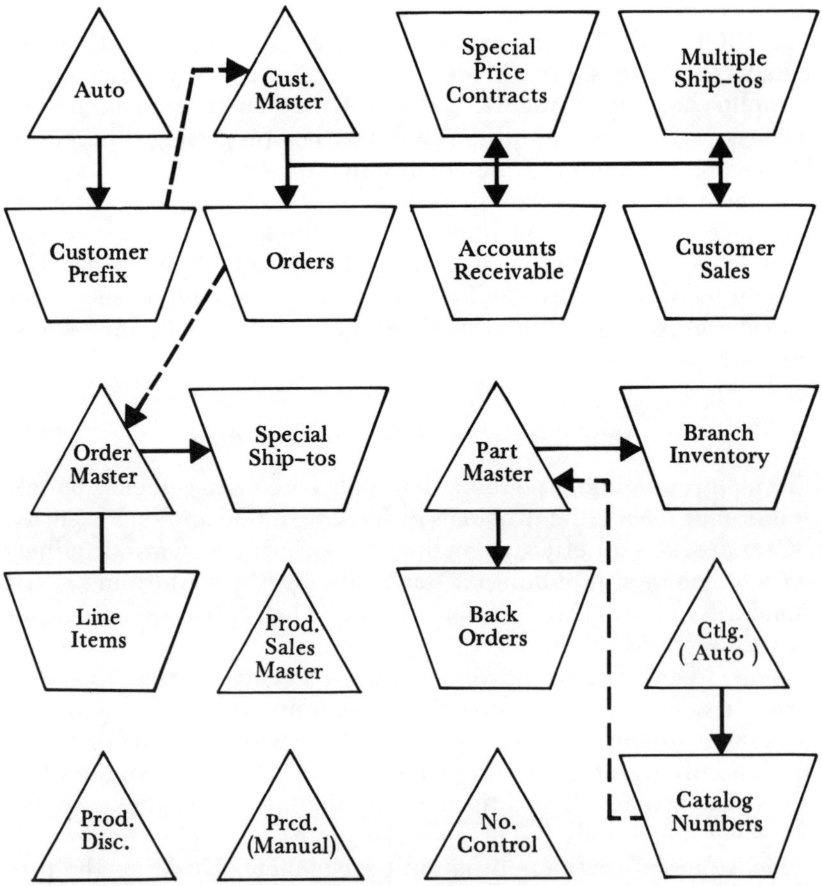

of one file at a time, which is typical of older methods of file management; he thinks in terms of all the files and the interrelationships that exist between them. Figure 15 is a typical order-entry data base. The triangles represent master files while the trapezoids indicate associated detail files. The solid lines indicate the interfile relationships, and the dotted lines depict indirect relationships. Looking at it, you don't see just one file. You see all the files functioning together. And this image becomes a constant reminder to the programmer of the environment that he is working in.

After working in a data base environment over a period of time, the concepts of collective file management become ingrained into the programmer's thinking. He no longer thinks in a conventional file manner; he thinks in terms of systems. And in the process, he expands his perception to other systems.

This is just what we are trying to accomplish in the development of program prototypes. But in a conventional file environment, there was too much to overcome to provide the technician with the kind of systems visibility that data base provides.

Hopefully, the days of tunnel vision are over. Between the concept of standard program design and that of data base, all the tools are available to create a powerful application library.

Standard Data Names

The last area to address is the integration of file standards that can be made practical and useful in the development of all application programs.

The most important standard to be set is that of common record descriptions. Before any programming can take place, the file organization must be defined. Conventionally, this is done through the preparation of record descriptions that identify the content of each file used in the system. In data base management, this is done through the preparation of a data base schema. Though data base management provides an effective method for accessing and updating file information, it does not ensure the standardization of record and item names within the application programs.

Many a system has been programmed where the same files have been given different descriptions from program to program. Using an order-entry application as an example, one program might define the customer number within the customer file as CUSTNO, whereas the very next program it is called C-NO or CUST-NUMBER. This kind of nonstandardization at the file level makes it extremely difficult for anyone to follow the usage of these items from one program to another.

Establishing common record descriptions solves this problem. The usual way to do this is to place each common record descriptor into a copy statement library. Then each program that uses any of these records simply copies the common description by specifying a COPY verb followed by the record name. This technique not only establishes a rigorous data definition standard but also saves unnecessary coding.

In a data base environment, this technique should be further enhanced by making sure that the data items within the data base schema or data base root file conform to the names defined in the common record descriptions. This will provide additional systems compatibility.

The use of a well-designed data base and a well-organized source statement library will minimize development time and assure high standards throughout the system. Systems conforming to this approach will automatically become more modular and easier to maintain. Developing program prototypes will further strengthen the quality and modularity of programs and will speed system development. An application built on these principles will become one of the organization's most important assets.

9

Building the Network: Intrastructures

Now that the issues of selecting the right computer system, choosing a unified systems design, and setting high-level standards are behind us, let's focus on the challenge of implementation. For the firm that is limiting its implementation to a single site, the task of distributing computer power is not a difficult one. But for the firm that is considering multiple installations and wants to derive the benefits of an integrated distributed computer network, the task is much like eating an elephant. It has to be done one bite at a time.

Consider the situation of a large multinational firm that has 20 or 30 independently operating profit centers. In an organization this size it's not unusual to find a little of everything. Some divisions may be performing their operations manually; some may be using antiquated equipment or outdated systems; some might be operating through remote job entry to a central computer or to a larger division's mainframe; others may be using time-sharing services or service bureaus; and there may even be a few that are using minicomputers or microcomputers.

Just how this evolved is unimportant. It could have been an inherited problem, resulting from a series of acquisitions. Or it may have been the result of a series of independent management decisions. What is important is to acknowledge the reality—and many a company finds itself in just this kind of predicament. Therefore, it may well be from such a heterogeneous structure that the network has to be formed. So the question arises: Where do you start?

The answer is not easy, but one thing is sure: you don't start by ignoring the present problems. A top-down approach has to be used. Determine at the outset what considerations or concessions have to be made in order to reunify this situation. Don't be intimidated or get demoralized by the scope of the project. Remember, it's an elephant, and it can only be devoured one bite at a time.

The ultimate goal should be to integrate all the data processing functions of the organization. It can be done. And, in the process, internal safeguards will be put in place to ensure that incongruous data processing practices and incompatible computer systems do not reoccur in the future.

The First Step—Isolating a Beta Site

To minimize the risk of failure and retain overall control, a test or beta site should be selected. If facilities are not directly available to the corporation, a preliminary study should be performed to determine which division within the organization would be best suited as an initial development site. This division will later act as the beta site and become the first entrant in the network. For those firms that have corporate resources available, development should still be done in conjunction with the beta-site division. A joint approach works more effectively and makes the divisions feel a part of the project.

Selecting a suitable beta site is important. The choice should be based on three key factors: (1) how representative the operations of the division are of the organization as a whole, (2) how useful the current systems of the division are, and (3) how much cooperation can be expended from the division's management.

Representativeness of the Site

The beta site selected must have operations typical of the other divisions within the corporation. Its internal procedures should be common to all of them. This means that the first concern is to find a "model division."

For firms that specialize in particular industries, this should not pose a problem. But for those companies that are extremely diversified, this may seem an impossible task. But don't lose faith. A closer look might show surprising similarities.

Applications generally conform to industry standards. So determine just how many truly unique applications there are. Then select a division that would serve as a good starting point. Even in diversified situations, a reasonable amount of commonality exists. Otherwise, all the software firms selling manufacturing-control packages, order-entry packages, and general accounting packages (accounts payable, accounts receivable, general ledger) would have been out of business years ago. Looking at their financial statements, the situation appears to be quite the contrary—they're thriving.

Don't pick a small division as your beta site. Pick a large one. Generally, the larger the division, the more respect it has from the other divisions. The psychology is in its favor. Smaller divisions look up to larger ones. And if the system works in the larger division, the smaller ones will feel more secure in trying it themselves.

Usefulness of the Systems

The next question is which of the beta division's current systems should be used as model systems. If more than one division qualifies as a beta site, then choose the group whose data processing systems best serve the overall needs of the corporation.

Users have no hang-ups on system design. Their interests are in information—how fast they can get it and how accurate it is. So, from a practical standpoint, if a current system works, use it. It will ease the transition and expedite the implementation.

But this is only a starting point. In the next step, the internal structure of the systems can be redeveloped, loose files can be consolidated into a data base, program elements can be modularized and recoded, systems can be expanded and integrated, on-line provisions can be added. The user does not have to see a difference. None of the reports should be eliminated, unless they have become obsolete.

So even though a redevelopment effort might be necessary to bring the system up to standards, it's considerably easier to redevelop and improve a currently used system than to develop a new one from scratch. And look at the benefits. The system can be standardized and the operations significantly improved without traumatizing the users. Day-to-day operations can still go on without major interruptions.

Nevertheless, the criteria for retaining current systems should be their usefulness to the corporation, their flexibility of design, and their level of processing efficiency. If the current application systems are antiquated and not worth retaining, then unquestionably a new system should be designed. Otherwise try to save them.

Divisional Cooperation

Another important consideration in the selection of the beta site is the amount of cooperation and support that divisional management is willing to give the project. Without this support the project will become a second-class citizen—progress will be slow and there will be increased risk of failure. If the story has been told well and sold well, there should be no problem. But if the divisions view the project as benefitting only the corporation and see no benefits to themselves, then circumstances will arise where other projects take priority and the network will never get off the ground.

So in the quest for a suitable beta site, be sure to choose a division whose management is supportive and willing to get involved, and above all be sure that the divisions realize the benefits they will receive by joining into a unified network structure.

Selecting the Beta Site Computer System

After the beta site has been choosen, the next major task is to select a computer system that is equipped to handle the needs not only of the first entrant into the network but of any entrant. The imporatnce of this selection is that the system sets the precedent for all other systems in the network. This decision should not be made lightly. In the hardware and software evaluation, don't make the mistake of limiting the study to a particular division. Be sure that the computer family selected has a sufficiently wide product range to effectively serve the data processing needs of all the divisions within the organization. And although hardware and software considerations play an important role, don't underestimate the significance of costs.

Networks almost always entail the purchase of new equipment. Very few have been put together using existing equipment. Therefore, the issue of cost is vital, especially in view of the fact that a network is not a one-system purchase. It entails the purchase of many systems. As illustrated in Appendix A, when making the evaluation, you should consider system cost a key factor in the analysis. Therefore, if during the evaluation you find that the cost of the system originally preferred is prohibitive, keep looking. You'll find one that offers the same versatility and yet is cost-effective. If you don't, you're doing something wrong.

The cost issue is what normally separates the minicomputers and mega-minis from the mainframes. The low cost of minicomputer technology has made distributed processing economically feasible. Many mainframe companies have tried to remain cost-competitive by offering a variety of different products. But don't allow the vendor to recommend a network solution that uses different types of computers. They will probably be incompatible, and result in the same incongruity with which you started. So, look for a family solution. Select a computer family that offers a wide range of products. Then each division can select an appropriate model that will serve its needs and yet fall within its price constraints.

The product-family approach also allows the corporation to negotiate blanket-order discounts. Corporations like General Mills and Ford have received discounts of 10 percent to 40 percent on equipment and software, not because they are larger corporations, but because most vendors offer significant discounts on multiple computer purchases. Therefore, not only does the network architecture benefit from choosing a single product family, but there are tremendous cost advantages as well.

A Brief Review of System Requirements

Implementing distributed systems can be quite easy if the proper hardware and software tools are available and the system is well designed. Placing video terminals and printers into user areas should be simply a matter of running wire and plugging in the units. Likewise, developing application software to allow the user to process his information through these terminals and printers should be easy. To ensure that it is, use this short checklist in your evaluation and have the vendor guarantee that the product family you select satisfies each of these critical on-line features:

- The computer must be able to support a variety of terminals in different manners.
- The number of terminals that a computer can handle simultaneously must not be so restricted as to seriously limit user access.
- The operating system must provide sufficient time-sharing or multiprocessing capability to quickly and efficiently service the on-line environment.
- The computer must have an effective terminal-communications subsystem for developing and implementing screen-oriented on-line systems (as discussed in Chapter 8).
- The computer must have a strong data base management subsystem for controlling and securing multi-user access to centrally maintained data files.

If the hardware features are not present, then the system is not practical. If the software features are lacking, then either additional systems software will have to be purchased (or developed) to overcome these deficiencies or the programmers will have to absorb the responsibility of incorporating such features into the applications programs. Since neither of these alternatives is good, take the time to evaluate systems carefully to make sure that the system you select satisfies *all* the features on the checklist.

Constructing the Data Base

After the computer selection has been made and the system has been ordered, normally there is a three- to four-month interval before the system is actually installed. This intervening period is an ideal time to review the present file organization and begin the design effort for the new data base environment. If a data base structure already exists, the time could be used to incorporate some additional features that have been planned but have never been implemented, or to expand or modify certain aspects of the current design.

Whether the data base is designed in a hierarchical, network, or relational manner is of secondary importance. Any of these structures will do the job, so the decision is really a matter of personal preference. What is important is that the company make a commitment to use one of these three data base approaches in order to organize and control its data files effectively. This will ensure file compatibility and provide a secure method through which multiple users can access information in the new environment.

During this phase, file conversion should not be a big problem. Conversion has become a way of life with most data processing people. But if everything goes well, this should be the last conversion for many years. The intention of data base is to arrive at a structure that obviates the need to perform future conversions. Usually this is achieved. However, if redesign is required, most data base management packages provide sufficient utilities to simplify the task of any further conversion efforts.

So, in constructing the new data base, don't be overly concerned with the conversion effort that may be required in order to change files from their current structure to the new one. Remember, this needs to be done only once. The emphasis should be placed on the practicality of the new data base structure. For that is what you're going to have to live with.

To be certain that nothing is overlooked, do a top-down study of the files. Gather all the record descriptions and place them in a three-ring binder, sectioned off by application. This will help in the organization of the new data base. Then determine the relationsips that exist between the various files in each application area. Eliminate redundant files by consolidating the information into one file. In the same manner, try to eliminate the reoccurrence of identical fields in multiple files, if they can possibly be limited to a single file.

Review the resulting file layouts with the users and make sure that all information requirements have been satisfied. If so, all that remains is to finalize the resulting files into a data base structure. This is done through the preparation of a data base schema, which is nothing more than a formal statement in data base language of the fields, records, and file relationships that will exist in the data base environment.

Data bases are collections of files. Since several data bases can be accessed at the same time, it doesn't really matter whether one giant data base is created or a series of application data bases are devised. However, from an operations standpoint, it's much easier to manipulate individual application data bases than it is to manipulate a large, obtuse structure. For that reason, companies tend to organize their files by application rather than consolidate them into one gigantic data base. This in the long run has proven to be a practical approach.

Standard industry applications have pretty much dictated the types of data base structures one would expect to find in a typical environment. In the case of our multinational manufacturing firm, the beta site might incorporate a data base structure similar to the one illustrated in Figure 16.

Although this exemplifies a manufacturing data base, similar structures are applicable to all industries. Some data fields may differ from one company to another; however, the overall data base organization tends to be consistent with the model: Order entry, accounts receivable, and sales could have been placed in three separate data bases, but that's really a matter of preference. What is significant is that this organization lends itself well to inter-data-base functions. By extracting information from the order-entry/accounts-receivable data base and the purchase-orders/accounts-payable data base, a cash flow can be projected. Similarly, through the use of order-entry and manufacturing data bases, the firm can perform an MRP (material requirements planning) analysis. Then again, by using the routings within the manufacturing data base and the labor distribution of the payroll data base, labor efficiencies can be derived.

Transactions can also be passed from one data base to another. As purchase orders are cut, journal entries could be passed to the general-ledger data base. In the same manner, receipt of goods through purchasing could update inventory. And in those companies where piecework determines what the employee is paid, as the

Figure 16. Typical manufacturing data base.

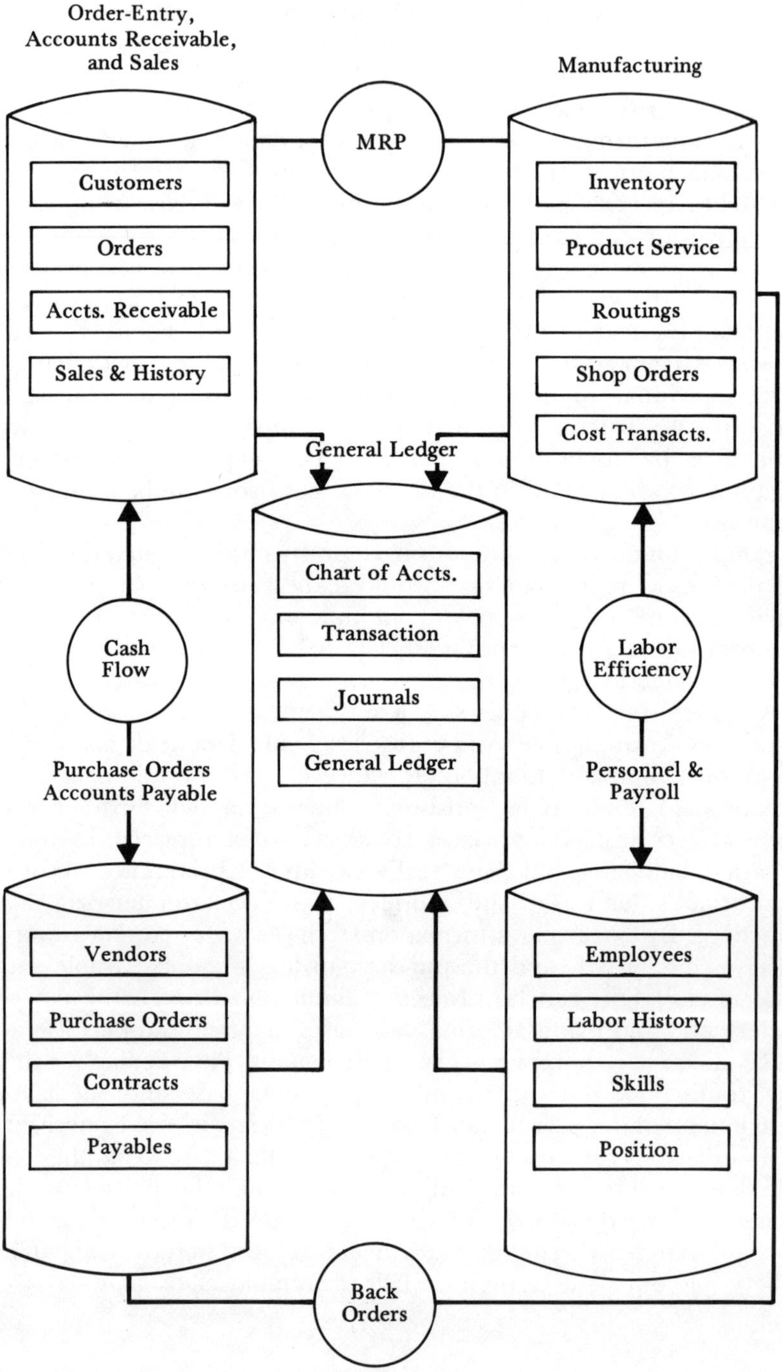

employee reports the completion of each assignment, the status of the shop order within the manufacturing data base could automatically be updated. At the same time, earnings could be assigned to the employee's record within the payroll data base.

So, even though the files have been organized in several separate data bases, information is still readily accessible. Structuring files in data base groupings makes a lot of sense, and it doesn't restrict or overly complicate the file organization.

Developing the Basic System Structure

After the data base has been defined, the next step is to develop new systems that can be used in a networking manner. If during the selection of the beta site it is determined that a good portion of the current application systems can be salvaged, then all that needs to be decided is what system to redevelop first. However, if it has been determined that there is no useful purpose in salvaging any of the systems, then the corporation has to decide which is more cost-effective—purchasing packaged systems or developing new ones. This decision can be further complicated by the fact that software firms offer general-purpose software that can be used as a basis for redevelopment.

Of course, in reality, things aren't black or white. Certain systems will be retained and others will be purchased or replaced. Combining purchased software with internally developed software does not pose a problem if system standards are upheld. However, don't lose sight of the fact that this is the opportunity to unify and integrate the systems once and for all. Quick, inexpensive purchased solutions can cause expensive long-term problems. So be careful.

Using Packaged Systems

Evaluate packaged software according to the same criteria that are used to evaluate current application systems. Once the sparkle and glitter are removed from some of the heavily promoted packages, you may find that some of these packaged systems aren't much better than the systems you're about to discard. A few cosmetic touches and some fancy advertising can easily cloud one's perspective. So look beyond the cosmetics and see if the package really addresses the requirements, or if it is just another antiquated system revived by a few clever on-line features.

If, after a thorough evaluation, a packaged solution is still seriously considered, be sure that the product conforms to network programming standards and that the company marketing the product is willing and able to turn over a fully documented package. Not only should user documentation be available, the system should be accompanied by a full set of current file layouts, program flowcharts, and functional narratives, describing the purpose and logic of each program module. Program listings and screen layouts should also be included, in case the software firm is not able to sustain itself in the marketplace or later decides to abandon the product.

After all these issues have been satisfied, determine the ultimate cost of the package. Since most software companies only license software and will not sell it, a multicopy agreement might have to be negotiated to limit the cost of using the product. And, of course, most firms require or encourage some form of maintenance contract. So this should also be taken into account in the cost analysis.

Normally in a buy-or-build decision, if a programming staff is available, it is more cost-effective to develop the system in-house. However, for sophisticated application systems such as manufacturing control and order entry, where development time is measured in man-years, a packaged solution might well be the answer—*if* the price is right. But remember, the primary objective is to build a library of application programs that every entrant in the network can use. Therefore, whether a packaged solution is used or a redevelopment effort is undertaken, do all in your power to ensure that the systems adhere to the same high standard. The final systems should be compatibly structured and integrated so that after a few years it will be difficult to distinguish the packaged systems from the internally developed ones.

Redeveloping Current Systems and Building New Systems

For those systems that are to be retained and redeveloped, review the way the system now functions. If the system presently operates in batch, identify which programs should be redeveloped as on-line functions and which should remain batch. Usually the transaction-processing programs are converted to on-line functions, while the mass updating and reporting programs remain batch operations. If the system is currently an on-line system, you have an opportunity to clean up any weaknesses in the current design and strengthen both the on-line and reporting operations. If the system is to be developed new, then a full systems design is necessary. The design should stress such areas as file creation, file maintenance, on-line inquiry, internal updating, and hard-copy reporting.

Whichever approach is taken, the first step is to develop a source library of file descriptions and commonly used coding techniques, which can be used in application program development through a copy or inclusion feature. This will effectively standardize the descriptions of all commonly used files as well as reduce program development time.

To achieve the highest level of standardization, the file descriptions placed in the source library should be consistent with those stated in the data set item list within the data base schema. By using the same item names in the file descriptions as in the schema, all item references will conform to a single standard. So whether the application programs use item lists or file descriptions, one common set of descriptors will prevail.

The next step is to develop a set of program models that can be used for all in-house programming. Remember, there are only half a dozen different types of programs. So set up a group of model programs that represent each of the various prototypes and incorporate them into your programming-standards documentation. They will provide excellent guidelines for the programming staff and establish a strong framework through which to achieve functional modularity.

In the development of these on-line prototypes, the importance of the terminal-communications subsystem comes into play. An on-line monitor similar to the one discussed in Chapter 8 is essential. Through the use of such a package, communications, verification, and data conversion can be practically eliminated as programming tasks. Removing these functions from the application program not only simplifies the on-line programmer's task but provides certain processing benefits as well. In particular, the application programs become smaller and easier to maintain. This, coupled with the use of versatile data base software, significantly reduces the programming effort required to adequately service a complex multi-user environment.

Since there are only five basic on-line program prototypes (an add module, a change module, a delete module, a display module, and a dual-entry module), it shouldn't be difficult to devise a model program for each of these functions and include it in the documentation. Because on-line programs normally use transaction screens, screen models should also be included in the program documentation. This will also provide an excellent vehicle for training new programmers in on-line techniques.

The same procedures should be used in establishing standard program models for the remaining batch prototypes—that is, a posting module, a sort module, and a report module. Since the new environment will be an on-line one, there is no need to establish program models for the older batch edit and maintenance prototypes. These functions have been replaced by appropriate on-line functions.

Of these remaining three functions, the sort procedure is frequently performed through vendor-supplied utilities. In fact, most internally coded sorts are just parameterized entries to a vendor sort utility. Therefore, actually only two batch program prototypes have to be modeled.

Of these two remaining batch functions, the report module is the most commonly used. Even in sophisticated on-line environments, there is a propensity to retain as much information in hard copy as possible. It is not unusual for companies that are committed to on-line processing to have more reporting programs than on-line programs. Companies still operate by reporting period and need more than just on-demand information to fulfill these requirements. So when you add up all the daily, weekly, monthly, quarterly, and yearly reports, they often outnumber the on-line functions. Therefore, of these two batch prototypes, the report program model is extremely important.

All new application programs should be patterned after the respective functional prototypes. If this practice is encouraged, development will go fast, and the by-product will be a reusable application library for future development. If this kind of approach is not used, the benefits will be only short-term.

Systems Implementation—A Case Study

In the mid-1970s, a Rochester-based multinational manufacturing corporation made the decision to advance into distributed processing and implement a worldwide network of homogeneous systems that could function in a fully integrated manner and provide the corporation with timely financial information.

The corporation manufactured and marketed products in two major markets: the automotive market and the building and construction market. It serviced these markets on a global basis by providing quality textile products, which were used as subassemblies by other domestic and foreign manufacturing firms. In some instances, the products of one manufacturing division were used as raw materials for another. Certain operations were performed continuously, while others were geared to customer orders.

Manufacturing facilities and warehouse locations were strategically placed in key geographic areas in the United States, Europe, South

America, Australia, and the Far East, in order to allow the corporation to quickly expedite products to any company in the world. Similarly, sales offices were established in key marketing centers throughout the world to provide corporate visibility and strong local representation.

Because of the different types of products and the different methods of manufacturing and marketing, it was originally felt that a standard systems approach would be impractical. However a six-month systems study revealed the contrary. Not only was it recommended that a standard system be developed for the corporation, it was further felt that the implementation of such a system would:

- In some instances result in substantial cost savings, due to a conversion to less expensive equipment.
- Make available a fully tested set of application systems and programs to divisons that had minimal or no data processing expertise, thus boosting divisional development efforts.
- Provide an environment that facilitated resource sharing among divisions. Compatibility and standardization would allow equipment, systems, and programs, and even people to be available in times of need.
- Provide central coordination and control over new projects, allowing the divisions to advance quickly as a group while minimizing the possibility of redundant efforts.
- Improve the company's competitive position in the market through better communication and a network structure that helped in analyzing strategies and implementing new corporate directives.

In reviewing the divisional operations, it was found that the Rochester division, which was the company's main division and performed two out of the three different kinds of manufacturing operations within the company, was ideally suited as a beta site for a new information systems network. It also served the data processing needs of many of the domestic marketing divisions, as well as the data processing requirements of the corporation.

In evaluating the data processing functions at the division, it was found that the division had just finished implementing a new on-line order-entry system. This system was state-of-the-art and was highly regarded by all the users. Therefore, there was no question that this system should be retained. In examining the manufacturing control system, it was determined that the system was outdated and provided little value to the corporation. As a result, the company decided to purchase a packaged design from which a new manufacturing system could be developed. Since the design was complete, the project immediately advanced to the development stages. In analyzing the financial packages, it was determined that although they were batch-oriented, they were adequate. Therefore, the decision was made to salvage them but to turn them into on-line systems, retaining the same reporting features that were provided in the original system.

A large-scale minicomputer system was selected to replace the division's medium-size mainframe. This reduced the annual data processing cost by $100,000. The new minicomputer had 512 kilobytes of main semiconductor memory, was error-correcting and error-logging, and had a battery backup that allowed it to recover from a power failure within a reasonable time. The older mainframe system had only 192 kilobytes of core memory and had no recovery capability.

The new minicomputer was actually configured to support 100 megabytes of auxiliary disk storage through the use of two 50MB drives, while the older system supported only 75 megabytes of storage, using three drives. Both the new and the old system used 600-lines-per-minute printers. However, the older system had four tape units whereas the new one had only one, since tape was used only as a backup medium.

On-line processing on the mainframe was supported through four video display terminals which were placed in the user areas: one in sales, two in production planning, and one in general accounting. This constituted the on-line environment. Since terminal processing was so expensive in this environment, all program development was done through punch cards. On the new minicomputer system, ten video terminals were ordered. Four were used to replace the four existing units, one was used as a system console, and two were used for program development (since the card reader was not retained). The remaining three terminals were scheduled for the new on-line function.

At this point, the various application data bases were devised and corresponding record layouts were placed in a commonly accessible library. Programming development was performed through three project groups: one for manufacturing; another for order entry, accounts receivable, and sales; and the last for payroll, accounts payable, and general ledger. Each project group was headed by a project leader, who reported directly to the project manager. Although each group functioned independently, the project manager oversaw the effort and made sure that the systems conformed to a high design standard. All programs were required to copy commonly used file descriptions and to conform to the appropriate program prototype.

To minimize interruptions of systems development by day-to-day operations, a separate staff of programmers was assigned the task of maintaining the ongoing systems. Therefore, good progress was made on the development of the new systems. And since the new systems were ultimately more important, the departmental users also cooperated in minimizing their data processing requests during the transition period.

Since the order-entry and accounts-receivable systems were the newest and most valuable, a decision was made to implement them first. Conversion programs were written to transfer the data from the old system to the new one. And since none of the original mainframe programs was retained, a comprehensive testing procedure was devised to test all the processing features of the newly developed system. Upon satisfactory completion of system testing, it was decided that a one-month parallel run should be performed to bring out any hidden bugs that might have been overlooked.

The parallel run was totally under the control of the department users. In each department that played a role in the one-month parallel run, a video terminal connected to the new system was placed directly next to the terminal used by the mainframe system. As each transaction was entered into the live system, it was immediately re-entered into the new one. Reports that were prepared and distributed to user departments from the live system were also prepared and distributed from the new one. All operations and processing functions that were done on the one system were redone on the other, right down to the nightly batch operations and weekly and monthly reports.

Each day, differences were analyzed. Some were due to data-entry errors, others to omissions, and still others to minor program bugs. Whenever possible, adjustments were made to synchronize the test system with the live system. It was agreed that if the parallel system fell behind due to an excessive amount of programming errors, the parallel would be stopped and resume the following month, after the programs were corrected and adequately tested.

But the parallel was more than just a system test. It was a vehicle to allow the users to become familiar with the new system and, in the process, to become confident that it was going to work reliably for them. Companies that have not done this have missed the real value behind it. The parallel process gives the users reassurance . If things don't go right, you continue processing on the old system. If they do, then the older system can be gradually phased out without radically affecting anyone.

One system after another was converted and implemented in just this manner. After the order-entry and accounts-receivable systems, the parallel began on the three financial systems: payroll, accounts payable, and general ledger. Concurrently with this (but after completion of the order-entry system) came the sales systems. The development-to-implementation cycle for these systems took less than a year.

However, during that time the new manufacturing system was still in development. Because of the complexity of the system designs and the amount of user training that was required, it was understood that full implementation of this system would take well over a year, which posed another problem. Inventory was not integrated with order entry. So, when the order-entry files were converted and transferred to the new system, the inventory still remained on the old system. Therefore, until the manufacturing system could be fully implemented and the inventory file would be available, the manufacturing applications had to remain on the old system. This meant that provision had to be made to transfer information nightly between the two computers in order to keep the inventory files current on both systems.

Such situations occur in many major conversion projects and must be adequately planned for. In this particular case, tape was used as the transfer medium. Transactions were written out to tape on the new system. This tape was then taken over to the mainframe system and processed as input transactions. Similarly, transactions were written to tape on the mainframe and subsequently processed on the new system. Had the systems supported 2780/3780 communication, a direct communications line between the two units could have been used.

After a little more than a year of development, the majority of applications had been converted in one form or another from the old system to the new one. All applications were data-base-oriented and on-line. The new manufacturing system was well on its way. Three of the six modules had been installed and placed in production, satisfying all processing needs of the departmental users at the time.

This represented the first step in building the distributed processing network. The structure chosen for the network was a "star" configuration consisting of a number of terminal stations strategically placed in user areas throughout the organization and connected to a central processor and a central data base (see Figure 17). Each of the terminal users felt that he had dedicated access to the computer system, when in fact they were sharing a common resource concurrently.

Figure 17. A star network with central data base.

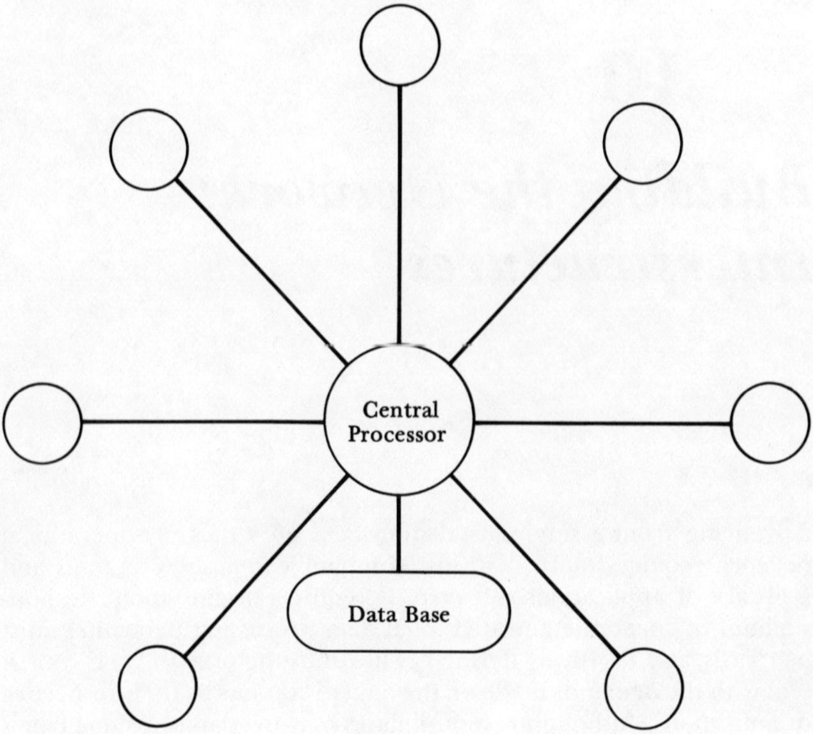

Although the outcome was dramatic, the way in which it took place was not. There were no upheavals, no forced installations, no premature failures, no disgruntled users. The transition was handled smoothly and methodically. Weekly progress meetings took place between the technical staff and the users. All design and implementation decisions were arrived at through consensus. Implementation schedules were agreed on in advance, and systems were put in at the rate the user could absorb.

From a technical standpoint, this concluded the major development effort required for a networking approach. All programs were then documented and placed by systems onto library tapes. User manuals were prepared for each system in the network library, which provided a thorough source reference, in user language, of all features available through the system. These manuals were used as training aids for new employees and sources of information for management.

10

Building the Network: Interstructures

Advancing from a single installation beta site to a fully operational network requires more than just compatible computer systems and a library of applications software. It requires organization. Responsibilities of corporate and divisional data processing personnel must be clearly and decisively defined. They must be practical and consistent with the demands made on the data processors by their respective organizations. Although responsibilities may overlap occasionally, it's important that the major responsibilities remain distinct and that the organizations complement one another.

In corporations such as the one cited in our case study, divisions are usually organized as independent entities with profit and loss responsibility. The corporation is not interested in supervising the day-to-day affairs of the operation. It only wants to be sure that the business is being properly managed and that management has the resources it needs to carry out its responsibilities and make a profit. Therefore, an organized approach would benefit both the corporation and the division. However, there are certain concerns that must be addressed.

In considering a network, the corporation's primary interest is in coordinating and standardizing its data processing functions. Therefore, it's reasonable that the corporation's data processing organization should be responsible for monitoring and scheduling the development activities of major new application systems as well as ensuring that current systems live up to a certain standard that is practical and desirable. Additionally, it is the responsibility of this organization to assist divisions that require data processing support but have insufficient data processing personnel or computer resources.

Looking at the other side of the issue, divisional data processing responsibilities are generally oriented toward user support. Where the corporate organization is more interested in the big picture, the divisional group is attentive to the departmental user and the details. From the time a system is developed and installed, maintenance becomes a perpetual activity. The majority of the divisional data processor's time is consumed in supporting ongoing systems and providing data processing expertise to departmental users. But divisional data processors are also concerned with issues that uniquely relate to the operations of their specific division. They're responsible for providing data processing support for such functions.

When friction occurs between these two groups, it's generally because one of them does not clearly understand the importance of the responsibilities of the other. Defining the responsibilities of the corporate and the divisional staffs at the beginning of the project will alleviate this problem.

The multinational firm in our case study resolved this problem by having the two groups work closely together in the initial beta-site installation so that each could understand the concerns of the other. Besides becoming codevelopers of the new system, each provided backup support to the other, and both shared the responsibilities of implementing the various application systems.

The project wasn't seen as a corporate project or a divisional project. It was a team effort, where both groups pitched in and carried their own weight. Although it was clearly understood that the corporate group would not remain involved after the project was completed, during the project both groups functioned as one. This was not only an effective method of managing such an important project, it was practical as well.

Since the divisional group was so actively involved in the development effort, no additional training was actually required in order for it to be able to maintain the system. Also, since the divisional people were so knowledgeable, they were able to help document the applications for network use.

The Second Entrant to the Network

During the last stages of the beta project, the controller of the Tennessee division, who was following the progress of the project quite closely, requested to be the next entrant into the new network. The division was at the time processing its payroll, accounts-payable, and general-ledger functions using a 3780 RJE station; but order entry, accounts receivable, and manufacturing were still being done manually. Although the division had annual sales of $10 million, it was growing at an astonishing annual rate, and its manual methods and procedures were being overburdened by the quickening pace of business.

Initially, it was decided to replace the RJE terminal, through which the division processed its financial information, with two video display units and a printer. These units would operate over long-distance lines to the Rochester systems where the data base would be held. All programs available to the Rochester division were by design available to any other divisional user. Therefore, no major development effort was necessary.

This, of course, required several pairs of modulation/demodulation (modem) devices to transmit the digital information as audio signals over the telephone lines, from the terminals in Tennessee to the computer in Rochester and back again (see Figure 18). The printer shared one of the terminal modems.

As is the case in most communications applications, the speed of the modem and the type of telephone service were based on the amount of time required and the kind of terminals available. Since it was anticipated that only 10 to 20 hours a week would be consumed in communications, originally it was felt that voice-grade WATS lines would be sufficient. However, due to the poor grade of the signal experienced and the increasing usage of the line, dedicated lines were found to be less expensive and more reliable in the long run.

Since modems had to be ordered in pairs and since the cost of the modem and the cost of the interfacing telephone dataset increased as the transmission requirements increased, it was determined that

Figure 18. Long-distance communications over modem lines.

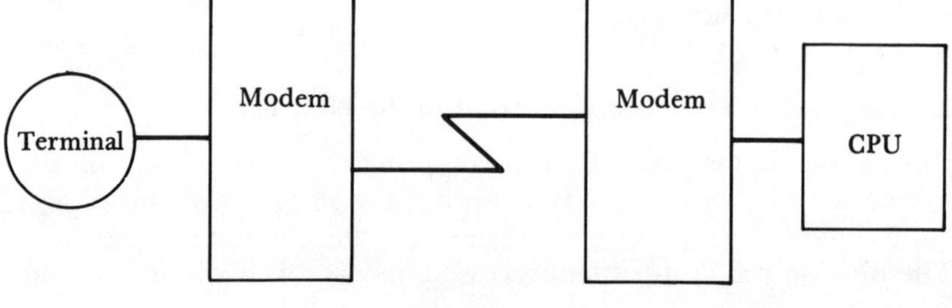

1200 baud (120 characters per second) was the most cost-effective processing rate. Although the terminals normally operated at 2400 baud (240 characters per second), the visual difference of the lower rate was hardly noticeable.

Although the Tennessee division was involved in a different type of manufacturing from the Rochester division, the newly developed manufacturing control system was found versatile enough in its design to satisfy the processing requirements of both divisions. And since both divisions served the same markets, the order-entry system was ideal for both. Therefore, though it took almost two years to implement the first divisional network system, the second installation, requiring only a few terminals, a couple of pairs of modems, and a small investment in user training, took only a few months.

In final preparation for the installation, the Rochester division had only a few additional accommodations to make. A space-requirement study had to be performed to determine the amount of disk space that was required to house the Tennessee division's data base, and on the hardware side two terminal ports had to be reserved for Tennessee communications use. Except for these two provisions, nothing else was needed.

After the data bases were configured into the system for Tennessee, any programs on the system were immediately usable by the Tennessee division, since the application systems were designed in a general networking manner. Upon signing on to the system, the Tennessee users had direct access to the same processing programs as the Rochester people. As a matter of fact, the very same programs were used for both divisions. But internally the system distinguished between the Rochester user and the Tennessee user. When data base service had to be performed, the program knew that it had to access the Tennessee data base for the Tennessee user and the Rochester data base for the Rochester user.

This was accomplished through the security subsystem of the on-line monitor software. When a user signed on to the system and requested on-line service, the on-line program determined (on the basis of the sign-on) to what data base the user wanted access, what type of access the user would be allowed, and what special processing capabilities the user would be given. This was done regardless of the terminal being used and the systems configuration. The software, not the configuration or the terminal environment, directed the operation. A Tennessee user could sign on to the system and access his information from any of the Rochester division terminals; likewise, a Rochester user could interrogate his own information from any of the Tennessee stations. This was true terminal independence.

From a technical standpoint, the software offered such a flexible network design that it took less than one-half hour to set up the processing environment of an entirely new division. Granted, user training and terminal installation required significantly more time, however, the versatility and flexibility of design cannot be overly stressed in considering a network structure.

Computer-to-Computer Communications

At the same time that the Tennessee division was being incorporated into the network structure, a user study was completed at the Rochester division. The purpose of the study was to determine if improvements could be made in any of the processing areas that had been recently implemented.

The results of the study revealed that the production planning department in the Rochester division spent two to two and one-half man-days per week updating automotive order releases within the system. These releases were received weekly from the major auto manufacturers and represented shipping requirements over the next six-week period, based on the current levels of production. Two

Figure 19. Remote communications through IBM 3780 protocol.

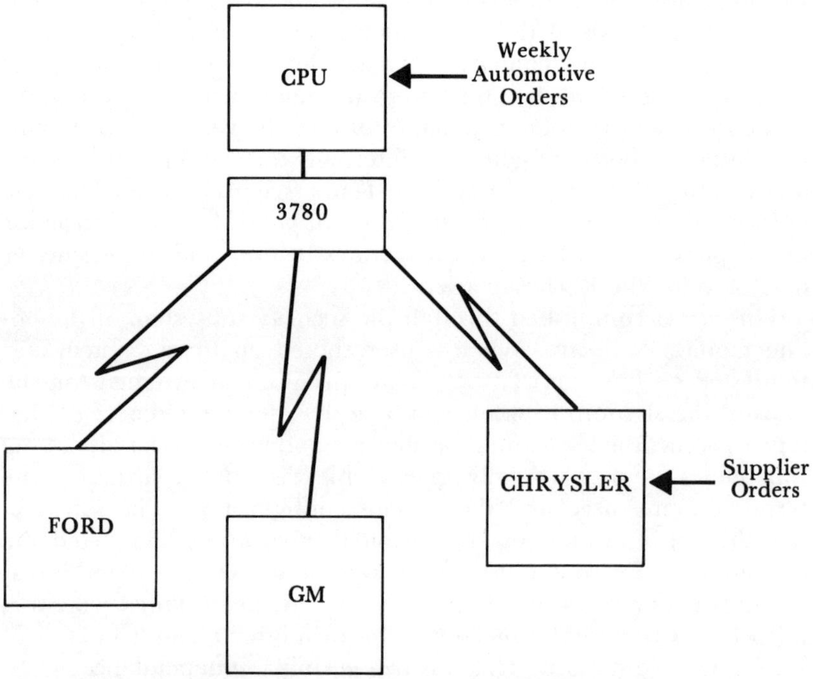

production planners would then dedicate a day of their time to enter these new schedules into the system.

In reviewing the process and making a few simple telephone calls to key data processing employees within the various auto companies, management discovered that the entire process for three of the four auto companies could be automated. Once a bisynchronous 3780 emulator was installed in the system, as illustrated in Figure 19, the weekly order releases were transmitted over the telephone lines from the computer systems at the various auto companies and entered directly into the order-entry data base. This not only saved two and a half days of employee time, it got the information into the system three days earlier than previously, and with 100 percent accuracy.

Although the justification for the 3780 emulator was based on savings of data-entry time and improved communications with the various automotive customers, the emulator was also useful in communicating with other companies that supported the same communications protocol.

Multiplexing to Save Telephone Line Costs

At the end of the second year, after the Rochester division was well in hand, the corporation relocated and needed four terminals moved to the new facility. Although it was within 10 miles of the division, it had to be handled in the same manner as if it were 1,000 miles. Telephone-line communication was the only answer. If the corporation had employed the same technique as that used by the Tennessee division, four modems and four telephone datasets would have been required to satisfy the communication linkage. Since the corporation chose to use dedicated lines in order to assure high data integrity in transmission, four dedicated lines would have been necessary. This would have cost the corporation about $4,800 in modems and an additional $360 per month in communication costs, just to be able to do what could have been done for free 10 miles down the road.

Unfortunately, that's the price paid for the ability to do remote processing. However, to lessen the pain, there was a better way called *multiplexing*. Multiplexing, as illustrated in Figure 20, is basically a technique developed to reduce telephone costs. It does it at the expense of higher front-end costs. But since it minimizes the recurring monthly communications usage fees, it pays for itself in a short time.

Multiplexing, as the figure shows, is a technique of organizing a number of independent transmission lines into a single line and, at

Figure 20. Combining transmission links through miltiplexing.

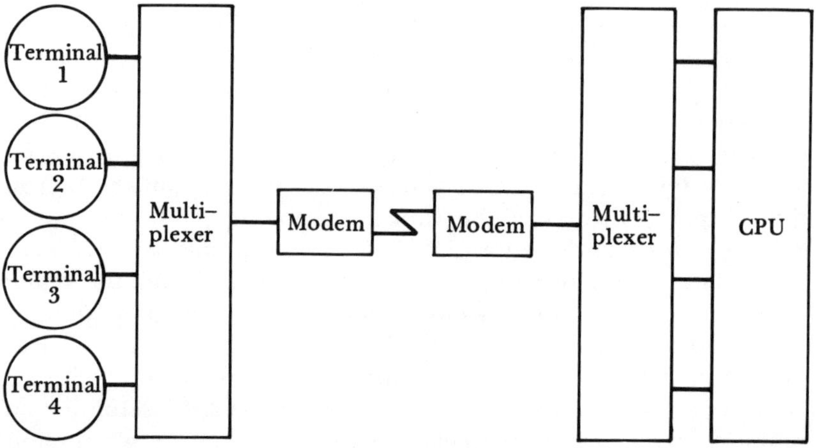

the other end, separating them again for processing. Like modems, these units must be purchased in pairs.

In using multiplexers, the corporation had to consider the line speed at which the communication occurred. As a rule of thumb, the resulting terminal speed was determined by the line speed divided by the number of active terminals processing over the multiplexer. If four terminals were to equally share the same multiplexer and the communication line was supported at 9600 baud (960 characters per second), then each of the terminals would at best be processing at about 2400 baud (240 characters per second). However, if the line speed were only 2400 baud as was the situation at the Tennessee division, then the terminals would be operating at only 60 characters per second, which might be tolerable to the program development group but would be too slow for the accounting users.

Therefore, although multiplexing minimized the use of multiple telephone lines, it required higher communications speed and more expensive modems in order to not degrade the terminal environment. To support only two terminals in such a manner was not cost-effective. However, three or more terminals definitely justified the cost.

In the corporation's case, two 9600-baud modems were purchased along with two multiplexers. And since the terminals were located in different departments, lines were installed from the multiplexer to the user areas for convenience of processing.

Using Multidrop Lines (Daisy Chaining)

Although it was never used, another quite popular communications option available at the time was the use of multidrop lines to service local and remote terminals. In the standard user configuration, terminals were directly connected to the system through the data communications port. This required a port dedicated to each terminal, and a line from each terminal back to the central processor. In multidrop or multipoint applications, as illustrated in Figure 21, a single communications line can support a variety of terminals.

In such configurations (frequently referred to as daisy chaining), the terminals are connected directly to the computer or can be linked by means of a modem. When terminals are connected through the use of modems, communication is usually synchronous. Lines that are locally connected to the system may be supported through either synchronous or asynchronous methods.

Each multidrop line is wired from terminal to terminal in the configuration. Each terminal is assigned a device number, which is used to identify the individual transmissions as they are passed across the line. Special multidrop software is required to encode and decode the transmissions that are made up and down the line. However, unlike the terminals in local point-to-point terminal environments,

Figure 21. Connecting terminals through multidrop lines.

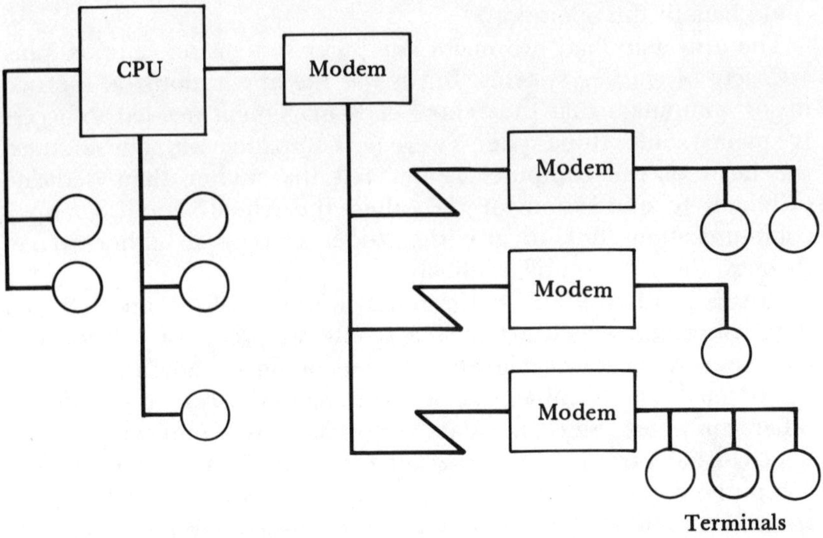

multipoint terminals can reside thousands of feet from the central processor and from one another.

In reviewing uses for this communication approach, the corporation originally considered a multidrop line to distribute data-collection terminals on the shop floor. It was felt that because of the long distances between production departments, this approach would be more practical than the point-to-point approach. First, it required considerably less wiring, since only one line had to be drawn out to the floor. Second, because of the distance to some of the remote departments, the multidrop line provided a more reliable communications path. In the final analysis, however, it was decided that the shop floor lines should be scheduled in another phase; thus the lines were never drawn.

Data Controllers and Data Concentrators

While reviewing other communications alternatives, one of the technicians in the Rochester division had heard that the University of Rochester had recently incorporated a data concentrator to handle its entire terminal environment. Management contacted the university's School of Management to learn more about this approach, and the assistant dean invited members of the corporation and divisional staffs to come over and see a demonstration of the operation. Since the university had selected the same computer system as the corporation, the corporation was interested to see how a data concentrator could benefit the operation.

The university had two major computer systems on campus, plus a variety of smaller systems. But it was the applications on the two major computers that the School of Management needed to access frequently. Since these systems were not compatible with one another, the head of the computer center felt that rather than dedicate terminals to one system or the other, the school should set up a communications link to give the students access to either system through the same set of terminals.

In this configuration, the terminals were actually connected to a data controller, which acted as a front-end processor for the two computer systems (see Figure 22). Depending on how the student signed on to the terminal, the student received access to one or the other computer. Since the data controller was a minicomputer, it kept constant track of the current terminal loads on each of the computer systems. If all ports on a requested system were busy, the controller notified the student and either placed him in a queue for service or terminated his request.

Figure 22. Connecting terminals through data controllers.

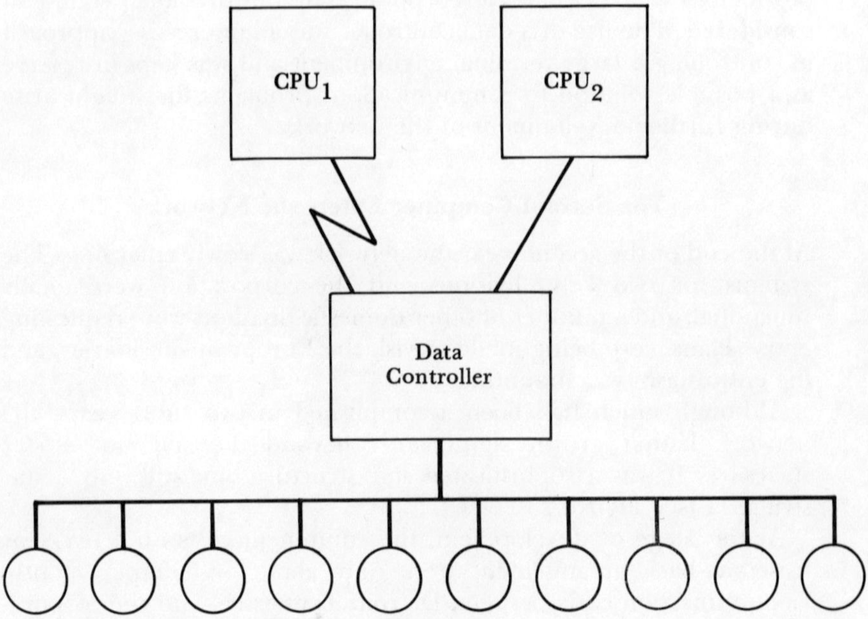

What made this approach intriguing is that it offered a variety of options to the communications specialist. Communications from the terminal to the data controller could be performed asynchronously through inexpensive low-speed terminals, just as at the university, or synchronously through high-speed units, if it was more practical. There were no restrictions on which types of terminal to use. The entry requirements were extremely general, and the terminal required only standard communications features.

The communications options available between the data controller and the computers were also quite numerous. In the university's case, the main processor was located on the other side of the campus, so communications were performed over telephone lines through high-speed modems, while a direct connection was used to the second computer, since it resided in the same facility as the controller. Mode of communications was again an open issue. All modes were supported. Point-to-point, multidrop, asynchronous, synchronous, and bisynchronous were all viable alternatives. The university selected two different communication media on the basis of availability of interfaces on each of the computer systems.

What the university had done was quite impressive and raised new possibilities that neither the corporate nor the divisional staff had considered. The use of a data controller was an interesting approach in controlling a large terminal environment and was kept in reserve as a possible solution to communications problems that might arise during further development of the network.

The Second Computer Enters the Network

At the end of the second year the network was slowly emerging. The systems for two U.S. divisions and the corporation were totally functional, and a number of other domestic divisions were requesting entry. Plans were being made to visit the European subsidaries, and the enthusiasm was mounting.

Although much had been accomplished in two short years, the network hadn't grown significantly beyond the stage of a star structure. It was a sophisticated star structure, but still only a star structure (see Figure 23).

At this stage of development, the equipment costs on a five-year lease/buy-back arrangement were only about $6,500 per month. Communication costs between Detroit, Tennessee, and the corporation were averaging an additional $1,000 per month. But considering that the annual sales of the two divisions were in excess of $70 million at the time, and that the entire operation was being managed through a combined data processing staff of fewer than ten people, the costs were well within reason.

However, during the six months while Tennessee was processing over communication lines, the division experienced severe growing pains. It had acquired a number of major contracts, and the paperwork and accounting procedures within the division practically tripled. Division management felt that rather than expand its communication costs, it should install its own in-house system.

A capital requisition was submitted to the corporation and approved. Division management, working closely with the corporation, arrived at a suitable initial equipment configuration, and the computer system was ordered. To retain compatibility within the network, management chose a smaller computer of the same family as the Rochester division's computer. Since this was the second computer to be purchased by the corporation, the vendor offered the division a discount.

Installation was scheduled, and preparations were made to install the new computer system. Since this was the division's first computer, a staff had to be recruited and trained. As in many companies that

Figure 23. Expanded star structure.

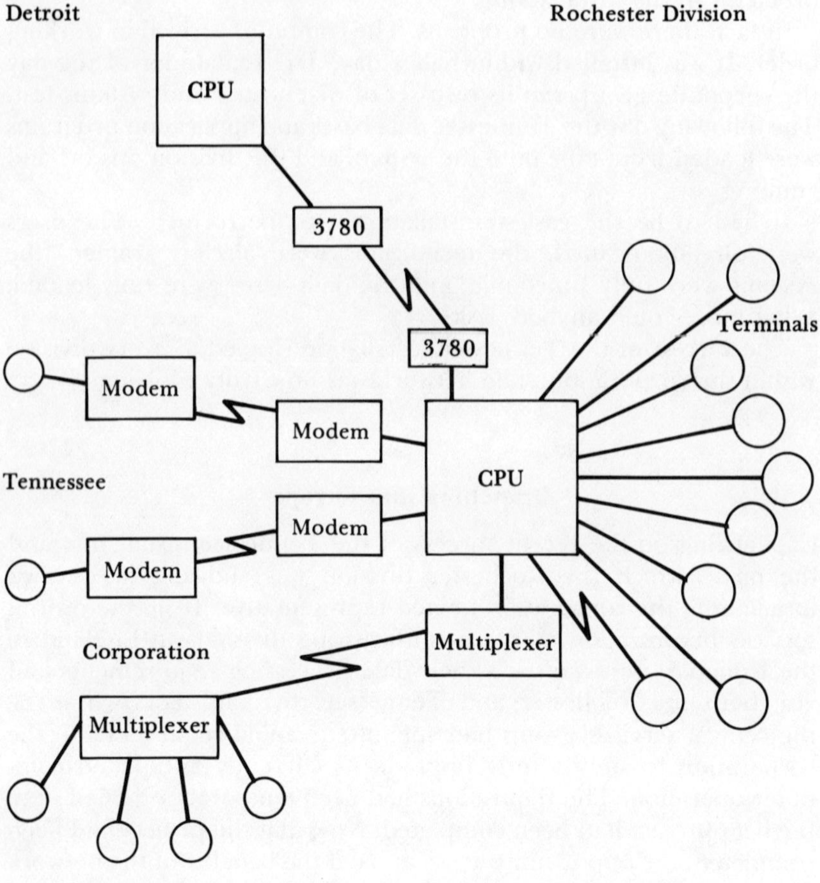

recruit from within, notice was given and first options were offered to the existing employees. One of the programmers in the Rochester division requested to be transferred to the new staff. The data processing manager's position was filled through a lateral promotion of a young Tennessee manager. The last position, computer operator, was handled through a professional recruitment agency.

Since the key programmer was totally familiar with the technical side of the operation, it was felt that no formal training was required. Corporate support was made available for as long a period as necessary to ensure an easy transition and a smooth operation. The system was basically the same that the division had been using for the last six months. Therefore, there was no reason to anticipate problems in the installation.

In fact, there were no problems. The computer arrived in working order. It was installed within half a day. The remainder of the day the corporate group ran its own set of diagnostics and systems test. The following day the Tennessee data bases and application programs were loaded from tape onto the system, and the division was off and running.

It had to be the easiest installation ever performed. The users were already trained, the technicians were already trained, the systems were fully functional, and the data bases were fully loaded. What more could anybody ask?

The success of the Tennessee installation rippled to every division within the corporation. The network was now truly evolving.

Branching into Europe

Capitalizing on the recent success of the Tennessee installation and the pride which the Rochester division was showing in its own installation, the corporation invited representatives from the central services organization of the manufacturing divisions in England to the United States to discuss their data processing requirements and visit both the Rochester and Tennessee divisions. For two years, the central services group had submitted capital requisitions to the corporation to significantly upgrade its currently antiquated computer operation. The requisitions had been temporarily denied until the beta project had been completed. Now that the project had been completed, the opportunity arose to see if the benefits of the network were attractive enough to alter the British division's direction.

After spending several weeks in the United States and witnessing the enthusiasm of the corporate and divisional people, the visitors were undoubtedly influenced by the experience. However, expecting such a short visit to change the convictions that the division's management had held for the last two years was definitely unrealistic.

The data processing manager at central services was a proud and knowledgeable individual. The corporation was pleasantly surprised to find that he approved of most aspects of the network project. He liked the on-line approach. He was extremely impressed by the data base concept. And, because of the small size of his own organization, he was easily sold on the idea of an application program library to allow resource sharing. However, he expressed strong dissatisfaction with the computer selected to serve the network. He had another model in mind for the European extension.

Solving such a problem by coercion usually results in more long-term disadvantages than benefits. Therefore, it was felt that a comparative analysis of the two units might provide a more objective approach and reveal which of the two computers really was the better.

To preserve a sense of objectivity, the same criteria that were used in selecting the original network system were used in the European study. Appendix A is the actual report that resulted from the study.

The analysis was based on five major issues: (1) hardware capabilities, (2) software capabilities, (3) vendor support, (4) ease of conversion, and (5) cost. Both vendors were interviewed and allowed to make a presentation to the review committee. The review committee consisted of the corporate MIS director, the central services data processing managers, the central services financial director, and the central services managing director.

As many meetings and interviews as the committee felt necessary were held. Statistics that appeared in the report were either gathered from industry-accepted journals such as *DataPro* or arrived at through genuine benchmarks. After the report was distributed, each vendor had the opportunity to refute the findings and state his case to the committee. One of the vendors insisted on a hearing and lost in open rebuttal before the committee. At the end of the review, with no pressure imposed by the corporation, a unanimous vote was made in favor of the original computer selected.

Establishing a European Consortium

Getting acceptance from services to implement a network link in the United Kingdom was a very important victory. It set the stage for the entire European expansion. England in effect became the beta site for Europe. And as Rochester was used to launch the American expansion, England was used to catapult the European expansion.

But there was a serious concern as to whether an adequate level of support would be available to guarantee the successful completion of the full European expansion. Transcontinental travel was time-consuming and not cheap. And if problems arose, they could not be responded to adequately on a long-distance basis because of the six to eight hours time difference. Local support was extremely important.

Besides the problems of distance and language, a more serious problem was the European programmers' lack of technical experience with on-line systems. Therefore, there was an immediate need for training of European support personnel.

The next problem, which was even more serious, was the rivalry problem. It's quite normal for divisions of a corporation to be rivals. However, with a European division, there is the added dimension of national pride. These two factors together can spell real trouble.

As an attempt to resolve both problems, the corporation decided that perhaps the scheduled computer installation in England should act as a training ground for other European installations. When this approach was proposed to the other two major European divisions, the reaction was extremely favorable: both felt that the experience their personnel would acquire would be tremendously beneficial in their own installations.

This accomplished two things. One, it consolidated the training of all major European processing personnel. Two, it placed all European technical people in a project situation where they had to work together to accomplish a common objective.

An implementation plan was prepared and distributed to all divisions that were scheduled to play a part in the British installation. The plan, a copy of which can be found in Appendix B, basically identified the scope of the project, the individuals who would be involved, the procedures that would be used to test the system upon arrival, and the content of the training program that would be administered early in the installation.

Three months prior to the installation, the British data processing manager was invited for an extended visit to the United States so that he could become familiar with the system in advance of his people, and in an environment where he would not feel the pressure of the installation. During that period, all the facilities of the corporation and the division were at his disposal. He had the opportunity to review the documentation in detail and discuss any aspect of the systems with either available technical personnel or the user staff. This period was totally reserved to reinforce his knowledge of the system prior to returning to England for the formal implementation.

Similar accommodations were offered to the Belgian and German data processing managers prior to their installations. But since they had already acquired much experience from the British project, these visits were not as critical.

Within eighteen months, two computer systems had been installed in England, another system was in the early stages of installation in

Belgium, and a fourth system was scheduled for shipment to Germany.

Retaining Control During Rapid Growth

While these installations were taking hold in Europe and other European installations were in the planning stages, movement was still underfoot to expand the network in North America. Systems were being scoped for three other U.S. divisions and one Canadian division. The technical problems were behind the corporation. The administrative problems prevailed. Visits were being scheduled to subsidiaries in Australia, Japan, and the Far East, with plans to incorporate these divisions into the network. The system was mushrooming.

As a precautionary measure, to secure the network and improve communications and support, a new position was established: the *network manager*. This responsibility was to coordinate the network and evaluate all development projects and systems modifications. Monthly, a news bulletin was prepared and distributed by the network manager to all functional divisions. The bulletin identified all systems modifications, new development activities, new reports, new on-line functions, upcoming training programs, seminars, trade shows, and the like.

The purpose of the bulletin was not only to inform but also to encourage a fraternity between the corporation and the operating divisions, and so prevent the structure from growing apart as it expanded. The bulletin credited individuals who had contributed application programs or full systems for inclusion in the network library. It also made these applications available upon request to any division within the network.

This form of network monitoring was extremely effective. The divisions viewed it not as an interference but as an aid. The divisional staff still had the freedom to develop applications that their divisions needed. The monitoring only provided a source of information that would have been more difficult to come by without centralized reporting. For this reason, most of the divisions freely cooperated with the network manager.

A second function of the network manager was to make sure that *no* applications were placed in the library that weren't suitably documented and developed according to system standards. For this reason, a documention specialist on the corporate staff was made available through the network manager to divisional personnel who, because of operational demand, did not have time to adequately document their programs but wanted them to be included in the library. Although some programs that were contributed to the library were not the best coded or the most useful, the fact that they were freely contributed is indicative of the excellent cooperation between the divisions and the corporation.

As the network developed, interdivisional communications that were previously handled through correspondence were considered for automation. Applications that were formerly done through telex and interoffice memos were considered for incorporation into the network application—much like "electronic mail." But more traditional procedures such as interdivisional billings and intercompany ordering or material requisitions were placed on a higher priority as networking applications.

The natural evolution from the star to the ring configuration allowed communications to be passed directly between peripheral systems, without requiring the assistance of a central unit. Figure 24 is an illustration of a typical ring configuration, where communication

Figure 24. Ring structure.

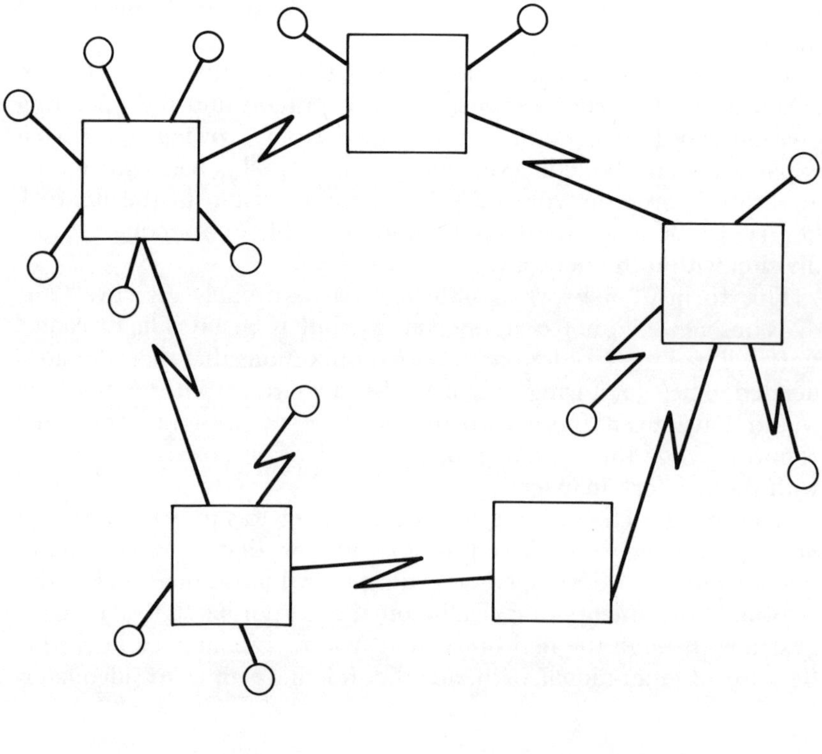

takes place in a designated circular structure from one node to another within the network. The ring, originally a communications structure, has tremendous application within a distributed-processing environment. Though not as constrained as in the communications environment, it frequently represents an open-ended line of communication between various nodes within the distributed-processing network.

Static ring structures are usually devised purely as efficient communications channels, while open rings provide an effective method of interdivisional communication. A good example of such an application is intercompany ordering and billing. Companies that treat their divisions as separate corporations require that interdivisional transactions be handled in the same accounting manner as transactions with external customers. This means that a stock transfer from one division to another must be recorded as a purchase to the division ordering the merchandise and a customer order to the division shipping the merchandise.

In a network application, where the systems are compatibly structured between divisions, the divisions can easily automate this order procedure. There can even be feasibility inquiry prior to ordering. This allows the business to operate more efficiently and cuts down the clerical overhead of unnecessary paperwork between divisions. But this is just one simple application that could be networked. There are many other potential applications.

Setting Up a Hierarchical Structure

For years, international corporations such as the one we've been discussing have been plagued with the problem of processing monthly financial statements. In most well-managed multinational corporations, once a month each subsidiary must submit a financial report to the corporation. This report represents the division's current status of business affairs and is usually measured against the division's budgeted financial projections. Upon receiving the information each month, the corporate accounting department usually is under immense pressure to assimilate the information and prepare various management reports as quickly as possible so that upper management can review the results and determine what directives to give the subsidiaries.

Upon completion of the analysis, another set of reports is prepared and distributed to the various divisions for review. Because of the time-consuming nature of the job, the reports are always untimely, and far too frequently the burden is left to the individual subsidiaries to translate the currencies from U.S. dollars back to their local currencies.

Whereas the analysis and management-reporting portions of the monthly process usually are computerized, information gathering and redistribution normally are not. The most unfortunate part is that for many subsidiaries, the information must be prepared several times: twice by the subsidiary (once in its local currency, the second time in U.S. dollars), and then again by the corporation as it receives the information.

Figure 25. Hierarchical structure.

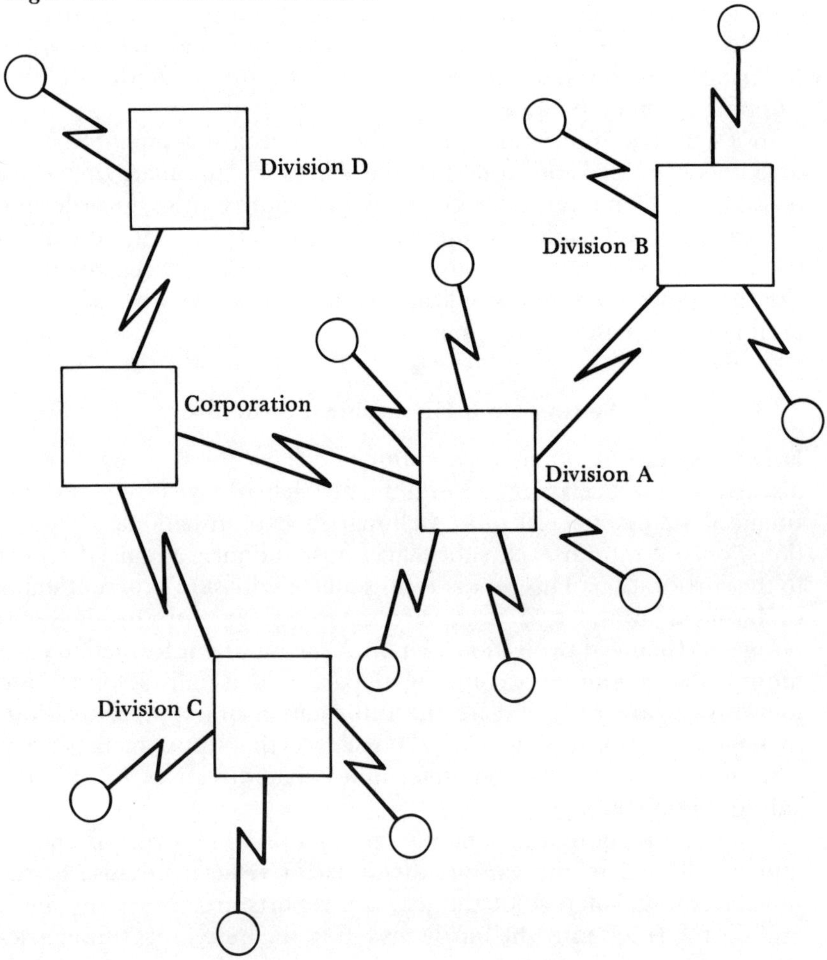

With a structured network, the solution to this kind of problem is obvious. The question is, though, at what point the manual system should be replaced by digital communications. In advancing networks such as the one we've been talking about, there is a point at which the improved timeliness of data and savings in clerical and computer time outweigh the cost of communications. And that is the point where the corporation should seriously consider automating the transmission and distribution process.

Although each division could directly communicate the information to the corporation through the network, setting up a hierarchical communications structure can significantly reduce the transmission costs. In analyzing line capabilities and line costs, one finds amazing differences from one country to another. Therefore, each application has to be analyzed on its own merit, with tariff rates and line capabilities in hand. Although a practical solution can be worked out, it will be unique in each case and may require alteration as tariff rates and communication capabilities change.

As is illustrated in Figure 25, a practical solution to this type of monthly reporting function might be for the corporation to set up a structure whereby the divisions that have poor communication lines can transmit their information at low speeds to a division that has better line capabilities. And from these divisions, the data could be forwarded to the corporation. However, because of the complexity of setting up such networks, structures of this nature tend to be iterative: you may have to go through several alternatives before finding the right one.

Summary

As noted in our sample study, distributed-processing networks can take many forms. The methods and techniques used by our multinational manufacturer might not be exactly what is appropriate for you. The important issues to be resolved are system compatibility and network standards. If these issues are properly addressed and the fundamentals are well developed, the rest becomes a matter of planning and installation.

The secret of a successful distributed-processing network is no different from the secret of a good computer system. It's got to be designed with people in mind. They are the final judges. And they are the ones that will decide if it will succeed or fail.

11

Security Issues

The advent of distributed processing and computer networks has significantly increased our ability to process decision-making information rapidly and disseminate it over a wide spectrum. But at the same time, increased distribution of sensitive information also creates greater security risks. Protecting information is much more difficult in a distributed computer system than in a centralized system. Distributed systems, quite simply, are inherently more difficult to control, because they have so many more information access points than their centralized counterparts.

Failure to protect sensitive information from unauthorized users can prove very hazardous to any corporation's fiscal health. Even from a legal standpoint, it pays to protect sensitive information. The Corrupt Practices Act of 1976 requires corporations to take reasonable measures to ensure that data are not misused.

Ensuring security in distributed computer systems is a hot topic for discussion today, with all the attention focused on computer clubs and youngsters with microcomputers in their homes. The key point here is access. Today's society is in the midst of an "access boom."

With computer access readily available to so many potential users, it is no wonder that security problems are reaching unprecedented proportions. As a result, security systems today have to protect computers against unauthorized users and ensure that unauthorized access is detected.

How Vulnerable Are Distributed Computer Systems?

Distributed computer systems are vulnerable to unauthorized access at several points: the host computer installation, any computer or terminal connected to the local area network, the local network itself, and long-haul communications over telephone lines or microwave links. Information transmitted over telephone lines, for example, can be accessed simply by tapping into a phone line. Computer messages can be tapped and recorded as easily as spoken conversations. And by tapping computer phone-line link-ups, one can easily determine what passwords and access codes are used by a particular system. These codes can then be used to gain access to other computer installations on the same network link-up. For example, in a corporate environment, someone with the right codes could gain access to division computers in another city or operations center.

Many on-line systems control access through programs that limit access of data base material to outside users. This is a good practice, since it limits the amount of material to which any potential information thief can gain access. Still, with the proper receiving equipment, anyone can record and print out material being displayed on video terminals or in a computer center.

In a distributed system, if someone breaks into one computer system in the network, then access to the entire network is possible. For example, someone who gains unauthorized access to a company's divisional computers in Denver could gain access to information in all divisions. Somebody who breaks into information networks can operate the systems from a home microcomputer with very little chance of ever being detected.

Although deliberate access attempts are rare, inadvertent access to computer systems is not. Often authorized personnel, through some quirk or mistaken use of a system, can gain access to areas that are regarded as off limits. Although it is unlikely that a mistake in one division could lead to destruction of computer material in another, the potential is there.

And as Hollywood has so aptly demonstrated in films like "WarGames" and "Superman III," there are an unlimited number of access routes for those who are creative. For instance, someone with little working knowledge of your system can easily gain access to confidential salary information, product data, cost and pricing lists, and corporate secrets, in the most unlikely ways.

All these cases, no matter how farfetched, illustrate important factors to consider when thinking about security. If you can envision any of these scenarios unfolding in your company, then it is time to consider a security system for your computer network.

How Much Security Do I Need?

To determine the amount of security protection your company or system needs, you must consider two major factors. One, if the data in your computers wound up in the wrong hands, what would be the consequence? Two, what is the probability of someone gaining unauthorized access to your company's computer system?

Whether you have an existing distributed-processing system or are planning to implement one, you should start your security system by preparing a computer security protection plan. This plan should include:

- A definition of sensitivity levels of data and identification of those who have access to data on each level.
- A definition of the perceived threat to security (including all possible unauthorized accesses to the system), and some assessment of the potential consequences of a break-in or violation.
- A security system design, including security protection elements and security procedures to counter any perceived threats.
- An estimate of the costs of implementing the security system.
- An estimate of continuous annual protection costs.

In addition, you must ensure that only authorized individuals will have access to information managed by the system's security controls. In other words, your security system must itself be secure.

The Department of Defense has defined the following requirements for a secure computer system:

Security policy—there must be an explicit and well-defined policy enforced by the system. This means there should be a set of rules spelling out who is authorized to use what information.

Marking—data must be marked or classified in a way that clearly shows how sensitive they are. For example, data may be marked "Officers Only," "Restricted," or "Unrestricted."

Identification—the person accessing information must be identified by an access code.

Accountability—audit information must be selectively filed so that actions violating security can be traced to the responsible party.

Assurance—the secure computer system must contain a hardware/software mechanism that can be independently evaluated so that it enforces the basic security requirements.

Continuous protection—the equipment and software that ensure computer security must be continuously protected against tampering and/or unauthorized changes.

Implementing Security Measures

A security system for a distributed-processing network can be implemented in phases. The protection effort should first address those security elements that can be implemented rapidly and that will have significant impact on overall security. The security elements relevant to distributed-processing systems are:

Security procedures.
Physical security safeguards.
System access controls.
Computer software modification controls.
Emanation protection.
Long-haul network security.
Data base access security.
Security logging.

Security Procedure

The computer network must be protected by a well-defined security procedure that is easily understood by everyone in your organization who comes in contact with the computer system. This procedure should cover the following items:

- Identification of security-administration personnel and definition of their job responsibilities.
- Control, use, and maintenance of password files.
- Assignment and control of access rights (who can access what data and programs).
- Physical access controls to computer system elements.
- Sign-on and sign-off procedures.
- Safeguards for system software when not in use.
- Storage and protection procedures for documented files, input/output products, and garbage.
- Software configuration control procedures.
- Testing and verification procedures for software security.
- Link-up and transmission procedures.
- Start-up, shutdown, and restart procedures.
- Controls for handling visitors and service technicians in computer operations areas.

Physical Security Safeguards

Physical security safeguards of computer elements at all locations should be implemented to protect against unauthorized access to the system, as well as to prevent tapping and adding of system penetration devices.

System Access Controls

Controlling access to your computer system is very important. It is in this area that security becomes troublesome, because of the large number of access points in distributed systems. Here are the best precautionary measures.

To begin with, a security administrator should use password access controls when allowing other users on the system. Of course, password assignments should be controlled by the administrator, and passwords should be changed frequently.

Visitors to the computer center should be controlled to prevent unauthorized users from installing programs that might allow access to sensitive information. One person should be appointed security supervisor with responsibility for maintaining the security of computer systems at each location. Security policies must be strictly enforced by this person.

Physical access to computer resources, particularly the host computer system, should be controlled on a 24-hour basis to prevent use by unauthorized personnel. Disk packs, magnetic tapes, and diskettes containing sensitive information (or containing programs that allow access to such data) should be securely stored.

The disposal of computer listings and storage media should be regulated. Intruders have broken into computer systems from printouts left in garbage cans. Carelessness in this simple area can turn out to be the most costly (and unnecessary) mistake in a computer operation.

Computer Software Modification Controls

Computer software modification should be controlled to prevent program alterations that could allow unauthorized users to bypass a security system. Controls should include screening of personnel responsible for implementing program changes, formal reviews of program modification efforts, strict software configuration control procedures, and thorough testing of modified programs to ensure that system security has not been jeopardized by any program changes.

Emanation Protection

Power lines may have to be shielded and filtered to reduce emanation of signals from computer equipment. Tests can be run to monitor signals from outside the facility to determine whether the levels are strong enough to allow an outsider to obtain sensitive information with listening devices outside the building.

Long-Haul Network Security

Unauthorized access to sensitive information transmitted over long-haul networks should be prevented at all times. Several techniques are available for protecting information during telephone transmissions, including the use of unlisted telephone numbers, sophisticated link-up procedures, and data encryption. Encryption devices provide the best security protection in this area.

Access Controls for Local Area Networks and Data Bases

Unauthorized access to local area networks (LANs) must be prevented. (Local area networks are discussed in some detail in the next chapter.) Physical security, password access controls, and data encryption are the most effective methods of protecting sensitive material transmitted over local area networks.

Data base access controls must be in place anywhere in the network where users are allowed to read and/or write information from the data base. These controls can be implemented through a combination of hardware and software techniques. Today there are several protection programs that operate on top of the host's operating system to limit user access.

Large companies and government agencies have spent considerable time and money on the development of secure systems to support many users with different access-level privileges. Unfortunately, so far these efforts have resulted in serious degradations in system performance.

Remember, it is much easier to implement security protection for a new system than one that already exists. Also, various levels of security can be obtained, with higher levels of security at a correspondingly higher cost.

Technology Outlook

A concept called "security reference monitor" has been developed as a model to define security protection requirements for multilevel-access systems. The monitor is assumed to be a "trusted" mechanism that enforces any desired access privileges every time the data base is used. The mechanism must be tamper-proof and have the ability to protect itself against invalidation. It should also be subjected to periodic analysis and testing.

In recent years, security advancements have focused on the development of a security "kernel," which enforces the reference-monitor concept in operating systems. With a security kernel in place, it is extremely difficult to tamper with a system. Currently, Honeywell, Inc., is successfully using a secure distributed computer system, called Multecs.

Soon, secure multilevel distributed systems will use a combination of smaller, less costly, and more easily verifiable components to permit secure network communications. The secure network will include trusted and untrusted elements to enforce multilevel-access security.

Multilevel-security communications networks will include the following major components: untrusted front-end processors, trusted front-end processors, trusted cryptographic authenticator devices, and untrusted DBMS. The trusted front-end devices enforce security policy, invoke DBMS commands, mask and filter output, validate input data markings, and handle exceptions. The untrusted front-end processor passes input queries and performs output formatting and post-data-base computations, such as counts, averages, and so on.

With this technology, DBMS security would be achieved as follows. When a data element or record is written, it is cryptographically sealed by a trusted device and the "authenticator" is added to the data record. The data record includes the sensitivity level. When the data record is subsequently queried by the user, the trusted DBMS front-end processor recomputes the cryptographic authenticator from the data and compares it to the authenticator attached to the record when it was first created. If they differ, the read is aborted and an "exception alarm" is signaled. If they agree, the integrity of the data record, including data sensitivity-level markings, is assured and the data can be further processed by the front-end processor.

This technology holds great promise for linking local area networks and subnetworks with wide area networks to provide secure communications at multiple sensitivity levels.

Summary

Security protection of a distributed-processing system involves the implementation of well-defined security procedures, the use of data protection equipment throughout the network, and the continuous monitoring of system security. Protecting information in a distributed computer system is much more difficult than in a centralized system, because there are so many access points to the system where physical access cannot be controlled.

Computer security protection should start with preparation of a security protection plan. The level of security protection should be dictated by the consequences of unauthorized access and the probability of such unauthorized access. The higher the level of protection, the greater the cost of the security system.

Since distributed systems are a relatively new technology, security protection of these operations is also in its infancy. However, computer security technology is advancing so rapidly that highly secure and relatively inexpensive multilevel-access networks will be available soon.

12

On the Horizon

Today, the movement to minicomputers has stabilized and most firms using minicomputer systems have structured their data processing environments to take full advantage of the possibilities of distributed processing. So the policies and procedures required for planned and controlled growth through a network design are in place. But another challenger has arrived on the scene—the microcomputer. These powerful devices pose an even greater challenge to data processing management than minicomputers, because of their virtually limitless potential.

Microcomputers have been available to the commercial business market since the mid-1970s. But for years, microcomputer sales hinged solely on word processing and worksheet applications. Micros, with their easy-to-use video screens, keyboards, and printers, are perfectly suited for word processing, and it was in this area that micros gained a foothold in American businesses. However, in the early 1980s, two young programmers developed a product called VisiCalc®, which led micros into a new world of automated spreadsheets. For those whose jobs entail updating budgets, accounting worksheets, price formulas, and other table-associated applications, this package was a godsend.

Between 1981 and 1983, more than 250,000 users purchased VisiCalc® programs. And because micros are designed for specific applications, many were purchased to take advantage of the VisiCalc® application. Indeed, until very recently, 60 percent to 70 percent of all microcomputer sales hinged on word processing and worksheet applications.

It wasn't until word processing became firmly entrenched in the daily activities of American business that microcomputers developed to their full potential. Micros should have become standard business tools much sooner, but data processing managers failed to recognize and promote the capabilities of these systems. As a result, micros got into many firms through the back door—and once they got in, their popularity spread quickly—because alert department heads ignored their in-house data processing managers and purchased micro systems to fit their own needs.

Too Many Micros

While this may have been good for micro manufacturers, it wasn't necessarily healthy for users. Because micros were so inexpensive and versatile, they became highly desirable; everyone bought a micro, even if he really didn't know what to do with one. A costly paradox soon developed—at a time when many firms desperately needed the convenience and advantages of a homogeneous system, they were actually building independent, heterogeneous systems containing numerous brands of micros incompatible with one another.

For example, in a round-table discussion held by *Computer Decisions* in January 1979, the distributed-processing manager from John Deere openly admitted that in an unofficial review, he had found more than 200 microcomputer systems being used in various areas of the company. These independently operating personal-computer systems had found their way into the firm under the guise of word processors, analogical and testing equipment, calculators, and other procurements. The company also found an equal number of micro systems being used as full-fledged computer systems. This fact could not be ignored.

Gradually, other companies woke up to the same problem. Micro proliferation had clearly developed into a problem of immense proportions, and industry started looking for answers. The questions on everyone's mind were: Should micros be controlled, as long as they are serving a useful purpose within the organization? And with everyone from the neighborhood store owner to the President of the United States buying micros, how could their infiltration be controlled?

Unfortunately, the spread of micros and the resulting organizational pains are no different from the minicomputer bulge experienced by the New York bank cited in Chapter 8. Without proper handling, these systems can become just as troublesome as minis.

Even though microcomputer systems are purchased for specific functions, their growth within an organization should be carefully managed. Don't be deceived by bargain price tags. Fifty or 100 micros costing $3,500 to $10,000 each represent a sizable investment. Assuming that these units are allowed to proliferate within an organization, what's likely to happen? Most micros are sold as single units housing a video terminal, a keyboard processor, and one or two diskette drives for storage. By design, each is a single-terminal system. Therefore, when another need arises, it usually means adding another terminal system. The same principle applies for adding peripherals. Peripherals that can be used with different microcomputer brands are rare. So if a user requires five systems, he has to accept the fact that he also needs five printers.

The constraints imposed by this single-terminal computer design have given birth to a new generation of microcomputer products and concepts. One popular idea, which has received considerable attention recently, is the Convergent Technologies workstation concept. This systems regrouping method, started by a number of former Intel employees, represents the first step toward changing micros from autonomously functioning units to network units. The workstation concept answers the need for powerful micro systems that share expensive peripheral equipment such as disk drives and high-speed printers. The concept also allows users to take advantage of economies of scale during expansionary phases. But it is not the only solution to networking problems.

A Powerful Solution: Local Area Networks

Besides Convergent Technologies, other visionary companies from California's famed Silicon Valley also heard industry's cries for help and began working on different solutions. It wasn't long before the appearance of high-tech linking packages with a unique answer: a marriage between micros from different vendors.

Many of the communication advances came out of the expansion to larger-scale disks. Thus companies like Corvus, which were originally in the market of selling high-capacity add-on disks to microcomputer users, found themselves in the local-area-networking market. To sell their disks, one of the major problems they had to solve was to develop the necessary interfaces between their disks and the various popular microprocessors on the market. Since it seemed foolish to restrict the interfacing of the disk units to only one microcomputer at a time, the manufacturers provided a communications control unit that allowed several micros access to the same disk. This in turn led to the development of local area networks (LANs), in which different micros that couldn't communicate directly with one another could communicate through the LAN structure.

This turned out to be a blessing for everyone, especially companies with computer portfolios resembling used-car lots. These high-speed links allowed micros to "talk" to each other and understand what the other micros were saying. Some of the best linking packages are produced by industry leaders such as Corvus, Wang, Xerox, Zilog, and Network Systems, among others. They are part of a multimillion-dollar field that is rapidly taking corporate computer systems out of the centrally oriented world of star structures and into the realm of independent local area networks.

The key to this approach to connecting heterogeneous microcomputer systems is an amazing innovation called "interface cards." They very much resemble credit cards and act as both filters and translators, allowing the micro systems to communicate with one another through their disk units. Corvus Omninet, for example, was one of the first systems to interconnect micros produced by different manufacturers. The Corvus system uses an interface card to provide communications and network management. Each micro is outfitted with an interface card and linked to an Omninet system and to other micros with coaxial or fiber-optic cable. With one of these systems in place, it's possible to form a network with several different computers, such as Apple, IBM, Xerox, Zenith, NEC, or Atari. Networks with as many as 64 varieties of micros are already possible, and bigger systems are likely in the future.

Today a number of microcomputer manufacturers are also offering LAN capability, but many of them limit the user to equipment sold by that particular manufacturer. True networking should not be so limiting. If you are interested in LAN capability, you will have many more options for expanding your network in the future if you are careful to choose a system that can handle different brands of computers.

Without network interfacing, intercommunication of incompitable microcomputers would still be a pipe dream. But at $150 to $300, the network interfaces are reasonably inexpensive, and their price will probably decrease as time goes on. Once the power of this concept is fully understood, local area networks will become the next major movement in distributed processing.

What's Involved in Local Area Networking

All local area networks that are available on the market fall within one of four basic communications structures: PBX, baseband, broadband, or hybrid. Each of these transmission modes offers a different type of communication service. PBX is the most primitive and the cheapest to use and install; broadband is the most advanced and sophisticated and requires a considerable investment. Lines usually have to be installed to support any LAN structure, unless the system is configured to use existing PBX internal telephone lines. However, most of the PBX systems lack suitable signal-checking features for ensuring the integrity of signals transmitted across the lines.

Most of the more commonly used systems are at least baseband-oriented. One of the major reasons for this is that the baseband environment offers some form of signal control, either through collision detection (referred to as CSMA/CD) or token passing. In baseband systems, only one band is set up, and all communications are transmitted over this band.

In the collision detection systems, the baseband network is available at all times for signal transmission between any two stations on the line. However, if during the process of communication, two signals from different sources happen to collide in transit, the system is intelligent enough to acknowledge the collision and request that each station retransmit its information.

The token processing system uses a more conservative approach. It polls each station in a cyclical fashion and allows only one station to transmit information across the line at a time. By controlling the communication flow, it eliminates the possibility of collision, making the probability of the information reaching its destination intact very high.

Because of its reasonable reliability and low cost of installation, baseband control has been adopted for most of the LAN networks on the market. Nevertheless, there are a number of broadband networks available. What distinguishes a broadband network is that it offers multiple bands on which to perform concurrent communications. Other key features of broadband networking are speed and high reliability—advantages that are due to the fact that many of the bands are radio frequency bands. One of the leading broadband systems is WANGNET, which offers four concurrent bands of communications in its network structure. The two highest bands are dedicated to Wang and Wang-compatible units, while a lower band is open for other units.

Local Area Network Configurations

There are three types of wiring techniques used in the LAN structures: star, ring, and bus. In the star configuration, the network structure is centrally oriented, with nodes positioned at the points of the star. In the ring configuration, the wiring is drawn in a daisy-chain fashion from one node to another. In the bus configuration, a line is drawn throughout the office, with outlets available every so many feet. The user simply plugs his unit into the closest outlet. Because of its flexibility, the bus structure is the one most commonly offered by the major LAN manufacturers.

Integrating LANs into Distributed-Processing Networks

In a typical minicomputer-based commercial on-line "star" system (as in Figure 26), the accounts and financial records of the company are retained on the mass-storage disks next to the central processing unit, while the video terminals are placed out at the user locations. Some of the terminals might have direct links into the system, while others might communicate through modems. The biggest weakness in this structure is that the users are not protected in the event of a

***Figure 26.** Traditional mainframe- or minicomputer-based distributed system arranged in a star structure.*

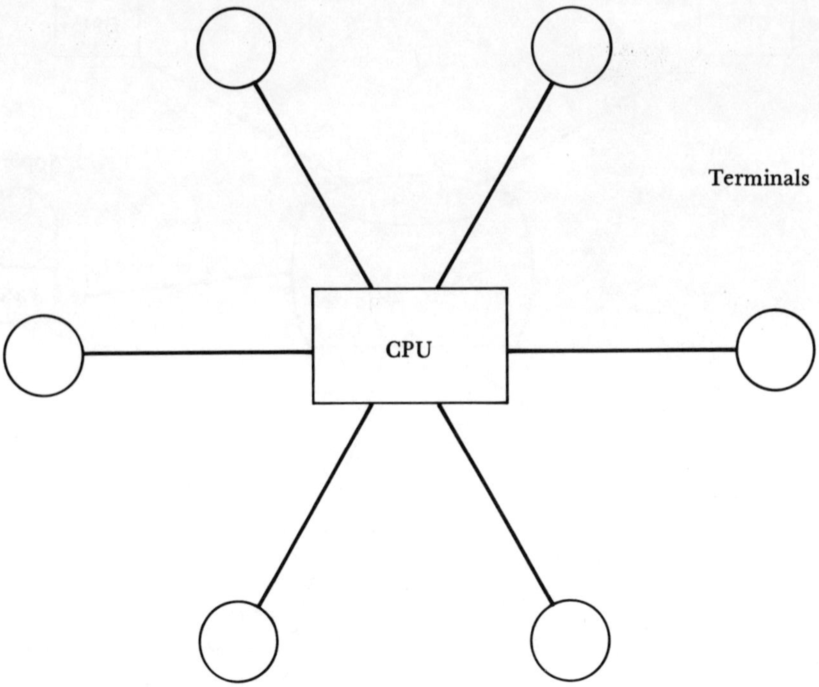

main processor failure. When the central processor fails, all outlying terminals also fail, because they are dependent upon the central unit and the information housed in it.

By contrast, the LAN structure (shown in Figure 27) is not dependent on a central processing unit. It is a network organized around a centralized data base and a number of independently operating microcomputer units. In this kind of configuration, the terminals are not totally dependent on the central processor. Each microcomputer has its own processor. Therefore, if one of the units fails, it will have little effect on the network—all the others will still continue to function. How is this possible? Each terminal is in effect a computer. Therefore, even if the data base is momentarily inac-

Figure 27. The new LAN (local area network) approach to micros.

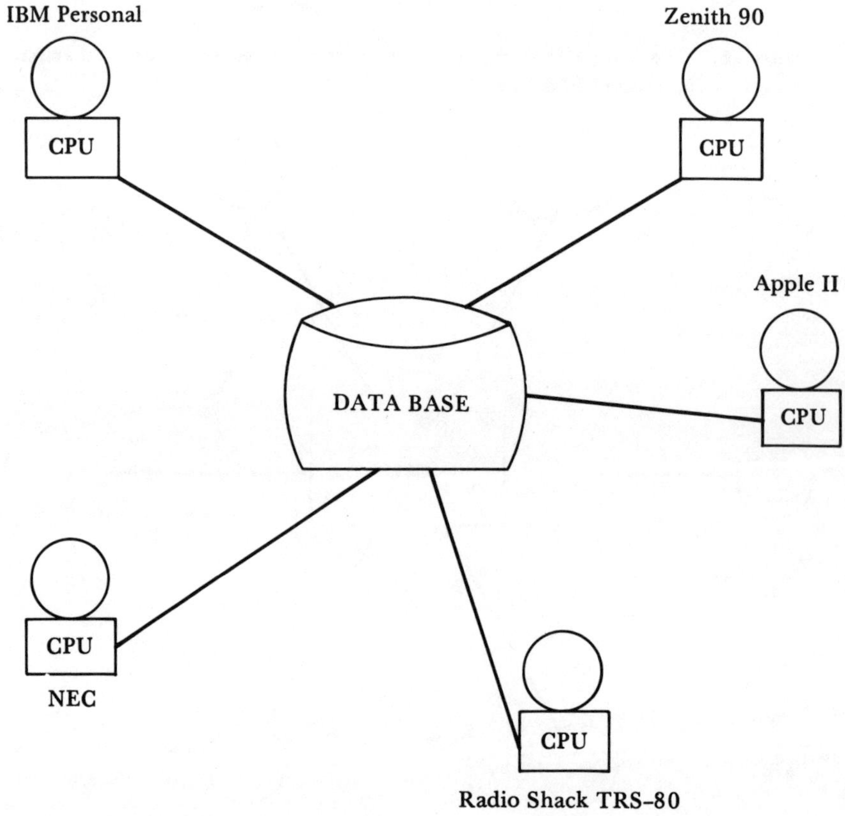

cessible, the computers can switch into a "local mode operation" and still be used to perform data entry and other processing functions. Systems software, of course, must be sophisticated enough to detect a breakdown. But today, as software is continually improving and becoming cheaper, this feature is reasonable and desirable, even if it is not essential in many areas.

Besides these benefits, a LAN system offers unique cost savings. By interconnecting individual systems, users can share expensive peripheral equipment. Also, LANs allow the central processing unit to perform other duties. Downloading the processing from a central computer to a microcomputer will undoubtedly improve response time. But the most important point is that the ability to switch automatically to local mode operations allows outlying operators to continue working without interruptions. For the first time, computer operators are working with a truly intelligent terminal—one that can regulate itself. In a data-entry environment, this is an ideal setup.

Pooling of Peripherals

When we view the long-range direction of systems architecture, it becomes obvious that autonomous systems will soon be a thing of the past. Integrated systems and networking are beginning to dominate the scene. This will undoubtedly have a significant impact on the future systems designer. In the past, data processing specialists who held this title were responsible only for designing the program specifications for a computerized application system. In the future, they will also be responsible for selecting and integrating the various hardware components into an appropriate distributed systems design.

The fact remains that from now on computer hardware will be procured on a networking basis—and justifiably. Firms such as Wang Laboratories are heavily promoting their microcomputer-based word processors, which use commonly available peripherals and offer communications capability to the central host. The expenses and inefficiencies of nonsharable peripherals are avoided by pooling peripherals. Networking and interfacing of large-scale disks and high-speed printers are rapidly becoming a common practice in larger organizations.

Many banks and *Fortune* 500 companies have implemented word processing systems that are integrated with the mainframe systems so that documents can be passed down to the host system, where they are printed on laser printers at a rate of up to 70,000 lines a minute. Not only is this now feasible, but it makes a lot of sense. The technology is definitely available, so why not use it?

Looking Ahead

What do these linked micro systems mean for distributed data processing in the future? The possibilities are exciting and will be dramatically far-reaching. Micro-to-micro link-ups have led to micro-to-minicomputer and micro-to-mainframe communications, which open up a host of new options to the designer of distributed systems.

Most micro systems support modern communications. The standard is asynchronous communications, and most units can handle transmission rates of 300 to 1200 baud quite comfortably. The more advanced units can handle even higher transmission rates. This turns the microcomputer into an asynchronous terminal look-alike, and therefore allows it to be interfaced to systems such as the DEC PDP II Series and Vax units, the HP 3000 units, the DG Eclipse units, and other terminal-oriented minicomputer systems.

An even more powerful option is interfacing micros to the larger mainframe systems, such as the IBM 370s, the 3033s, and the 4300s. Special communication hardware and software products have been developed to allow a wide variety of micros to communicate as 3270-compatible units or even through SDLC protocol. To strengthen this linkage, some microcomputer vendors are even offering direct hookup to the 3784 controller over fiber-optic or coaxial cable.

The future will be dominated by "strings"—a new concept that combines the best distributed-processing techniques of the star and the ring with a few new twists of its own. Under a string setup (see Figure 28), interface cards similar to those in a LAN structure can be used to link micros and mainframes. Accompanying software packages will allow information to be easily communicated over the 2780-to-3780 spectrum from mainframe to micro and back. Therefore, microcomputers will no longer be considered simple terminals. With the necessary modifications, they will become miniature (but highly powerful) central processing units, capable of handling many of the functions of a mainframe, at a fraction of the cost.

Already, a new California-based firm called Datalux has begun marketing several software packages that enable popular brands of personal computers to perform standard data-entry functions, transmitting batched data to a mainframe or large computer. The company is hoping the concept will appeal to beleagured corporations that don't know what to do about having too many desk-top microcomputers. Besides Datalux, other companies like Cullinet are developing data base communications software that can download portions of data bases (or full data bases) from the mainframes to the micros for decision support and update, and then put the results back in the mainframe system.

Figure 28. The future: "string" networks.

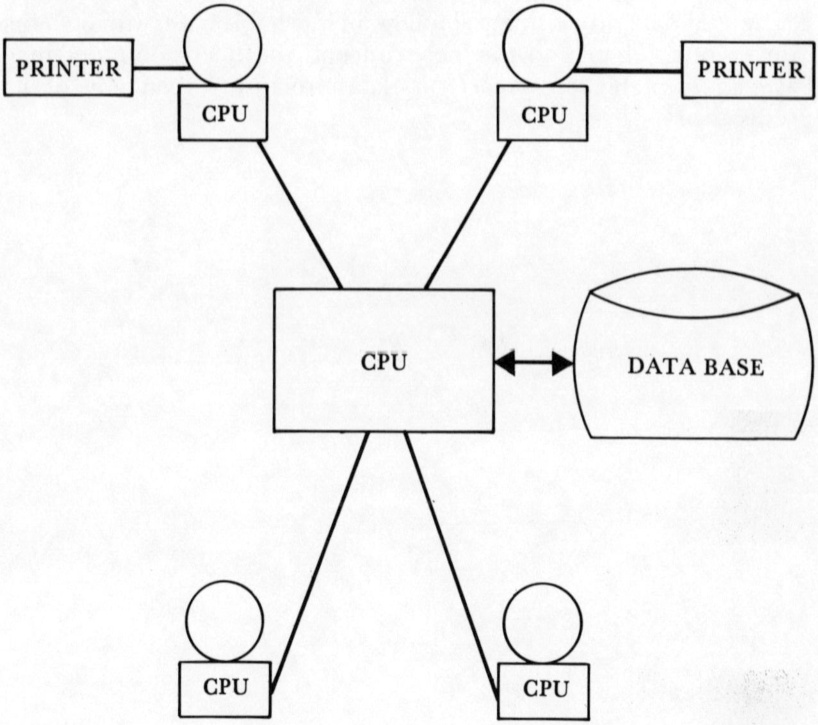

Where will all this lead? With the development of string networks, micros will further promote the concepts of distributed processing throughout organizations of all sizes. For those who think distributed processing is in a cooling-off period, consider the next 500,000 microcomputer units that will be purchased this year for business. Corporate executives will do their own work on a micro either in their office or at home, without having to depend on mainframe availability.

Eventually, micro and minicomputer networks may evolve into supersystems capable of replacing mainframes completely. A complex string system could prevent a total breakdown of the information network if the main system should fail. Given the low price of microcomputers why are we still using dumb terminals? It seems clear that we should replace them with intelligent, networked micros in order to eliminate the problems caused by overloading our centralized computer systems.

Of course, the string concept is still on the drawing board. But at this point it is reasonable to assume that microcomputers and distributed data processing will follow an inevitable path, with benefits to everyone. Thanks to this new concept, the microcomputer may have an even bigger impact on data processing than any of its predecessors.

Appendix A

Comparative Analysis of Two Computer Systems

Contents

Section 1
Introduction

1.1 Scope
1.2 Objective
1.3 Systems Evaluation

Section 2
Technical Discussion

2.1 Hardware Capabilities
2.1.1 Hardware Evaluation Criteria
2.1.1.1 Memory Requirements
2.1.1.2 Type of Memory Available
2.1.1.3 Processing Time
2.1.1.4 Separate Input/Output (I/O) Processor
2.1.1.5 Firmware Capability
2.1.1.6 Hardware Registers
2.1.1.7 Arithmetic Capability
2.1.1.8 Support of Peripherals
2.1.1.8.1 Mass-Storage Disks
2.1.1.8.2 Nine-Track Tape
2.1.1.8.3 Video Terminals
2.1.1.8.4 Teletype Printers

2.1.1.8.5 High-Speed Line Printer
2.1.1.8.6 Card Reader
2.1.1.9 Communications
2.1.2 Hardware Critical for the Corporation's Network
2.1.2.1 Memory Requirements
2.1.2.2 Wide Range of Processors
2.1.2.3 Supporting Peripherals
2.1.2.4 Medium-Speed Printer
2.1.2.5 Communications
2.1.3 Hardware Comparison of the Two Computer Systems
2.1.4 Hardware Summary Analysis
2.1.4.1 Hardware Summary for C1
2.1.4.2 Hardware Summary for C2
2.1.4.3 Comparative Hardware Analysis
2.2 Software Capabilities
2.2.1 Software Evaluation Criteria
2.2.1.1 Operating System Software
2.2.1.1.1 Terminal Independence
2.2.1.1.2 Multiprocessing
2.2.1.1.3 Re-entrant Applications
2.2.1.1.4 Reusable Memory Management
2.2.1.1.5 Virtual Memory
2.2.1.1.6 Dynamic Program Loading
2.2.1.1.7 Common Subroutine (Run-Time) Library
2.2.1.1.8 Data Stacking
2.2.1.1.9 Logical I/O Handling
2.2.1.1.10 Spooling
2.2.1.2 Data Base Management
2.2.1.2.1 Data Base Access
2.2.1.2.2 Multithreading of the Data Base
2.2.1.2.3 Multiple Chains
2.2.1.2.4 Network Data Management
2.2.1.2.5 Data Base Security and Recovery
2.2.1.2.6 Query Language
2.2.1.3 Terminal Transaction-Processing Monitor
2.2.1.4 Support for Low-Level Languages
2.2.1.5 Support for Higher-Level Languages
2.2.1.6 Password Protection and User Control
2.2.1.7 System Utilities and Recovery Routines
2.2.2 Communications Software
2.2.3 Software Comparison of C1 and C2
2.2.4 Software Summary Analysis
2.2.4.1 Software Summary for C1

2.2.4.2 Software Summary for C2
2.2.4.3 Comparative Software Analysis

Section 3
Support

3.1 Hardware Support
3.1.1 Hardware Support for C1
3.1.2 Hardware Support for C2
3.1.3 Hardware Support Summary
3.2 Software Support
3.2.1 Software Support for C1
3.2.2 Software Support for C2
3.2.3 Software Support Summary
3.3 Education and Training

Section 4
Conversion

4.1 Analysis of Method 1—Convert As Is
4.2 Analysis of Method 2—File Conversion Only
4.3 Analysis of Method 3—File Conversion with Limited Program Conversion
4.4 Conversion Summary

Section 5
Cost

5.1 Quotations for C2
5.2 Quotation for C1
5.3 Cost Summary

Section 6
Summary

1
Introduction

1.1. Scope

The scope of this report is confined to five basic areas of our computer selection criteria:

Hardware capabilities.
Software capabilities.

Support.
Conversion.
Cost.

For each area, we will discuss the strengths and limitations of the two computer systems. The discussions shall be detailed enough for suitable evaluation in technical as well as business terms.

1.2. Objective

The objective of this report is to evaluate two computer systems, C1 and C2, on a hardware and software basis in order to select a suitable system for the corporation's operation. We must consider what plan of action should be taken to ensure that:

- Equipment is selected that can successfully handle both the present operation and the future on-line operation.
- The conversion effort will involve minimum restructuring of file information and application programs and limited system development.
- A unified effort will be made by all personnel involved to ensure successful transition.

1.3. Systems Evaluation

Evaluation data have been compiled for two computers, C1 and C2. Each has been reviewed by DATAPRO Research Corp., the foremost data processing research consultants in the country. The C1 system was rated in a lower performance class than the C2 system. C1 was compared to the IBM System 3 product line, while C2 was placed in the mainframe class of the IBM 370, Model 135.

The C1 product has been on the market for over ten years, in which time it has maintained one compatible set of operating software which has been thoroughly field-tested and continuously enhanced to meet market demands. C2 is a relatively new product line resulting from the manufacturer's recent policy of establishing a compatible set of products that could address the entire business market. From a hardware standpoint, C2 is an excellent system; however, from a software perspective, it has been in a developmental evolution since its inception, and although it no doubt is a very promising product, it will require time to mature.

2
Technical Discussion

2.1. Hardware Capabilities

In order to decide which of these systems would be most suited for the corporation, criteria of evaluation have been established which represent the corporation's basic requirements and clarify the most important features.

2.1.1 Hardware Evaluation Criteria

The following paragraphs itemize the basic hardware requirements that the system must have in order to serve the corporation and the network.

2.1.1.1 Memory Requirements

Systems must support memory of at least 256,000 bytes with expandability to 512,000 bytes, using hardware memory mapping or direct addressability. To support the ongoing system requires 256,000 bytes of memory; however, additional memory could improve throughput, if throughput becomes a problem.

2.1.1.2 Type of Memory Available

Memory must be semiconductor to adequately meet the processing demands of a high-performance on-line environment. The advantages of semiconductor memory are:

Less power required to maintain it.
Less space required to house the unit.
Direct isolation of defective memory components.
Greater long-run reliability.
Extremely fast execution (200-600 nanoseconds).
Extremely inexpensive.

Within the next five years, memory will be found only in the semiconductor form, primarily due to these six advantages. All vendors offer semiconductor memory within their product lines in one manner or another. Today, it is principally being offered as interchangeable with or in combination with core memory, but core will soon be obsolete.

2.1.1.3 Processing Time

The processing unit must have high-speed memory in order to ensure adequate response time to the user. This requires a processor with memory cycle time no greater than 700 nanoseconds (.7 microsecond). It is difficult to evaluate processing throughput on the basis of statistics alone, but the statistics do provide some guideline. Such factors as the instruction size, the capability to fetch the next instruction while the present one is executing, the number of bytes of information transferable per fetch (the data path), and the time required to execute each instruction are as important in analysis as the speed of memory. Benchmarks (configured test environments) tend to resolve the problems of theoretical analysis.

2.1.1.4 Separate Input/Output (I/O) Processor

To relieve the input/output (I/O) burden of having to service multiple low-speed devices by the central processor, the system the corporation selects should have an internal I/O processor. This unit usually shares the central processing unit. The result of this configuration is a substantial improvement in throughput.

2.1.1.5 Firmware Capability

Computer manufacturers have expanded their machines' instruction capabilities in order to satisfactorily handle the kind of processing indicative of commercial applications—that is, high-precision decimal arithmetic, rapid flow of strings of data, data string comparison, and extensive table manipulation. This was achieved by adding "firmware" or microprogrammable high-speed memory (normally 20 nanosecond cycle time) into the central processor to execute instructions. By contrast, instructions of the older form were kept in hardware and were inflexible to modification. Because the firmware area is accessible to the user, frequently used subroutines can be placed there, reducing memory requirements and increasing throughput. A firmware-oriented machine is required to satisfy the type of processing taking place at the organization.

2.1.1.6 Hardware Registers

The system the corporation selects must contain a comfortable number of hardware registers in order to minimize the overhead factor or bottlenecking of data manipulation. In general-purpose systems, 8 to 16 general registers and 2 to 3 index registers is sufficient. For stack-oriented machines, fewer general-purpose registers and more index or stack registers are required.

2.1.1.7 Arithmetic Capability

The corporation is not interested in the strong scientific capabilities of these machines, such as complex arithmetic or trigonometric functions; but it is concerned with the machine's ability to do high-precision, high-speed integer, and floating-point arithmetic. These functions are dependent upon the machine's resources to perform 32-bit to 64-bit, 10-digit to 15-digit accuracy in addition, subtraction, multiplication, and division through hardware registers rather than through slow software manipulation. The decimal arithmetic refers to the firmware capabilities of the machines to handle what is conventionally known as packed-decimal arithmetic, developed by IBM in the construction of its COBOL compilers. Packed-decimal arithmetic, on the norm, takes ten times longer to execute than binary or floating-point operations. Since a good portion of the systems presently require considerable arithmetic calculations, it would be extremely important from a performance standpoint that these operations take place in binary or floating-point form rather than packed-decimal form. This is an internal function and does not affect programming in any way.

2.1.1.8 Support of Peripherals

The system should support a wide variety of peripheral equipment in order to satisfy the corporations requirements for:

Mass-storage disks.
Nine-track tapes (industry standard).
Video terminals.
Teletype printers.
High-speed line printer.
Card reader.

2.1.1.8.1 Mass-Storage Disks

The system must be capable of high-speed data transfer to support the large-scale units. Overlap-seek capability would be desirable and definitely increases the throughput and optimizes the response time (overlap seek allows two users to retrieve information simultaneously from two different disks). Normally, the vendor provides a controller that is capable of supporting up to eight individual disk drives. This interface is placed in the computer manufacturer's central processor, and is directly linked to either the CPU (central processing unit) or the I/O processor. Different manufacturers' disk units possess different storage capabilities:

C1—50 megabytes of storage.
C2—100 megabytes of storage.

The price of the unit is related to its storage capacity.

2.1.1.8.2 Nine-Track Tape

Nine-track tape is an industry standard in the field of commercial data processing. This standard has been set by IBM in its 2400 series, and has become a standard method of off-line communication between large mainframes such as the 360/370s and the newer processors such as C1 and C2. Presently, to maintain compatibility we require a density of 1600 bits per inch (bpi) and a velocity of 45 inches per second (ips). This would allow interchangeable use of tapes across all computers in the network.

2.1.1.8.3 Video Terminals

In a true on-line environment, these devices are the direct interface between the various departmental users and the computer. Therefore, it is important that they have as many user-oriented features as possible to minimize the time required for training and adjustment. The key features expected of a good video display terminal are:

High-speed performance (960 characters per second).
Reliability (less than one failure per quarter).
Low cost.

Terminals vary in capability from low-speed 30-characters-per-second glass typewriters to 960-characters-per-second menu-oriented screen communications devices. These devices fall into two classes of communications:

- Asynchronous—where information is transmitted character by character to and from the processor.
- Synchronous—where information is transmitted as a block or a page of characters to and from the processor.

Asynchronous terminals are low-cost terminals and are excellent for program development. The transmission rate of these units ranges from 30 to 240 characters per second. For transaction processing, it is advantageous to operate in a synchronous manner, using a screen menu format for entry of information, and requiring computer processing only upon transmission of the entire block. These terminals require additional features not usually found on asynchronous devices, such as screen-formatting capability, cursor addressability, dual intensity to differentiate input from menu, line-drawing capability, tabbing, transmit identification, and others. They also operate at rates ranging between 240 and 960 characters per second.

The advantage of using synchronous instead of asynchronous terminals in large terminal environments is that the synchronous terminals reduce the servicing load on the processor and improve throughput.

2.1.1.8.4 Teletype Printers

These devices operate like low-speed asynchronous video terminals, but can do the additional function of providing hard-copy output. Terminals of this type can be located in the warehouse for preparation of bills of lading, packing slips, stencils, stock status reports, and the like. These devices can also be connected to a video terminal, bypassing the need for a direct connection to the computer.

2.1.1.8.5 High-Speed Line Printer

The corporation must have a high-speed line printer, connected to the central unit, for the production of program listings and batch reports. This printer must be capable of speeds no less than 600 lines per minute, otherwise the system will be backlogged in reports.

2.1.1.8.6 Card Reader

Initially, development must take place through the video terminals and through program card units. For this reason, a medium-speed card reader is required. After the on-line system development effort levels off, this device will no longer be necessary, because all entries will be made via the terminals.

2.1.1.9 Communications

The corporation will be interested only in the area of terminal communications, which has been discussed in paragraph 2.1.1.8.3. Communications with other divisions are discussed in the paragraphs relating to the corporation's network.

2.1.2 Hardware Critical for the Corporation's Network

The European portion of the corporate network needs to communicate with Europe as well as relay information back to the Corporate Headquarters. We must not only be concerned with the European operation but must also consider hardware requirements to support its role in the network.

2.1.2.1 Memory Requirements

In order to satisfy a worldwide network, additional memory modules might be required. The memory would be dedicated to the expansion of I/O buffers and the capability of executing more routines simultaneously. The present configuration accommodates the execution of eight concurrent tasks. With the additional requests made by the network, and the final load of the division, a configuration of 16 tasks should be adequate.

2.1.2.2 Wide Range of Processors

It would be extremely desirable, but not required, to select a manufacturer which has a series of processors that support a wide range of application models, small to large, using one set of systems software, that is, one operating system, one data base manager, one terminal processor, and the same set of higher-level language compilers. This could reduce the cost of the programming development by establishing one set of programs that can act as the standard for the system. Keeping the application programs confined to small program units will ensure that these programs can be used in both the host and satellite systems. This can be adequately accomplished only if the system software is the same for both processors.

2.1.2.3 Supporting Peripherals

Added to the complement of peripherals must be the single-cartridge disks, which would be configured for the smaller satellite systems at other corporate facilities. These devices have a capacity of 10 megabytes per unit.

2.1.2.4 Medium-Speed Printer

The satellite systems do not require high-speed line printers (600 lines per minute) but should be satisfied with inexpensive 200 lpm printers or the medium-speed 300 lpm printers.

2.1.2.5 Communications

Through the use of the 2780 emulator, communications can be supported at all levels over the network. Users in the European divisions could have direct access to information in the system over a switched network hookup, which displays the information on the user terminal seconds after the request. For computer-to-computer communications, the corporation's satellites will be able to transmit and receive information to/from other satellites within the network, or to/from the host computer at headquarters. The expense of the network will depend primarily on the cost of the common carrier. The expense for the equipment within the computer system will be small compared to the total cost of the system.

2.1.3 Hardware Comparison of the Two Computer Systems

The hardware features of the two systems, C1 and C2, are summarized for comparison in Table A-1.

C1 has a limited capability of instruction overlap (the loading into the CPU of the next instruction while the present one is in execution). C1's architecture can accommodate only the loading and interrogation portion of the operation code of the next instruction and not the entire instruction. This is due to the fact that the instruction is operated on by the firmware and not the CPU; therefore, the instruction must be held until the firmware has completed the present instruction and is ready to receive another.

Although there is no dedicated stack registers or dedicated multiprocess management hardware, there are sufficient general-purpose hardware registers to support a good multiprocessing operating

Table A-1. Hardware comparison of the two computer systems C1 and C2.

Hardware Capability	C1	C2
1. *Main Storage (Memory)*		
Storage type, semiconductor	CMOS	NMOS
Quoted capacity, bytes	256,000	256,000
Incremental memory size, bytes	16,000	16,000
Maximum capacity (512,000 bytes required)	1,000,000	512,000*
Speed of memory, nanoseconds (10^{-9} seconds)	525 ns.	350 ns.
Bits reserved for error check and correction	1†	5
Error checking	Parity†	Fault control
Error identification or logging	Standard	Standard
Error correction	No	Standard
Multiprocess hardware protection	Standard	Standard
Battery backup	No	Standard
Storage protection	Software	Hardware
2. *Central Processing Unit*		
Type of system	General-purpose	Time-sharing
Firmware instruction capability	Standard	Standard
No. of instructions in processor	186	209
Data path, bits	16	16
Instruction size, bits:		
stack instructions	—	8
register—register instructions	16	16
register—immediate instructions	32	16
memory—register instructions	32	16
memory—immediate instructions	48	16
memory—memory instructions	48	16
Instruction overlap capability	Partial	Total
Hardware registers		
no. of accumulators	29	38
no. of index registers	8	1
Add time, nanoseconds	2 ns.	5 ns.
Hardware multiply/divide (32 bit)	Standard	Standard
Hardware floating point (64 bit)	Optional	Standard

enhanced version was offered, using semiconductor memory and expanding the memory capability to 512K bytes. In 1978, the company announced another memory expansion to its C2 users, which accommodated 2 million bytes of main memory. However, since the 1973 announcement, the essential design of the C2 system has not been altered. Periodic enhancements have expanded memory and I/O capabilities, but these have been done within the framework of the initial architecture. It is anticipated that further enhancements will be made as the product grows in use.

The C2 is a stack-oriented computer system, with hardware designed specifically to operate in multi-user on-line environments where multiprocessing is a standard function. Stack management is meaningless in a single-process operation. The concept has evolved over the last 15 years as the most efficient answer to the problem of supporting a large multiprocessing operation. Those companies, like C2, which have selected to use these principles in the design of their systems, have further benefitted by implementing many of the stack functions directly in the computer hardware as an ultimate optimization factor. Like C1, C2 is also a firmware-oriented machine. However, the width of all 209 instructions can be accommodated within the 16-bit data path that C2 uses; therefore, full instructions are loaded for each memory fetch made. This coupled with the instruction overlap capability, whereby the entire next instruction is loaded while the present one is being processed, means that the instruction fetch time (the time required to transfer an instruction from main memory to the CPU) does not have an inhibiting effect on the processing of the C2 system. This is concluded simply by the fact that the fastest operating instruction (a load register) takes twice as long to execute (1.6 μs) as an instruction fetch takes to complete (.7 μs).

Studying the C2 design further, we found that the manufacturer has taken advantage of the C2's stack architecture by implementing high-speed 8-bit operating instructions that execute directly off the special stack hardware, which has been incorporated into the system to optimize standard multiprocessing techniques. By making use of these stack instructions, C2 is able to minimize the size of object (load) programs and substantially cut down the processing time, because two of these stack instructions can be retrieved for each 16-bit fetch. Also, by using the stack instructions, the overlap capability is doubled.

The operating system heavily uses the stack hardware to perform its multiprocessing functions. It can branch from one routine to another (establishing a new stack frame) within 25 microseconds through the use of a hardware branching procedure. This almost falls within the execution range of the more complex machine instructions.

In the area of input/output, a separate IOP (I/O processor) has been designed into C2 to assist the processor by allowing I/O to process concurrently with the CPU. When memory is required for I/O servicing, cycles are stolen from the CPU to satisfy the memory management functions. Otherwise, the operation is totally exclusive. C2 uses the IOP as a high-speed .9 megabytes/second multiplexer channel and supports all its peripherals, with the exception of the disks, onto this channel. A separate 2.8 megabyte/second selector channel has been implemented to support the large disk units, and free them from channel contention. The disk unit C2 is supplying with the C2 is a relatively new product to the line. These units are manufactured directly by C2, whereas previous units were manufactured by other peripheral suppliers and interfaced into the system. In reviewing the track record, we find that most users have been totally satisfied with them, praising their reliability. This attitude is also reflected in the DATAPRO reviews.

The area where C2 appears weak is that of synchronous terminal communications. C2's manufacturer has demonstrated to date its leadership in the asynchronous terminal environment, and is in the development of synchronous support. Although it manufactures some of the most sophisticated and reliable video terminals on the market, including an excellent 4K-memory-based synchronous terminal, it has not supported synchronous communications in the past. Presently, it is about to announce its first synchronous terminal controller in both the U.S. and Europe. In speaking with one of the C2 communications experts, we have found that this is an empty announcement and that further refinements are to be expected in the next year—converging to the ultimate goal of supporting large terminal environments (64 terminals) on a synchronous multidrop-line capability.

2.1.4.3 Comparative Hardware Analysis

From our analysis of the two computers, C1 and C2, the following results have appeared:

1. C2 is a substantially faster executing machine than C1, taking into account memory speed, instruction execution times, instruction overlap capability, extent of the instruction set, special stack hardware, and number of hardware registers.

2. C2 offers a power monitor with automatic restart, which suspends processing during power failures and resumes automatically when power is restored. This feature is not available on C1.
3. C2's maximum I/O transfer ratio is 2.5 times that of C1. This means that C2 can process 2.5 times the input/output load of C1.
4. C1 offers six overlapping I/O ports through which input/output devices can be attached. C2 offers only three channels, or half the amount of channels that are on C1.
5. The C2 disk drives offer more storage than the comparable C1 units.
6. From the terminal information that has been supplied, it would appear that the C2 terminals support more features and provide greater capabilities than the comparable C1 terminals. In this area, C1 is in the process of improving its product line. Again, we have no information on the capabilities of the terminals.
7. Synchronous communications hardware has been offered on C1 for over two years. It is a recent addition to the C2 system, which has in the past exclusively used an asynchronous terminal controller (ATC) to handle all terminals within the on-line environment.
8. Both systems offer excellent IBM-compatible 3780 emulation hardware for intercomputer communications.

2.2 Software Capabilities

The method used in the evaluation of software capabilities will be the same as was used in the hardware portion. Establishing evaluation criteria is essential in determining which system is most suited to Europe.

2.2.1 Software Evaluation Criteria

In order for a system to qualify for Europe, it must possess these minimum software characteristics:

Operating System Software:
- Terminal independence.
- Multiprocessing.
- Re-entrant applications.
- Reusable memory management.
- Virtual memory.

Dynamic program loading.
Common subroutine linkage.
Data stacking.
Logical I/O handling.
Spooling.

Data Base Management.
Terminal Transaction Processing Monitor.
Support for Low-Level and Higher-Level Languages
Password Protection and User Control.
System Utilities and Recovery Routines.

Each of these areas shall be addressed in subsequent paragraphs.

2.2.1.1 Operating System Software

A good operating system is measured by the amount of sophisticated features it offers and the ease or transparency of their use. Conventional systems required a high degree of sophistication on the part of the user in order to employ or manage such features. Modern systems tend to shelter the user from this requirement and provide operating software which internally manages these functions.

On most of the minicomputers on the market today, the operating system does not require sophisticated knowledge on the part of the user or programmer. The present direction in operating software is away from extensive use of job control language by allowing the system to perform as much management as it can without requiring operator intervention.

2.2.1.1.1 Terminal Independence

As shown in Figure A-1, an on-line system monitors and maintains communications between many independent users and the central processor without requiring scheduled intervention. This is the exact opposite of batch processing. Instead of *one* scheduled request coming into the processor for servicing, calling a lengthy operation to execute to completion before turning control over to the next scheduled request, dozens of requests are being fed into the processor simultaneously, and each is being serviced independently of the other. Normally, this is accomplished through the use of video display terminals; however, other devices such as teletypewriters and low-speed keyboard printers are also frequently used.

Figure A-1. Terminal independence.

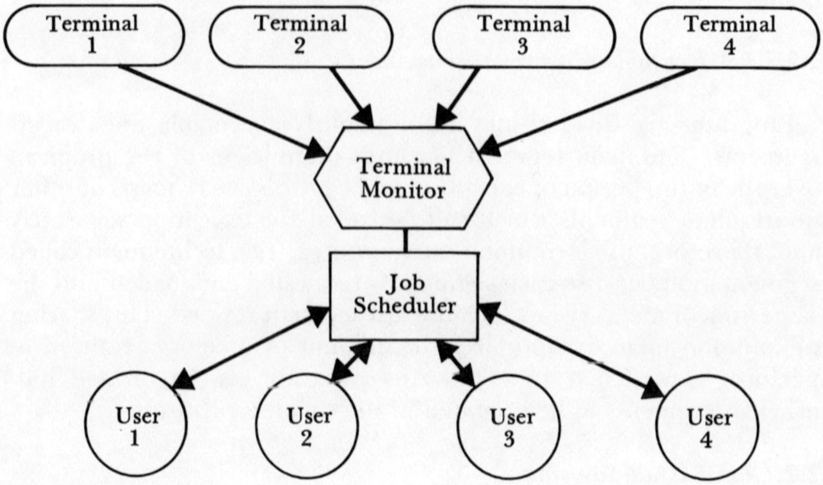

2.2.1.1.2 Multiprocessing

In mainframe systems, multiprocessing is supported only in the large units such as the IBM 360/40 and 370/155. However, in the minicomputer field, even the smallest systems offer multiprocessing. Multiprocessing is the ability of the processor to perform many operations at the same time. This is done by partitioning memory into user application segments, loading the various applications into the computer, and running them simultaneously. In an on-line environment, this allows the system to service many user requests at the same time; ideally, a process is reserved for every user terminal in the system.

2.2.1.1.3 Re-entrant Applications

In order to optimize memory, frequently used routines or applications should be coded in such a way that many users can access them concurrently without requiring separate copies of the program to be in memory—that is, only one copy of the program needs to be in memory at the time of execution. The concept of re-entrant applications is meaningful only in a multiprocessing environment, where many processes require servicing by the same routine. If the system does not have this feature, then additional copies of the routine must be present in memory, inflating the memory requirement.

2.2.1.1.4 Reusable Memory Management

Programs are divided into autonomously executable units called segments. The main segment becomes the nucleus of the program over the entire period of execution and controls the requests of other nonresident segments which can be called for execution separately and, therefore, use a common memory area. The technique is called segmentation because each segment is requested and loaded into the same area of memory in which the last segment resided. This sharing of common memory optimizes the amount of memory required to perform a particular function. Any program can be divided into efficient segments to be executed in the smallest processors.

2.2.1.1.5 Virtual Memory

In order to augment the capability of the memory manager within the central processor, a concept of virtual memory was instituted. Virtual memory allows the computer system to process programs that exceed the processor's hardware memory capacity by maintaining portions of the program or entire program units in an auxiliary memory area on disk. When a memory-based process is completed or interrupted (perhaps due to I/O servicing), it is removed from main memory and placed into virtual memory, and the next-highest-priority virtual-memory-based program section is moved into main memory for execution. The concept of transferring active processes between main memory and auxiliary memory is called virtual-memory management. It allows the processor to handle a program significantly longer than its main memory can accommodate.

This feature is extremely useful in a multiprocessing environment, where the processor is kept as busy as possible without requiring operator intervention for continuous scheduling. Low-priority batch jobs would be rolled out to virtual memory when high-priority on-line functions required servicing; after which the batch function would be rolled back in to resume execution. This is automatically handled by the memory manager in the computer.

2.2.1.1.6 Dynamic Program Loading

Up to recent years, only time-sharing systems were capable of dynamic program loading. But since the fever of on-line systems has spread, the real-time system manufacturers have modified their operating systems to support this feature. The idea is to use any available memory upon demand without establishing fixed partitions in the memory, but protecting the area where a program is loaded. This is a function of memory management, and the more advanced processors allocate and maintain their available memory through hardware functions, freeing the operating system from added overhead.

2.2.1.1.7 Common Subroutine (Run-Time) Library

The more efficient systems have used the technique of creating one common library of subroutines which are all re-entrant codable applications and are loaded into memory in one central area to be used by multiple user programs. The user application, most frequently the result of a compiled program, accesses the routines in the run-time library through branch and return functions, passing parameters to and from the common functions. This technique definitely conserves memory while improving throughput. It is essential that data base management software be located in such an area.

2.2.1.1.8 Data Stacking

Like overlay management, data stacking provides a common area of memory which can be used as a scratch pad by multitask user

Figure A-2. Subroutine library.

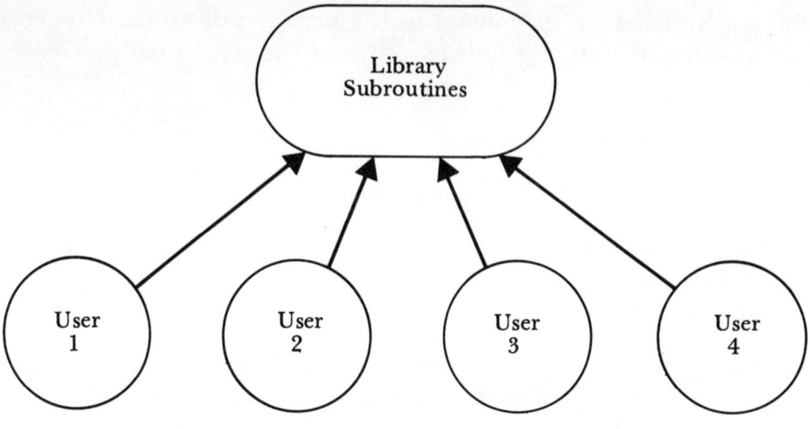

functions. The area is dynamically assigned to a task at execution time and freed upon completion. New data stacks overlay old used data stacks, placing the new interim task data values into a reusable stack area to conserve memory requirements and allow re-entrancy of code. The more critical memory becomes, the more important data stacking is. As a note of interest, the large-scale systems never offered this feature.

2.2.1.1.9 Logical I/O Handling

The purpose behind logical I/O handling was to remove the application from the restrictions of having to identify the physical I/O devices before use. Under the logical method, the application program specifies a run-time device by providing a symbolic identifier, which is later equated to a physical device. This gives the system greater flexibility at run time and simplifies the task of device reassignments. In the large-scale IBM 370 systems, this feature is only offered in the "Cadillac" of operating systems—OS.

2.2.1.1.10 Spooling

One of the most common bottlenecks within a computer system is the printing of reports or listings. The computer operates in nanoseconds (10^{-9} seconds), but the printer functions in seconds. In the past, the throughput of systems was inhibited exclusively because of this slow-speed device. Toward the end of the 1960s, the technique of spooling was developed, which allowed the operating programs to function at computer speeds, while the listings lagged behind. This was accomplished by placing the report information in a temporary disk file. A separate I/O processor concurrently read this file and transferred its content to the printer. All efficient systems use spooling. It costs very little in overhead and substantially increases throughput.

2.2.1.2 Data Base Management

The key ingredients in a true on-line real-time system are:

Multiterminal access.
Multiprocessing.
Integrated data base.

The integrated data base requirement leads to data base management. Often this feature alone is considered the foundation of on-line systems, since without it the system could not survive. The concept of a data base is to create a structure that centralizes information in a related fashion, eliminating the redundancy of data found in conventional file systems. However, it does require more space to structure the information. The purpose of the data base manager is to provide a traffic controller that supervises the accessing and updating of information within the data base. The following paragraphs discuss what is required to support the corporation's data base.

2.2.1.2.1 Data Base Access

Presently there are two types of data base access methods: a multi-key ISAM method and a master–variable file method. The latter technique is the most widely accepted today. It consists of a master-record lookup through the algorithmic calculation of a key, followed by the reading of related chained records called "variable" records. This technique makes on-line inquiry possible and eliminates many of the requirements of large batch passes of the files and pre-sorts for reporting. Both C2 and C1 offer the TOTAL data base management package.

2.2.1.2.2 Multithreading of the Data Base

Due to the extensive data base accessing required to service an on-line system, it is extremely desirable to allow many users access into the data base concurrently, as long as the integrity of the data is preserved. This feature is called multithreading. Many systems simplify data base processing by allowing only single-threading, which provides data base access to one user at a time. This works quite satisfactorily under normal conditions, but multithreading eliminates the possibility of bottlenecks.

2.2.1.2.3 Multiple Chains

Any sophisticated application requires the ability of the data base manager to perform multiple chain processing. This means that variable detail files can be accessed via different masters; for example, we might want to keep routings by part and also keep routings by work center. Also, master files would have the capability of supporting multiple detail linkages; for example, the customer master would support the invoice file, the price file, the ship-to file, the special-

Figure A-3. Hierarchical and network data management.

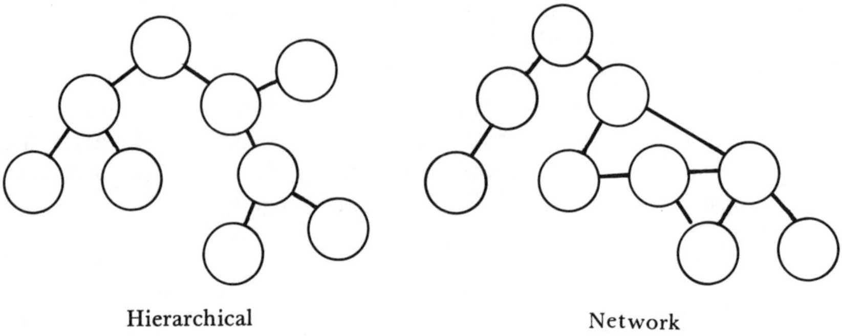

instructions file, and so on, and access could be performed at any time through any path.

2.2.1.2.4 Network Data Management

There are presently two accepted forms of data management: hierarchical and network. The first permits the user to access data down a chain of related files, such as customer to order to item to special instructions, whereas the network approach allows the user to access information by crossing over the range of data. Figure A-3 shows a hierarchical and a network structure.

The flexibility of a network structure is extremely valuable in the formation of a manufacturing data base. The best example of this is the bill-of-materials processor (see Figure A-4). Its data base structure is totally network-oriented.

Figure A-4. Bill-of-materials processor (BOMP).

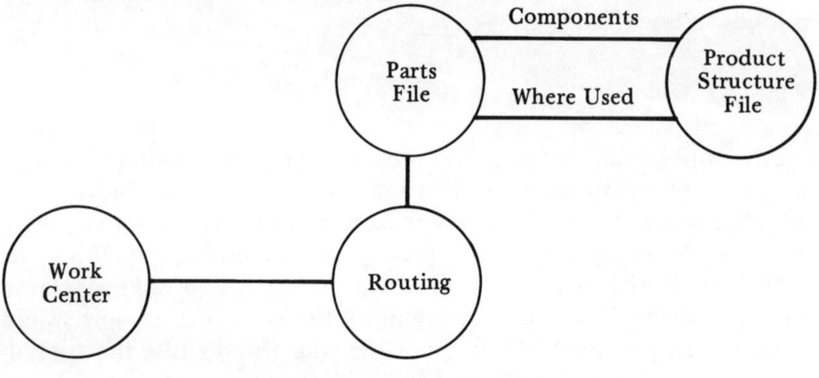

In sum, a network data base manager is a definite requirement for the corporation.

2.2.1.2.5 *Data Base Security and Recovery*

Due to the centralization and accessibility of confidential information, it becomes necessary for the system to have extensive security provisions. This is to prevent unauthorized use of the data base. Advanced data base managers are able to restrict access on the basis of the item rather than the application or the entire record. Take the example of two clerks wishing general access to the personnel/payroll files. The one might have authority to access salary data, whereas the other might be allowed only name and address data. In this circumstance, the data base manager would void the employee's record, filter out the data by replacing unauthorized data with blanks and pass the information to the respective users. Therefore, control of the system is directly a function of how rigorously the security is maintained.

Recovery is another feature of extreme importance. Each of the systems under evaluation must have excellent provisions for data base recovery to minimize the amount of time required to restore the data base in the event of a system malfunction.

2.2.1.2.6 *Query Language*

The development of query language is directly dependent on the establishment of data base management system. The function of a query language is to allow nontechnical (nonprogrammer) users to independently select information from their data bases and report it in a manner they specify. This is done directly at the user's terminal. Becoming proficient in using a query language requires only a few hours of training.

What this does for the corporation is reduce the turnaround time and communications problems between the data processing department and the various users. One-time applications should definitely be done through a query language, while the data processing department remains responsible for larger, systems requests.

2.2.1.3 *Terminal Transaction-Processing Monitor*

The purpose of establishing a transaction-processing (TP) monitor is to centralize the processing functions of supporting the entire online user environment through one powerful software routine. The responsibilities of this routine are to:

- Satisfy on-line requests by displaying appropriate transaction menus (screens) for entry use.
- Perform detailed front-end editing of inputted transaction information.
- Secure access to the system through user password provisions.
- Limit access to the data bases through acknowledged user capabilities.
- Allow only validated transactions into the system.
- Invoke the user application programs required to service the on-line environment.

This function should be capable of monitoring and controlling the entire on-line environment in a complete multiprocessing manner. To adequately support such a function requires the use of a centralized screen data base which houses the entire screen domain, accessible through English-language titles. The screen layout should include the transaction input description for front-end editing and the identification code of the particular application required to perform the processing. When a qualified user makes a request through his video terminal to the monitor to perform an application function, the monitor simply retrieves the appropriate transaction screen from the screen data base and displays it on the user's terminal, then waits for the transaction to be entered. Upon entry, the monitor turns control over to a detail editor, which uses the transaction input descriptors to identify which fields are being entered and which edits must take place against them. When all editing is satisfactorily completed, control is returned back to the monitor, which then invokes the appropriate application program for processing.

Consider this process taking place simultaneously over the entire terminal environment. All processing will be occurring concurrently. This is the function of a TP monitor.

2.2.1.4 Support for Low-Level Languages

The trend in today's technology is the development, on the one hand, of language of higher and higher levels, converging toward the query language approach; and, on the other hand, of more and more efficient lower-level-language support. In years to come, the necessity of intermediate languages will become less significant. Lower-level languages include assembler languages, macro-assembler languages, and microprogramming languages.

Assembler languages are in one-to-one correspondence with the hardware to execute various machine functions, such as loading registers, adding registers, and moving data from one location in memory to another location. No higher-level language will achieve the efficiency of a good assembler program; however, selecting what programs shall be written in assembler is critical. *No* user application programs should ever be coded in assembler language. But the subroutines used in the higher-level languages, such as data conversions, I/O processing, and intricate bit manipulation, should most probably be assembler routines.

One level away from the assembler languages are the macro-assembler languages, which were designed to ease the effort of writing assembler code. These macro-assemblers can be very sophisticated. For example, the macro-assembler language used in the computer C2 resembles a high-level language. Using a macro-assembler language definitely improves productivity.

Many processors are offering programmable read-only memory (PROM). This is a highly efficient semiconductor memory that operates at a speed well in excess of that of standard memory.

However, to use this feature requires that the programmer write in a language called micro-code. Only highly trained technicians can adequately write micro-code programs, due to the degree of technical knowledge required. Micro-assembler languages have helped tremendously in the development of firmware codes. This technology has become a common practice among technicians in the microcomputer field.

2.2.1.5 *Support for Higher-Level Languages*

The corporation's system must be able to support COBOL and FORTRAN. It would be desirable but not necessary for the system to also have such languages as BASIC and RPG II. COBOL would be useful to support the initial phase of conversion from the current system. COBOL has been an industry standard for the mainframe systems for years and is quickly becoming a standard in the minicomputer field as well. The other compilers available to the systems are merely frills to satisfy external applications.

2.2.1.6 *Password Protection and User Control*

When on-line systems are implemented, control of the processing function is removed from the EDP area and distributed out to the user departments. In order to ensure the integrity of the data base, it is essential that adequate security be built into the system. This security function can be instituted at a number of levels. Without becoming excessive, the better the security features, the safer the system. In a true on-line environment, security checks should take place at the following levels:

User identification level.
User account level.
Data base levels:
—No access to data base.
—Only partial access to data base.
Program level.

In the current systems of the corporation, management can restrict or totally inhibit access to the on-line systems by employing security checks on one or more of these levels. We would want to maintain this capability in the European system.

2.2.1.7 System Utilities and Recovery Routines

A complete set of vendor-supplied operating software should include a package of system utilities and recovery procedures. By system utilities we are referring to a set of general-purpose routines that allow the EDP staff to perform daily system functions without having to program these functions themselves. These utilities would handle such functions as file copying, data base buildup, system backup, library maintenance, and so on.

In an on-line system, when program development is also being done on-line, a strong text editor function is required. Through the text editor, programs can be entered and maintained in the system through video display terminal, eliminating the need for a card reader.

Recovery procedures must be at the disposal of the EDP department in the event of a system or data base malfunction. The more efficient the recovery operation, the more valuable the utility. It is imperative to minimize downtime in an on-line environment because of the effect it has on the user. These recovery procedures are crucial to maintaining a high-performance environment.

2.2.2 Communications Software

Both systems support various levels of communications software. The software to support the terminal environment allows both asynchronous and synchronous communications between the video display units and the processors. All major minicomputer manufacturers offer powerful interprocessor communications software that is an inexpensive enhancement to the present equipment.

2.2.3. Software Comparison of C1 and C2

The software capabilities of the two computer systems C1 and C2 are summarized in Table A-2.

Table A-2. Software comparison of the two computer systems.

Software Capability	*C1*	*C2*
1. *Operating System Capabilities*		
Terminal independence	No	Yes
Terminal reassignable	Yes	Yes
Multiprocessing	Yes	Yes
Re-entrant applications	No*	Yes
Reusable memory management	Yes	Yes
Virtual memory	Yes	Yes
Dynamic program loading	Yes	Yes
Common subroutine linkage	No	Yes
Data stacking	No	Yes
Logical I/O handling	Yes	Yes
Spooling	Yes	Yes
Implemented into firmware	No	Partially
2. *Data Base Management Support*		
Access	Master/ Variable	Master/ Variable
Product	TOTAL	IMAGE
Multithreaded	No	Yes
Multiple chain	Yes	Yes
Network access	Yes	Yes
No. of unique items	—	255
No. of detail files supported	30†	99
Password security	No	Yes
Recovery provisions	No	Yes
ISAM capability	Yes	Yes
Query language	No	Yes
Implemented in firmware	No	Partially
3. *Terminal Transaction-Processing Monitor*	Limited	Yes

Table A-2. (Continued)

Software Capability	*C1*	*C2*
4. *Lower-Level Languages*		
Assembler-codable	No	Yes
Macro-assembler-codable	No	Yes
Microprogrammable	No	No
Implemented into firmware	No	Partially
5. *Higher-Level Languages*		
COBOL	Yes	Yes
FORTRAN	Yes	Yes
BASIC interactive	No	Yes
BASIC compiler	No	Yes
RPG II	Yes	Yes
Implemented into firmware	No	BASIC FORTRAN partially COBOL partially
6. *Communications Software*		
Asynchronous terminal	Yes	Yes
Synchronous terminal	Yes	Yes
2780 emulation	Yes	Yes

* Programs are re-entrant codable, but the application processes are not.
† This will be upgraded to a capability of 66 data files.

2.2.4 Software Summary Analysis

This portion of the analysis discusses the strengths and weaknesses of each vendor's software, and how they affect the system and the user in an on-line multiprocessing environment. The following paragraphs provide highlights of each system and a summary comparative analysis.

2.2.4.1 Software Summary for C1

The basic operating system in C1 is NET, a multiprocessing, operating system which uses dynamic memory management and the virtual-memory concept. Previously, the system was constrained to 16 processes. Presently, as many separate program processes can be executed concurrently within the system as are requested for servicing, limited only by the amount of physical main memory present in the system. Each process requires a mimimun of 28K-34K main memory in which to initiate a program. All programs on the C1 are structured in a segmentation manner, maintaining the data and the code in separate segments. The manufacturer refers to this as its "Segment 0—Segment 1" technique, as illustrated in Figure A-5. The combination of these two segments makes up a "process." These segments are variable in size, depending upon the requirements of the program, and it is the memory management software in the operating system that is responsible for dynamically allocating sufficient contiguous memory in which the program can execute. For each process that requires initiation, the memory manager reorganizes memory to make it available if sufficient contiguous memory is not available to accommodate the segment size. This function, due to its critical nature, should not be performed by operating software alone but should be supported by hardware within the CPU.

This segmentation approach allows C1 to optimize its memory management through the use of defined program segment routines and virtual-memory program storage. By making all program segments re-entrant in processing, the conventional swapping technique used in C1's virtual-memory management software is minimized to require only the swapping in of segments from virtual disk storage to main memory. The need to swap inactive segments back out to disk is eliminated. This feature is consistent with the better operating systems.

Figure A-5. ***"Segment O—Segment 1 technique" for Computer C1.***

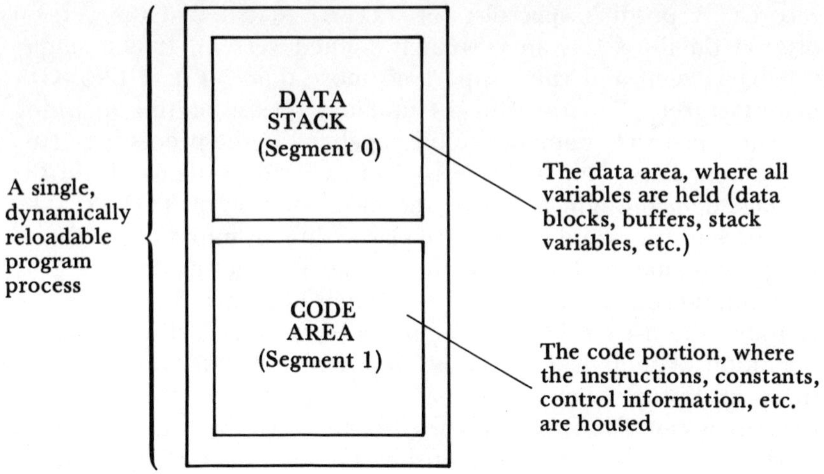

One concern that was noted in our analysis was that the C1 does not have re-entrant application capability, even though all its program segments are re-entrantly constructed. This means that multiple copies of a program are brought into memory whenever the program is executed in a multiprocessing manner. The manufacturer acknowledges this weakness and is in the process of modifying its operating system to eliminate the redundancy and conserve memory.

Spooling is a relatively new feature on the C1 and presently requires a user process in which to execute. In time, C1 will integrate this function into its operating system and thereby improve the throughput of the spooling operation and relieve the multiprocessing load on the user tasks. Further optimization could be accomplished by placing the spooler in firmware. This would definitely augment system performance.

Another area of concern is the data base capabilities of the C1. To adequately support the European on-line environment requires the use of powerful data base management software. Although the C1 offers flexible file management software, it is not sufficient to adequately support a responsive 12-terminal on-line environment. The manufacturer has recently announced that a version of the TOTAL data base management system is available on the C1 and can be purchased through Cincom, Inc., the founder of the package. However, this is a newly developed package, and DATAPRO implies that "TOTAL Universal, available for C1 systems, is designed for small-scale implementations." This comment is disturbing, because the corporation's European offices will not be a small-scale implementation. It will be supporting five to six data bases with over 40 data files. Any particular data file might consist of 5,000–20,000 records. A product specialist for TOTAL stated that the version offered on the C1 is an extremely limited version. It is a single-tasking version and can support no more than 30 data files. C1's manufacturer plans to offer an updated release of the operating system which will augment the file capability to the processing of 66 concurrent files. This upgrade is a direct result of demands on file management brought about by the incorporation of TOTAL. The data base routines and buffers are placed directly into the application program segments. Therefore, the probability of losing data integrity in a multiterminal, multiprocessing environment is very high. To consider the use of TOTAL would be very risky in the European operation. Although TOTAL is supported through C1's manufacturer in Europe, limitations have been placed on the extent of support it can give in this area. Also, there is no local support on TOTAL. Because of this relationship, no optimization can be implemented by the manufacturer, and the manufacturer accepts no responsibility for the use of TOTAL.

C1 offers several terminal transaction processors that function through C1 communications supervisor software; however, each one has a limitation that makes it unusable for the corporation. The principal limitations are:

1. The TP monitors which are offered require that terminals be assigned exclusively to particular application functions, which limits their usefulness.
2. For each group of application functions defining a terminal configuration, one monitor program is created which acts as a single process within the multiprocessing operating systems. Therefore, the monitor is not taking advantage of the multiprocessing systems but is restricted to single-phase processing.
3. A further limitation resulting from the single-phase monitor is that, although the monitor is supporting a multiterminal environment, it can handle the processing requests of only one terminal at a time.
4. None of the TP monitors which are offered provide detail editing of incoming data.

Therefore, the corporation would have to design and develop its own terminal transaction-processing monitor in order to best use the C1 system.

The manufacturer originally offered only COBOL on the C1. Although it has an assembler language, it was not released to C1 users. Since then the manufacturer has added FORTRAN and RPG II to its compiler library. The COBOL and FORTRAN compilers on this level are quite advanced. Although the use of COBOL would be restricted to supporting those programs which we elect to convert as is, the COBOL version implemented on the new C1 is one of the best versions we've noted on a medium-size computer. The FORTRAN offered is also a very good version, enhanced with character manipulation capabilities, bit manipulation capabilities, and double-precision integer (32-bit) and double-precision floating-point (64-bit) arithmetic, all supported in firmware instructions.

2.2.4.2 Software Summary for C2

The heart of the C2 is its multiprocessing operating system. This system is an enhancement of the operating system offered originally. To quote DATAPRO, the system "provides concurrent processing for multiprogrammed batch, time-sharing, and transaction processing." It includes a command interpreter, file management system, input/output system, virtual-memory manager, segmenter, (dynamic) loader, job session scheduler, process dispatcher, user trap manager, spooling facility, disk space manager, utility (and performance) intrinsics, initiator, configurator, system console manager, automatic power fail/auto restart feature, accounting facility, and logging facility. The operating system also offers a backup/restore facility, APL, and support for hard-copy microprocessor diagnostics. Selective operating system functions have been placed into firmware to enhance system performance. Other salient features of the operating systems include utilization of the machine's hardware-implemented stack architecture, recursive/re-entrant code, spooling of both terminal and batch devices, and remote processing via off-site video terminals through the use of telephone lines and modems.

The operating system is structured in functional segments so that only 8 percent or 40K bytes, of the operating system are resident in memory at any one time. The inactive portions remain out on disk in virtual memory until they are requested for processing. The cumulative size of the operating system is in the neighborhood of 500K. It is extremely modular in form and is table-driven for maximum flexibility.

Features that have been recently redesigned in the operating system include the local memory compression algorithm, the memory allocation function, and the program dispatcher. These features are directed to the optimization of the dynamic memory management function within the system. The C2, like the C1, allows program segments to be variable in size, depending upon the code requirement of the individual programs. This imposes an added burden on the processor at load time, since it is not dealing with standard-size segments. Therefore, memory frequently must be rearranged in order to create enough continguous space to accommodate the new programs' processes. The local compression algorithm functions to keep user segments tightly together by executing large block moves within memory whenever necessary, reducing the need for frequent onlays. The manufacturer states that the new dispatch function is three times faster than the previous model.

Other improvements in the operating system that have increased the capabilities of the system include improved file control intrinsics, files that can cross volume boundaries, more efficient multiterminal capabilities (increasing the size of the terminal environment that can be supported), and a power fail/auto restart that does not require human intervention.

In the area of data base management, C2 has the best vendor-supported data base management software on the market today. This is reflected in the DATAPRO report addressing data base management systems available on the minicomputers. This package consists of three parts: a data base definition language, data base access commands, and data base utilities. The data base commands are interfaced into all compiler languages: COBOL, FORTRAN, BASIC, RPG II, and a macro assembler. Access can be performed in any one of the following ways: serially, calculated (through the algorithm using a master key), directed (by a random record number), or chained (forward and backward through the detail record chain). Security is provided at the data-base, data-set, and data-item levels as defined through the data base schema. Eight different access modes are available to the IMAGE user, and many users may access a data base concurrently.

The only weakness in the DBMS is the manner in which it preserves data integrity in a multi-access update environment. Currently, the software can perform a data base "lock-out," a data set lock-out, and record lock-out during the update process, which in the final two cases inhibits other users from accessing information until the update is completed.

The query language on the C2 is excellent. However, when in use, it seriously affects the responsiveness or performance of the system, and, therefore, should be used discriminately. It is a very powerful tool, and further optimizations will take place in subsequent versions.

The FORTRAN language offered on the C2 is a full implementation of ANSI FORTRAN. It is further supported through a TRACE programming aid for program debugging. Such features as bit manipulation, character string definition and manipulation, high-speed subroutine linkage, double-precision integer and double precision floating-point arithmetic are all standard features in FORTRAN. Compilation time for commercial programs ranges from 10 to 30 seconds on the average. FORTRAN requires no minimum memory configurations.

The COBOL compiler implemented on C2 is based on the ANSI COBOL X 3.23—1968 and lacks only the Report Writer option. Language extensions include interprogramming communications, note lines, current data hookup, and multiple redefinition of programmed variables.

Under the title of communications, C2 offers both asynchronous and synchronous communications between the terminal environment and the CPU, and interprocessor communications between the C2 and other IBM 3780-compatible processors. C2 has also recently launched into the field of distributed system networks. The distributed software package provides the C2 user with the capability of communicating concurrently with a remote C2 in a full multiprocessing environment. In a network, any computer can at any time interchange information simultaneously with as many as seven other computers while supporting its own on-line environment.

Note: Although C2 offers a forms library (DEL) package, it was not found suitable for use as a terminal transaction-processing monitor. Therefore, the organization elected to develop its own TP monitor package, which it uses successfully on its present networked systems. This package is a complete implementation of the specifications discussed in section 2.2.3.

2.2.4.3 Comparative Software Analysis

The following conclusions can be reached from our analysis of the software provided on C1 and C2.

1. Both systems are addressing the software requirement of a strong on-line, multiprocessing environment. However, it would appear that the C1 operating software is still in the development process, whereas well-tested C2 operating software is readily available on the C2 today. As we stated in the introduction, the C2 will require time to mature.
2. Many features that are being performed in software on the C1 system have been placed into the high-speed firmware of the C2 system.
3. The C1 system will require more memory than the C2 to function in the same multiprocessing environment. This is primarily due to the fact that the C1 system does not utilize its re-entrant code to the extent that C2 does.
4. Neither system offers a complete terminal transaction-processing monitor. However, one has been developed internally by the organization, and it functions very satisfactorily on the C2. A similar one would have to be developed for the C1.
5. The data base management software on the C2 system is well reputed in the industry (as noted by DATAPRO) and is supported directly by the vendor. C1 uses Cincom's TOTAL package, which is supplied by an outside vendor.
6. C2 has one remaining weakness in its DBMS package. It still uses a data base and data set lock-out suspension of processing for other users requiring access.

7. C1 has had synchronous communication software for several years. This feature is new to the C2 but has been added as an extension to the 3780 emulator, which is C2's high-speed synchronous controller for computer-to-computer communications. C1's manufacturer is in the process of optimizing C1's synchronous communications software. Currently, the performance of the C1 synchronous package is comparable to C2's asynchronous communications package. Therefore, in both systems we can expect continuing performance advancement in the area of terminal communications.
8. An existing COBOL program, presently operational at the organization, was used as a benchmark test to determine the performance of the C1 and the C2 systems in a COBOL environment. The program was run under identical conditions on both systems. Both systems were dedicated to the batch execution of that single program and all output was spooled. No optimizations were made to the program that would have taken advantage of each computer's COBOL features. Both systems completed processing in the range of 15 minutes. This means that existing batch COBOL programs can be converted to either machine with equally good results.
9. For both C1 and C2, the manufacturers recommended the use of FORTRAN for processing speed and efficiency when developing systems that are to be used in a multiprocessing environment. The FORTRAN offered on C1 is relatively new to the manufacturer's C1 library of compilers, and we have no performance statistics on it. No major differences have been identified, but a number of minor differences have been noted.
10. C2 has development network software that allows C2 systems to flexibly communicate with each other, as though the network were one system spread out over the world. Today, C1 does not offer comparable capabilities, but allows intercomputer communications on a batch basis through an IBM-compatible 3780 emulator.

3
Support

After the installation takes place, the future success or failure of the system rests on two factors: reliability of the hardware and software, and local vendor support. The last factor can make or break our installation. It is extremely important that adequate local support be available in Europe.

Support will consist of the following areas: hardware support, software support, and training.

3.1 Hardware Support

To support the on-line environment demands that a field service representative be available and on-site within four hours' notice (preferably sooner). Local support minimizes the commuting time.

3.1.1 Hardware Support for C1

C1's manufacturer has extensive worldwide coverage, providing maintenance through 143 U.S. offices, 15 British offices, and 235 remaining international offices. However, not all offices have field service engineers trained on the C1. There is a field support center located four miles from our British facility from which the unit will be serviced. This center has one full-time maintenance engineer permanently assigned to support C1 installations within that area. However, if engineering support should not be available from this center within a reasonable time, support would be dispatched from one of the other centers.

We did not have sufficient information to gauge the reliability of the C1. According to the manufacturer, the disk problems of the past have been corrected, and the main processor is equipped to identify memory malfunctions should they occur.

3.1.2 Hardware Support for C2

Maintenance is covered through 53 U.S. offices, 9 Canadian offices, 5 British offices, and 116 other international offices. The manufacturer has a major C2 time-sharing operation in a community near our facility in England. Support would be dispatched from a field service engineering center approximately 15 miles from our facility. Four full-time field service engineers are permanently stationed on-site to provide engineering support to that installation and any other C2 installation in the surrounding area. Therefore, it is possible that a field service representative could be dispatched and on-site at the organization within an hour.

The organization's U.S. divisions selected the C2 system because of its much heralded record of reliability. Within the last two years, the eastern division has experienced only three hardware malfunctions. The southern division has not experienced its first as yet.

3.1.3 Hardware Support Summary

Both C1 and C2 would provide adequate support to the British division. It would appear that C2's manufacturer, at present, is better staffed in the immediate area. However, C1 is better represented in the United Kingdom, considering the total number of maintenance offices. Nevertheless, both organizations maintain full backup kits at each center for most frequently used parts. In a worst-case situation, any unit (or the entire system) could be totally replaced and made operational within 24 hours, since a full set of inventory is maintained in Switzerland for C2 and in Italy for C1.

3.2 Software Support

This area, though not as critical as hardware support, does require that qualified systems engineers representing the computer vendor be on call to resolve systems and programming problems that arise in the early stages of the installation. Also, it is the responsibility of the systems engineer to isolate problems occurring in vendor-supplied operating software. However, if the latter becomes the principal activity of the vendor representative, serious doubt is shed on the practicality of the computer system. Reliability of the operating software is essential in an on-line environment. The effects of downtime due to inadequate operating software are felt immediately throughout the organization. Therefore, our emphasis should not be on software engineering support but on software reliability. In the corporation's case, software engineering support could best be used in the areas of training and education.

3.2.1 Software Support for C1

C1's manufacturer offers system engineering support on the C1 throughout the United Kingdom. The organization has experienced excellent service from the C1 representatives assigned to the division's facility in England. It is anticipated that this relationship will continue should the corporation select the C1.

3.2.2 Software Support for C2

C2's manufacturer also offers systems engineering support throughout the United Kingdom. Currently, it does not have as many support centers as C1's manufacturer; however, three options of software support are available to the organization: (1) support through the manufacturer's British subsidiary, (2) support through a well-established C2 software consulting house, and (3) support through the corporate systems staff. Between these three organizations, the corporation would have more than adequate support.

3.2.3 Software Support Summary

Of the two companies, at the present time, C1 is better represented in the area of software support. However, both the C1 and the C2 system are selling well in the United Kingdom, so it would be expected that both C1 and C2 will be even stronger in software support in the coming years.

3.3 Education and Training

The manufacturers of both C1 and C2 offer a wide range of training programs, on-site as well as at their regional training centers. Both companies offer formal classroom training, supplemented by hands-on workshop sessions, training manuals, operating manuals, and exercises built directly into their systems. It is during the period after formal classroom training, when the staff is becoming familiar with the new computer system, that the vendor software representative could be most helpful. It is important that adequate on-site vendor support be provided during that period.

These features are covered through a software maintenance contract offered by each of the computer companies. This contract is definitely worth having.

4
Conversion

Several alternative methods of conversion are available to the organization and are presently under evaluation. It is the function of this portion of the analysis to discuss each of the proposed methods and determine which would be the best for the corporation. From our earlier analysis, and on the basis of the benchmark tests performed at the request of the organization by both manufacturers, it appears that the actual method of conversion can be determined independently of the computer selection. This is possible only because of the similarity between the two computer systems. This is not to suggest that there are no differences between the two computer systems. There are, and they will have to be accounted for as part of the conversion effort. However, these differences would not effect the method chosen for conversion. To date, there are three methods under consideration:

Method 1: Convert everything as is. This can be accomplished by converting all the files and programs from the existing system over to the new system, so as to preserve the same manner of processing. The new on-line system would then have to be developed as a separate project.

Method 2: Convert only the files. This method would minimize the conversion effort by limiting the interprocessor conversion to just data files. Equivalent programs within the corporation's network library would be used in place of the original programs. This would limit new development to programs not available through the library.

Method 3: Convert files and selective programs. This method would be similar to method 2, but would provide for the conversion of all application programs that do not have corresponding entries in the network library.

4.1 Analysis of Method 1—Convert As Is

We have received quotations from both manufacturers as to the amount of effort that will be required to transfer existing files and programs from the present system into each of the proposed new systems. The conversion will be done in two parts: (1) file conversion and (2) program conversion. The files, as defined in this method, will be converted to function as they do today, with no alteration. The file conversion process is quite straightforward but does require the use of multiple computers, since the currently used disk packs are not compatible with either the C1 or the C2. Therefore, an interim conversion must be made in order to transfer the information to a medium that is compatible. This can be accomplished using a GE computer, resulting in a 1600-bpi tape that can act as an intermediate medium to both the C1 and the C2. The balance of the conversion simply involves transferring the content of the tape(s) onto the respective C1 or C2 disks. Regardless of which conversion method is selected for final conversion, this procedure is a requirement that must be satisfied. Additionally, although a portion of the file conversion can be staggered over a period of time, the final conversion of critical information (present inventory-on-hand, accounts-receivable outstanding, and so on) must be accomplished within a 48-hour period or less.

Most of the effort will be spent converting the 300 existing COBOL programs. Some optimization might take place during this effort;

however, there is little chance that any significant modifications will be made to take advantage of the new system. The conversion will be a COBOL-to-COBOL conversion, resulting in the same batch operation previously performed on the current system. To expand from this position into an on-line, user-oriented environment will require a significant amount of new development, well in excess of the conversion effort.

C1's manufacturer has projected that the program conversion will take approximately 400 man-days to complete, and has offered the organization six months of full-time systems engineering support to assist in this effort at no additional cost. C2's manufacturer has negotiated with a large systems consulting house to provide similar services, at a price that would be compensated for by discounting the system. The discount provides for the same period of engineering support, but with a guarantee of completion within that period.

Both offers are very generous, but are directed to the fulfillment of a short-term solution—allowing the corporation to move laterally from one piece of equipment to another. However, the major effort is yet to be addressed, and that is the development of on-line systems for the organization. It is this effort that precipitated the "request for proposal" and formed the basis of our evaluation. If we only wanted to accomplish the conversion of what presently exists, we could have selected a computer far less expensive than the ones presently under evaluation. However, that is not our intention, and the support could be best used in the accomplishment of our long-term objectives.

Conservatively, it will cost the corporation in the neighborhood of $40,000 to complete the conversion as spelled out in method 1. Considering that these programs will shortly be replaced by on-line programs, this approach does not seem justified.

4.2 Analysis of Method 2—File Conversion Only

The second alternative available to the corporation is to convert only the files and to use programs from the organization's network library that are similar in function to the original programs. This would accomplish three things:

1. It would eliminate the need to convert any of the existing programs.
2. It would minimize the amount of program development, since most of the programs are available in the network library.

3. It would advance the compatibility of application systems functioning within the corporate network.

These are impressive benefits. However, this alternative cannot be seriously considered unless a reasonable correspondence exists between the current application systems of the British division and those in the network library. For this reason, an analysis was performed of all currently active systems of the British division. Through program-by-program comparison, we were able to determine the extent of correspondence, along with the amount of modifications and new development required to satisfy the differences. Strong correspondences were found in the following areas: the delivery schedule system, accounts receivable, stock system, stock valuation, weekly stock level analysis, proposed production program, bill-of-materials processing, cost of production, sales, and purchase ledger system.

However, there were also applications in the British organization that do not have corresponding programs in the network library. These would have to be preserved through new programming. Fortunately, these represent less than 20 percent of those in operation. Such applications as interdivisional MRP fall in this class. The redevelopment of this system will require 14 new programs, which is not a significant effort. But the result of this redevelopment can be used by the U.S. divisions. The remaining applications that would have to be redeveloped consist of the payroll system and a set of 40 special programs. We have discussed the possibility of using the C2 software consulting house to assume the responsibility of reprogramming the payroll system should we select C2. C1's manufacturer will absorb the same responsibility should we choose the C1. The reprogramming of the Belgian costing systems does not seem warranted at this stage, and is the biggest weakness in total redevelopment approach.

This approach definitely has benefits over the first method discussed, since through it the conversion and development effort is immediately directed toward accomplishing the long-term objective. This will shorten the total project time by as much as 50 percent. Another benefit is that the system will not be burdened by placing the new development activity on the same system on which production is running, as would be the case if method 1 were used. The last benefit is that we will not have to perform two conversions: the first to the new computer, the second to the new on-line system. The two conversions would require two sets of files, two sets of programs, and so on. This would be very taxing to both the computer and the personnel involved.

4.3 Analysis of Method 3—File Conversion with Limited Program Conversion

This method is very similar to method 2. But, unlike method 2, it does account for the conversion of programs that, due to their limited use or effectiveness, do not warrant redevelopment. These programs and their associated data files could then be converted in their present form, and remain in that form until they are phased out or scheduled for redesign and implementation into the mainstream. Of the three methods discussed, this method is the most practical, and, therefore, the best. It offers latitudes that are not found in the other two methods.

It is recommended that the programs definitely be handled in this manner. Possibly the payroll system and other batch systems could also be converted in this manner in order to limit the scope of new development required at the front-end of the project. A firm project management plan must be prepared identifying (1) the method used to transfer each of the existing systems and (2) the new development schedule.

4.4 Conversion Summary

The purpose of this summary was not to work out a detailed implementation schedule but to determine the best method of conversion. The computer selection will have a direct effect on the development requirements. C1's manufacturer will provide more system engineering support than the manufacturer of C2, and this support will be required if we are to perform the alterations necessary to allow our network library programs to function on the C1.

Regardless of the technical conclusion, support is a big issue and cannot be ignored. C2's manufacturer through its software consulting house, will assist in the file and program conversion; however, its continuing support will be costly to the corporation. Therefore, it is worth reviewing the major development needs in consideration of each of the computer systems.

Function	*C1*	*C2*
On-line operating software	Available	Available
Data base management software	TOTAL	DBMS

Terminal transaction–processing (on-line) monitor	Must develop	Available
Implementation of current network programs	Requires modification	No modifications needed
Convertibility of current programs	Easily convertible	Easily convertible
Implementation of current programs	Requires minor modification	Requires minor modification

Considering conversion and development from a broad perspective, it would appear that it could be handled with less effort on the C2 than the C1. However, due to the lack of support or expense of consulting support, should we select C2, it would require that the corporation operate more independently in the C2 environment than in the C1 environment.

5
Cost

The computer system presently at the British organization's facility is an outdated, limited-capability system consisting of 10K memory, two 5-megabyte disk units, a card reader, and a 200-lines-per-minute printer. The computer system proposed for the replacement of this equipment represents a significant upgrade to this system and can be justified only on the basis of long-term benefits. For that reason, it seems most practical to equip the initial replacement with a minimum configuration. In our cost analysis, we have chosen to configure the system with 256K of memory, two 40MB to 50MB disk units, video terminals as entry devices, and a printer with a speed of 300 to 600 lines per minute. The exact configurations have been itemized in Table A-3. It would be possible to establish an initial configuration even smaller than that. However, a smaller configuration would be more sensitive to expansion requirements in the near future than the one proposed.

The remainder of this section analyzes the detailed quotations supplied by each of the vendors.

5.1 Quotations for C2

Table A-4 lists quotations for the equipment configuration described in Table A-3, supplied through different C2 offices. The

Table A-3. Proposed system configurations.

Description	*C1*	*C2*
Hardware Quotation		
CPU and memory	256K	256K
2 disk units	40 megabytes/unit	50 megabytes/unit
1 tape unit	—	1600 bytes/inch
1 line printer	400 lines/minute	600 lines/minute
4 terminals	2400 baud	2400 baud
Software Quotation		
Assembler language	Not available	Standard
COBOL	Optional	Optional
FORTRAN	Optional	Optional
Communication software	Required	Standard
Data base software	TOTAL	DBMS

Table A-4. C2 quotations.*

Description	*OEM*	*Field Office*	*Main Office (Port of Export)*
Equipment			
C2 computer:	$102,131†	$118,218	$109,296
128KB fault-control memory			
1 magnetic tape unit			
1 50MB disk unit			
16-port interface			
2,400 baud video terminal			
Memory expansion to 256KB	7,634†	9,028	8,170
Additional 50MB disk unit	15,342	17,080	11,500
600 lpm line printer	20,399	20,709	20,788
3 2,400 baud terminals	10,849	12,078	9,693
Software			
Data base management system (DBMS)—	—	3,660	2,700
COBOL	—	1,830	1,440
	$156,355	$182,603	$163,587

* This was computed using a conversion factor of $1.87/£.

† These prices have been computed on the basis of a 15 percent discount. The original quote was for a processor with 320K of memory, which put the price in a higher class.

main office quote provides sale of the C2 exercising our 8 percent equipment discount, 11 percent video terminal discount, and 20 percent software discount. However, to take advantage of these discounts, the manufacturer will provide us only with quotations which extend to:

1. A U.S. port of export (we will have to arrange shipment, absorb import costs, and assume liability for transport to the British facility).
2. Switzerland (a Common Market location), where again we will have to arrange shipment, absorb import cost, and assume liability for transport to our facility in England.

By the nature of the terms stated in the present C2 multi-user agreement, the discount arrangement, which we have presumably agreed to, does not provide for shipment directly to any of our foreign subsidiaries. Due to the sensitivity of the equipment and the distance which the equipment must travel, the organization is not in a position to assume the liability for, or accept the risk of, damage in shipment. Even if the system is adequately insured, should anything happen, it might take several months before a settlement could be reached. We cannot afford the time that would be consumed in this process. Therefore, unless we can renegotiate our multi-user agreement, it appears that we should consider only the quotations that represent shipment to the British division.

Two of the three quotations received for the C2 system qualify for this solution. The main office is the sales office through which we established our multi-user discount arrangement. However, due to the new price announcement, the main office was considerate enough to supply us with updates to the original quotation we received from the field office. Therefore, the price quoted in the table under field office represents the newly revised discounted price list.

The second quotation is from another office, which currently has an OEM arrangement for C2. Due to the volume agreement it holds with the manufacturer, it has the ability to sell the same C2 equipment to the organization at a discounted price arrangement over the prices quoted by the field office. It is interesting to note that the field office not only encouraged this but even introduced the OEM's people to the corporation. This policy of independent quoting is unheard of in the mainframe computer market but very common in the minicomputer market. It offers a greater latitude of competitive bargaining, resulting in an increase in sales volume and market share, as the minicomputer companies view the situation.

There is a question as to the actual price that the OEM has quoted the corporation on the basic system, since the comparison used a calculated figure based on the discount multipliers computed. This price will have to be confirmed, but seems quite realistic for OEM negotiation.

Therefore, it appears that the OEM price, if accurate, is the best of the three, and will provide substantial savings over both the field price and our own multi-user discount price. However, to take advantage of this, the OEM would like us to contract the conversion to them. At present, we have not decided exactly how much of the current system will be converted; therefore, we have not solicited a price. Their original price for a total conversion—files and programs—was $40,000. Both the figure and the approach were unacceptable. We are contemplating a conversion effort that will cost no more than $20,000, and include a payroll package. But this still has to be negotiated.

5.2 Quotation for C1

C1 is structured in the tradition of an established mainframe company. Its system of communications between the U.S. and European offices is excellent. Since the manufacturer does not operate

Table A-5. C1 quotation.

Description	*Price*
Equipment	
C1 computer:	$132,998
256KB memory	
Console terminal	
2 40MB disk units	47,340
400 lpm printer	40,180
Synchronous communications controller	10,049
4 video terminals	23,333
Software	
Data base management system	
(TOTAL)	25,200
	$279,100

through an OEM base, the procurement of equipment is localized to the manufacturer's office nearest to the customer's site. Therefore, the quotation was prepared and presented by the corporation's office. It is shown in Table A-5.

In discussing these prices, the local C1 representative stated that we could expect a sizable discount on this quote, but he would not be able to quote a figure in time for the completion of this report. The manufacturer had originally offered a $40,000 discount off its original quotation in December to match the quotation submitted by the field C2 office. Recently when we reviewed the price of the new configuration with the local C1 representative, he stated that he feels confident that the company will discount the price to be competitive with the new C2 quote. Therefore, we shall assume that a discount in the same range would be forthcoming.

The manufacturer also offered the corporation a discount of 10 percent on all European systems that would be ordered to satisfy the requirements of the corporation's European offices.

5.3 Cost Summary

From our review of the quotations, it would be fair to incorporate the $40,000 discount we anticipate from C1's manufacturer. Since the figure for C1 absorbs a portion of the conversion cost, it seems also justified to subtract from the C2 price the $20,000 discount we are anticipating from the OEM. Therefore, the summary costs that we arrive at are as follows:

	Best Quote	*Maintenance*
C1	$239,100	$1,206/mo.
C2	176,355	1,375/mo.

Presumably, the corporation would elect to establish a leasing arrangement to finance the systems. At these present prices, assuming that the lease can be negotiated for a rate in the neighborhood of .02, we should anticipate monthly costs of:

	System	*Maintenance*	*Total*
C1	$4,782	$1,206	$5,988
C2	3,527	1,375	4,902

Final prices will not be known until we have concluded our negotiations.

6
Summary

The following list summarizes the results of the comparison between the C1 and C2 system in each of the functional areas under evaluation.

Area under Evaluation	*C1*	*C2*
Hardware strength		X
Software strength		X
Local support		
Hardware	X	X
Software	X	
Ease of conversion	X	X
Lowest cost (comparable systems)		X

It would seem that C2 is the better system for the corporation's British operation.

Appendix B
Installation and Training Procedure

Introduction

The order for the purchase of a new British computer system was formally submitted. This order was based on the specifications and configurational requirements derived from a comprehensive evaluation of both technical and user needs. The computer selected was C2.

At the start of the evaluation process, the two vendors under consideration were high in their price quotations. However, as is normal in a competitive situation, as the evaluation process proceeded, the corporation was offered various discount considerations. When the decision was finally made, the price at which the order was placed was less than half of one of the original prices quoted.

The second major criterion in the evaluation was the capability of the computer system's hardware and software to comfortably perform in an on-line multiterminal, multicomputer environment. What this means is that the computer selected for the U.K. cluster operation should be able to function as well in an on-line, stand-alone capacity as in a network capacity, where user information can be transferred upon demand through video terminals directly to the computer's data bank or (in the future) to any other computer within the network. Both the on-line multiterminal support feature and the computer-to-computer communication feature required special systems hardware and software that many computers do not have. It was very important that the computer which was selected satisfy those requirements. It was noted that C2 was one of the few computers, regardless of price, which had both of these capabilities.

The third evaluation criterion was software compatibility. Between the U.S. divisions and the corporation, over 500 programs have been developed that could be available to the U.K. cluster. This is only possible if the computer system resulting from the selection contains compatible operating software through which these programs can function. This, of course, was satisfied by selecting the same computer as that at the U.S. divisions.

The fourth criterion was reliability. Past experience with C2 had a considerable bearing on this factor. Within the last three years, very few serious hardware problems have occurred at existing corporate installations (average was one a year per division). Under operating conditions of 24 hours a day, 7 days a week, this kind of record is unheard of. Therefore, it was extremely difficult to evaluate any other product on a higher level.

The last criterion was the timespan over which the conversion effort would take place. It was decided that the existing U.K. files would be converted at the outset of this project into a data base form in order to facilitate the advancement of the U.K. cluster into on-line processing. This approach required creation of a series of conversion programs to accomplish the file transfer. Upon completion of the data conversion, consideration was given to the immediate use of the following network systems, due to their compatibility with present systems: accounts payable, accounts receivable, general ledger, and inventory control (bill-of-materials processing). The order in which these systems shall be put into effect will be based upon the following three factors: (1) the complexity of the system, (2) the amount of training required to support the system, and (3) the degree of difficulty anticipated to implement the system.

Approach

Effectively, upon completing the implementation of the new on-line systems, the British subsidiaries will operate very much like a subnetwork within the overall corporate worldwide computer network. Therefore, the approach that will be used in implementing these systems is very resemblant of the approach the corporation is using in developing the overall network.

At present, the subnetwork will consist of the following organizations: Central Services, Plastics, Elastomers, and Textiles. Each of these organizations reports with equal representation to a central services chairman. Functional responsibilities have been divested to the individual operating units in order to achieve a high level of operating efficiency and flexibility, while administrative functions common to each of the units, such as accounts receivable, accounts payable, and general ledger, have been consolidated and are handled through Central Services.

The computer system, which was originally purchased by the British subsidiaries, was used to support Central Services and to perform primarily financial functions. However, in recent years, attention has been directed to the development of integrated inventory control and production costing systems to assist Central Services and the Plastics division in the monitoring and analysis of the intracompany business, such as intracompany ordering to meet production's impact on sales contributions from material cost changes, activity of material within the warehouses, and the like.

Although general accounting operations still remain an important part of the monthly processing cycle, more and more emphasis is being given to the development of manufacturing and marketing support operations to improve business operations, and it is in these areas that the need for more computer power necessitated the upgrade to a new computer system.

Concurrent to the computer upgrade was a request for a change in the method of processing. Since the original computer had exhausted its product life, British management wanted to take advantage of the on-line data base features offered in the new computer systems. Therefore, no longer will information be filled out on keypunch forms which subsequently must be turned over to the computer room by a scheduled time for processing each day. This will be replaced by the strategic placement of video display units (VDUs) in the user departments, through which the user will enter his own information *directly* into the computer—not according to any scheduled time period, but whenever the user deems it necessary. This will eliminate the passing of information from hand to hand, propagating the possibility of data errors even before the information is entered into the computer. It will also eliminate the time required to pass the information from the user department, through the keypunch department, to the computer room, back to the user department in the form of an edit report. And lastly, it will eliminate the finger-pointing exercises of trying to determine who is at fault when errors do occur. The user knows his information best, and is ultimately responsible for it in any event. Therefore, it is only right that he should have total control over his own information.

But to make this new system and "new environment" a reality requires a *commitment.* Without this commitment, the system is destined for failure. This involvement or commitment is essential, not only on the part of the technical staff, but on the part of everybody involved with the system: technical personnel, user personnel, and management alike. Although the technical staff is responsible for conversion and program support, it is the user who is responsible for making the new system work.

Therefore, to emphasize this need and encourage management and user involvement early in the project, a User Implementation Committee (Management Steering Committee) has been established, separate from the Technical Installation Team, through which decisions will be made as to:

- Which systems will be implemented at which divisions.
- Which system goes first, and where.
- When training classes will be given and who will attend.
- Who will have access to the system, and what level of access.

All of these are user problems requiring user decisions. They also involve critical management decisions, and therefore require representation from individuals high enough in U.K. management to feel comfortable about making decisions. Therefore, it was recommended that the committee consist of two managers from each operating division, two from Central Services, and a chairman.

This committee has met twice, and is actively addressing the processing needs of the British divisions. The chairman has already given a presentation to the committee on the benefits derivable from on-line systems, but the chairman's role on the committee is only to provide guidance and technical support. It is the decisions arrived at by the committee as a whole which will direct the manner and effectiveness in which on-line systems are used in the U.K. It is intended that this committee shall meet no less than once a month and remain in power over the entire implementation phase, conceivably continuing as a governing body even after the system is totally operational. As systems are planned for divisional implementation, divisional user committees will be formed to initiate involvement on a local level. These divisional committees will consist of members who will be directly involved with the installation, and will be chaired by an associate holding a position on the Management Steering Committee. These committees will provide excellent representation and communication channels throughout the implementation phase.

The entire project will be directed through two organizations: (1) a Technical Installation Team and (2) a User Implementation Committee.

We addressed the purpose of the User Implementation Committee but did not discuss the function of the Technical Installation Team. This organization will be responsible for such functions as site preparation, computer installation, computer testing, data conversion, program conversion, technical training, systems analysis, program development, systems testing, systems integration, and documentation. It is at this point that responsibility will shift to the User Implementation Committee to schedule systems implementation. Only after the systems have been adequately tested and fully documented will the User Implementation Committee proceed to schedule training and implementation. The Technical Installation Team will consist of members from Corporate Information Systems, the U.K. Information Systems staff, and technical representatives from the other European divisions that are expecting installations.

It is anticipated that this team shall remain in existence for a period of three to six months, after which the corporate and European constituents shall return to their original organizations and the U.K. staff shall remain self-sufficient. The diagram in Figure B-1 illustrates the shift in technical responsibility as the project matures.

Figure B-1. ***Shift in technical responsibility during initial period of the conversion project.***

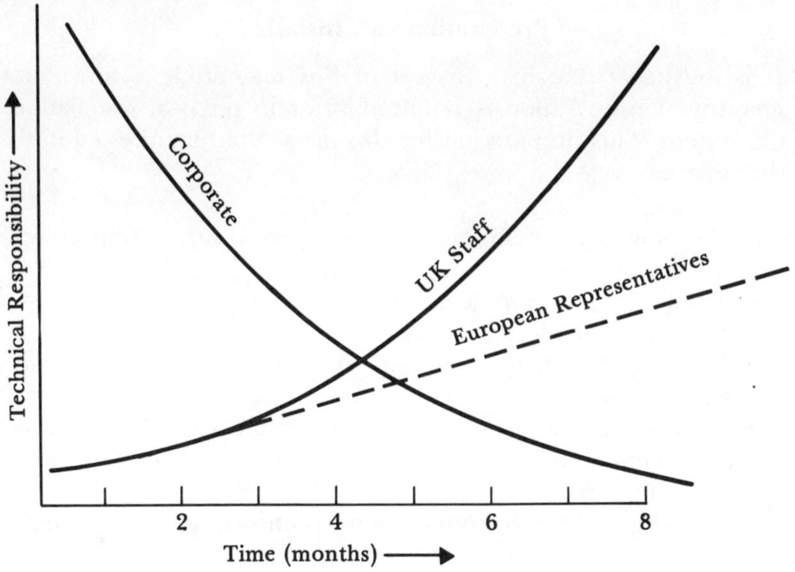

Due to its experience with the C2 computer and the network systems, the corporate group will assume initial responsibility for conversion and training. This phase will comprise the first three months and consist of:

- Acceptance testing of the new computer system.
- Installation of the corporation's system software and network programs.
- Technical training to support program development and network systems maintenance.
- Systems training to acquaint the U.K. staff and European representatives with network systems.

At the completion of systems training, it will be the responsibility of the U.K. staff to work closely with the User Implementation Committee so as to determine any enhancements or changes which must be incorporated into the application systems. The result of this analysis will dictate the amount of new program development required before systems implementation can occur. Also, all changes or enhancements to the network system must be reflected in the user documentation prior to user training.

It is felt that after the first four systems have been implemented, the U.K. staff will be well equipped to support and sustain successful operations.

Preparation and Installation

It is inevitable that in a project of this magnitude a considerable amount of preparation is required prior to physical installation of the system. This preparation for this project has manifested itself in the form of:

- Planning and scheduling tasks required to successfully complete the installation.
- Establishing a complete set of data conversion specifications through which to direct the conversion effort.
- Developing a strong training program for U.K. and European technical personnel.
- Organizing and assembling a thorough set of programming documentation on all network-supported systems within the program library.
- Revising all user documentation to conform to the new network policies and procedures.

The Manager of Data Processing for the U.K. cluster has made several visits to the United States to acquaint himself with the programming techniques used to support on-line processing. Substantial amounts of time were also spent during these visits early in the year to allow both corporate and U.K. organizations to become acquainted with the system each was supporting, in order to determine the extent of compatibility between the U.K. systems presently in operation and the corporate network on-line systems. Major processing differences between the two systems were noted and discussed. It was agreed by U.K. management that the following network on-line systems would be implemented in place of the existing batch U.K. systems, due to their close compatibility:

Accounts receivable
Accounts payable
General Ledger
Inventory control

Very little program development is required for the first three systems in order to support present U.K. operations. However, augmentation is required to the inventory control system in order to properly monitor stock activity at the ten off-site locations used by the U.K. cluster for raw-materials and finished-goods warehousing. Most of the new program development has been identified but, as yet, is unscheduled. A tentative schedule has been established for the training and development necessary to implement the accounts-receivable, accounts-payable, and general-ledger systems. This schedule carries into March, at which time the conversion process for the inventory control system will begin.

It is planned that the final recruiting shall be completed during early January, at which time it will be known when the remaining U.K. members and the two European representatives shall participate in the project. Until we have committed dates for their participation, it is difficult to plan or discuss their involvement. However, this situation should be resolved by early February, at which time a schedule shall be submitted.

The completion of the preparation phase is coincidental with the beginning of the installation phase. This phase is usually a hectic phase, and for that reason, we have placed considerable emphasis on support and preparation of this event. Formal installation is scheduled for the week of December 4, even though delivery will take place in early November.

The various visits made between the U.S. and England by corporate

MIS and U.K. MIS personnel allowed sufficient time for U.K. management to become familiar and comfortable with the new on-line programming and operating environment. Upon delivery, two tasks remain essential prior to advancing to systems conversion: (1) acceptance testing and (2) technical training.

The following section discusses the approach that will be used to conduct the technical training program in the U.K., but key to the successful installation of the new system is the thoroughness with which the equipment is tested. The C2 system will be subjected to two batteries of system tests. The first will be a rigorous sequence of system tests devised and executed by the computer manufacturer, which are intended to exercise the system to the fullest of its capabilities. Any malfunctions noted during this procedure will be logged for evaluation and resolution. The second battery of tests has been devised by the corporation to exercise the system in a manner consistent with the kinds of processing which it will be expected to perform during normal daily operations. This test will be given by the corporation's technical personnel. The satisfactory completion of all these tests shall be the criterion of acceptance.

Technical Training Program

Below is a detailed agenda for staff training of U.K. personnel in the subjects necessary to support the new C2 computer system. This program has been divided into three phases. The first phase, scheduled for early December, is a preliminary program, to be used to address programming fundamentals and data base concepts. The purpose of this program is to acquaint the staff with basic tools needed to perform normal data base operations. The second phase, scheduled for early January, is the continuance of the technical training program, addressing in a comprehensive manner all subjects required to support on-line systems development and processing. The last phase of the program is a detailed review of the structure and design of all network systems delivered to the U.K. Each system shall be handled as a separate study, and given in priority of installation.

Agenda for Technical Training Program

Preliminary Training

Date	*Time*	*Subject*
Dec. 4	9:00–12:00	Introduction to the C2 Computer
	1:30–5:00	Use of On-Line Editor/2

Preliminary Training (*cont.*)

Date	*Time*	*Subject*
5	9:00–5:00	Introduction to Programming Language NEW
6	9:00–5:00	NEW Language Workshop
7	9:00–5:00	NEW Language Workshop (*cont.*)
8	9:00–5:00	NEW Language Workshop (*cont.*)
Dec. 11	9:00–12:00	Introduction to Data Base Concepts
	1:30–5:00	Data Base Access
12	9:00–5:00	Data Base Programming Through NEW
13	9:00–5:00	Data Base Programming Workshop
14	9:00–5:00	Data Base Programming Workshop (*cont.*)
15	9:00–5:00	Data Base Programming Workshop (*cont.*)

Upon completion of the preliminary training program, there will be a three-week lapse before the next phase of the training will commence. This will allow sufficient time for the U.K. staff to absorb and practice the skills learned. It will also build up their basic confidence level and place them in a positive frame of mind for the comprehensive training session scheduled for January.

Comprehensive Training

Date	*Time*	*Subject*
Jan. 8	9:00–5:00	Network and C2 Environment
9	9:00–5:00	Introduction to the MPX Operating System
10	9:00–5:00	Comprehensive On-Line Editor/2 Wrap-up
11	9:00–5:00	Data Base Definition Language & Utilities
12	9:00–5:00	Introduction to Systems Programming Language
Jan. 15	9:00–5:00	Introduction to On-Line Design
16	9:00–5:00	Introduction to On-Line Programming
17	9:00–5:00	C2 Utilities
18	9:00–5:00	Systems Workshop
19	9:00–5:00	Systems Workshop (*cont.*)

At the end of this two-week program, the technical staff will be acquainted and equipped with all concepts and programming techniques necessary for productive systems development in the corporation's C2 environment. Furthermore, they will have a fundamental, conceptual knowledge of how each of the network systems has been designed and programmed, which will assist them in supporting the on-line user environment. A third training program has been established to discuss and review in detail each network system that is to be implemented in the U.K.

Course Content

Preliminary Training Program. The purpose of this program is to provide fundamental programming information which can be related in a straightforward manner and used almost immediately to reinforce comprehension of the C2 programming environment. The session is designed as a workshop. Major topics will be introduced using slide presentations, supported by a formal flip-chart presentation of principal points, and concluded with demonstrations, discussions, and workshop exercises.

The program will cover four major subject areas: (1) introduction to the C2 computer, (2) use of on-line Editor/2, (3) introduction to programming language NEW, and (4) introduction to data base concepts. The following paragraphs briefly discuss the content of each of the major subjects.

Introduction to the C2 Computer. This shall commence with a short slide presentation on the architecture of the C2. Hardware features shall be discussed in conjunction with a tour of the computer facility. The tour shall be followed by a brief demonstration of the system's capabilities, after which the class will resume in the meeting room to discuss fundamental system concepts that must be understood in order to perform basic programming operations. This will cover such topics as account structure, sessions and job streams, user sign-on, terminal commands, the use of the video terminal, and so on.

As is suggested by the time allotted for this subject, this will address only basic operation concepts. The subject will be handled in depth during the comprehensive training program in the course titled "Network and C2 Environment."

Use of the On-Line Editor/2. The on-line editor utility Editor/2 is a fundamental piece of operating software in the C2. This utility allows programmers to create and maintain programs through the use of video display terminals. After taking this course, programmers will be able to sit down at a terminal and type their own programs directly into the computer, with full capabilities to store, retrieve, modify, and delete program source.

The course addresses the essential Editor/2 commands and techniques that a programmer will require to prepare and modify his program source. This will encompass such functions as retrieval of existing source, storing of new source, addition or modification of programs, preparation of hard-copy listings, and so on.

Introduction to the NEW Programming Language. The NEW programming language was developed by the corporation to provide an efficient commercial programming language for the C2 which at the same time establishes a base language through which all network development will take place. This language is extremely similar to COBOL. Because it is a translator language, the "object code" produced is the most efficient for the computer in which the language functions.

The course is introduced with a pre-narrated slide presentation, which discusses the basic structure and characteristic of the language. A simple program exercise is included in the presentation to demonstrate the manner in which a typical NEW program is prepared. This provides valuable and background experience for the technical instruction phase of the course. To ensure that the participants have a thorough understanding of the language, a three-day workshop has been included in the session. The workshop will consist of a series of exercises which have been prepared to correspond closely with the kinds of assignments expected in a normal on-line commercial environment.

At the conclusion of the first week, a strong foundation should have been established from which to proceed into data base management and on-line systems concepts.

Introduction to Data Base Management. Since on-line processing requires data base management, and since all application systems within the network library are based on this concept, it is important that this subject be thoroughly covered and clearly comprehended. For that reason, a one-week course has been prepared to discuss the concepts and programming techniques required to support data base processing.

The first day of the course shall be dedicated to a formal classroom session in which the structure, organization, and access methods of data base management systems shall be discussed. An in-depth discussion is planned for the afternoon, when each of the data base interface commands will be reviewed in detail.

The second day will be devoted to a discussion of programming conventions which must be followed to interface effectively with the data base and perform such functions as record retrieval, record update, new record entries, record deletion, and data base security. The recommended use of structured programming techniques shall be noted, which will effectively increase development efficiency and improve program documentation.

The remainder of the week shall be reserved for a programming workshop, in which data base access assignments will be distributed that correspond to normal update or inquiry requests expected in a daily operational situation.

Comprehensive Training Program. This program shall be given several weeks after the preliminary program has been completed. The time between should be used to become comfortable with the new system and the new language. By the time the course commences, the programming staff should be curious about the more technical aspects of the computer with which they are becoming familiar. It is the purpose of this session to answer these queries in a formal set of presentations which will encompass the first week. Active participation in group discussion is encouraged during the first week session. Subjects to be discussed are as follows:

The Network & the C2 Environment
Introduction to the Operating System
A Comprehensive On-line "EDITOR" Wrap-up
Data Base Definition Language and Related Utilities

Upon conclusion of this first week, all of the major aspects of the C2 system and its associated operating software shall have been covered. The second week will be completely dedicated to the techniques and related software used by the corporation in the development of on-line application systems. This is the most important phase of the training program and is essential for the staff to be able to perform productive on-line program development. Topics discussed in this session are: the use of the on-line Monitor Package, the preparation of transaction screens, the preparation of transaction editors, design considerations to support on-line processing, and the programming techniques required to handle on-line operations. A two-day workshop is used to review and make modifications to an existing on-line system. This exercise will provide the participant with an overall knowledge of the system requirements necessary in preparing and maintaining a complete on-line operation. Correlations between on-line and batch operations will also be discussed.

At the conclusion of this two week period, the staff will be cognizant of the basic C2 operating environment and the methods used in the development of on-line systems. However, to reinforce what has been learned, it will be necessary that provisions be made to practice the skills.

Subsequent to this program, a detailed review program of each network on-line system delivered to the U.K. shall be scheduled as the third phase of training. The following is a description of the content of each of the major subjects within the Comprehensive Training Program.

The Network and the C2 Environment. The conversion to the C2 not only represents a computer upgrade for the U.K. cluster but also adds a further link to the corporation's new worldwide computer "network." Therefore, it is appropriate to discuss the U.K. system and its related importance in the network. Also included in the network discussions will be the universality of program software and relative independence of hardware. These two factors provide greater flexibility and cost-consciousness in the decision-making process for new equipment, along with the assurance that, in the future, existing equipment will be easily upgradable in a modular manner, with little concern about program conversion. The remainder of this discussion will relate the various features offered by C2 computer. This will be handled through a slide presentation as a systems overview which briefly, but comprehensively, relates all capabilities of the C2 system. It will begin with a review of the hardware architecture and systematically advance to the operating system, the on-line editor, the file management system, the data base management system, the job control cards, the system utilities, and the communications capabilities. Each of these areas will be addressed individually in separate presentations over the remainder of the week.

Introduction to the MP Operating System. A programmer-oriented discussion will be given on the C2 operating system during the second day of the program. This course will elaborate on the features cited in the systems overview. The purpose of this discussion is to provide information necessary for the staff to function adequately in a multiprogramming environment. Both interactive processing and computer-controlled batch job-stream execution will be discussed.

A Comprehensive On-Line Editor/2 Wrap-up. A half-day session on the third day of the program will be reserved to answer questions on the Editor/2 instruction set covered in the preliminary training program. After this review has been concluded, there will be a discussion of advanced instructions offered in the Editor/2 along with the expanded Editor/2 language commands usable in conjunction with batch-processing streams.

Data Base Definition Language and Related Utilities. The afternoon of the third day shall be reserved to discuss the data base schema and subschema concepts in conjunction with the data base definition language. During this presentation, an actual data base will be defined and constructed from start to finish. The participants will learn how to use password protection to secure individual items, data sets, and even the entire data base. They will learn how to develop the interrelationships between master and detail files as well as define principal keys and sort keys within the data set. This session will be concluded with a discussion of the major support utilities and how they are used.

The On-Line Environment. One full week will be devoted to the policies and procedures required in the design and programming of on-line systems. Special systems software has been developed by the corporation to support the use of multiple terminals distributed throughout the organization for the purpose of on-line processing. By on-line processing we mean that type of processing that allow the users direct access to information within the computer system through the use of video terminals located in their departments. Although the concept is simple, it requires a change in thinking from the manner in which systems were designed and programmed in the older batch method. This course will be used to discuss these differences and provide a firm foundation for the staff to develop and support their own on-line systems. Subjects discussed during this week will encompass:

- The use of the on-line monitor.
- The use of the screen utility to prepare on-line transaction screens.
- The preparation of the systems transaction editors.
- The design approach for on-line systems.
- The programming techniques required to interface between the transaction input and the application data bases.

This will be a "hands-on" session, accompanied by a case study of a complete on-line system. Included in the study is the recommended interface method between on-line and batch process operations. Through the case study, the staff will have the opportunity to review in depth the design and programming techniques required to support on-line processing. These techniques have been consistently practiced for the development of all network systems.

Although only two days have been dedicated in the training program to cover these concepts in a workshop manner, it is highly recommended that an additional week be set aside between the completion of this program and the start of the network systems training program to allow the staff to practice the techniques at their own pace before advancing into the review of the network on-line systems.

Systems Implementation

The final stage of conversion will be the actual systems implementation. This will involve a technical systems review of each system planned for implementation, followed by a systems integration phase. Commencing in late January, the first of the four systems selected for installation, namely, the accounts-receivable system, will be installed. This system shall be used as a study program, to acquaint the U.K. staff with the manner and techniques used by the corporation in the support of on-line data base processing. Emphasis will be placed on the methods used by the corporation to:

Develop video display screens.
Edit input transactions.
Recognize and indicate entry errors.
Process data base information.
Perform display inquiries.
Handle report requests.

The review shall first address the user aspects and functions of the system. This will be done through a step-by-step demonstration, discussing all input documents used and reports produced by the system. After the demonstration, attention will be directed to the system structure, identifying and discussing each of the operational programs in detail. The purpose of a detailed study is to familiarize the staff with the program documentation so that they will feel comfortable using the network programs.

The rest of the month will be used to identify and implement any additional programming features required to totally fulfill the accounts-receivable needs of the U.K. cluster. Since this is the most straightforward system in the group, it should be an ideal learning exercise in on-line processing. The techniques that will be used in the development of the new accounts-receivable functions will be typical of those required to support any of the on-line data base systems. Therefore, at the end of this month, the staff should have reached a level of competence in this mode of processing to allow us to accelerate the implementation program while retaining full control of each installed system.

It will be left to the User Implementation Committee to decide exactly when these new on-line systems will be placed into the different user organizations. Once those decisions are made, it will be the responsibility of the U.K. technical staff to direct the training of U.K. user personnel.

Index

access codes, 152
accessibility of systems and
  information
  as advantage of decentralized
    computer processing, 11
  on-line systems as tool for, 29–30
add module, in on-line
  programming, 121
Apple computers, and LANs, 159
Apple II, 68
applications driver function, of
  monitor, 100
applications editor function, of
  monitor, 99
asynchronous mode of terminal/
  computer communication, 75
Atari computers, in LANs, 159
Autocoder, IBM, 37, 50

baseband transmission mode, for
  LANs, 159–160
BASIC
  evaluation of, 107
  use of, in minicomputers, 17
Basic Assembler, IBM, 37
Basic Four, as software system
  developer, 44
batch processing
  changes in, 38–39
  history of, 37
  monitors for, 102–103
  as primary function of early
    computers, 35
  and stack management, 71
  standard program models for,
    121–122
  standards for, 102
beta site
  computer system for, 114–115
  criteria for, 112–114
  selecting, 112
broadband transmission mode, for
  LANs, 159–160
Burroughs Corporation, computer
  manufacturer, 47
bus LAN structure, 160–161
Business Week ("Moving Away from
  Mainframes"), 45

cathode-ray tube (CRT)
  and computer selection, 66
  development of, 35, 40
  use of, for on-line functions, 96
central control bus structure, 64
centralized computer processing
  advantage of, 14
  cost of, as disadvantage, 15
  definition of, 12
  delays as disadvantage of, 15
  disadvantages of, 3–5, 15–17
  inaccessibility of data as
    disadvantage of, 16–17
  inaccuracy of data as
    disadvantage of, 6
  organization effects of, 14
  remote data entry in, 12–13

centralized computer processing (continued)
  system failure vulnerability as disadvantage of, 15–16
  untimeliness of data as disadvantage of, 17
central processing unit (CPU), 64–66
change module, in on-line programming, 121
CICS
  as monitor, 96
  software package, 59, 73
Cincom, software company, 31
COBOL
  advances due to, 37, 38
  evaluation of, 107
  use of, in minicomputers, 17
code segment, 71
collision detection (CSMA/CD), in baseband transmission, 160
communication(s)
  asynchronous mode, 75
  computer-to-computer, 132–133
  cost of, 23–24
  data controller and, 137
  development of, 18, 29
  difficulties with, in decentralized computer processing, 12
  in distributed-processing systems, 23–24
  intercomputer, 83–84
  interdivisional, 144
  intracompany, 55
  network manager and, 143
  news bulletin for, 143
  software, 6–7
  speed of, 130, 134
  synchronous mode, 75
  terminal, as function of monitor, 99
  use of DDP in, 52–53
compiler, development of, by user, 56–57
component approach to program development, 103
COMPUTATIONAL computer languages, 57
Computer Decisions, 5, 157
computer equipment, evaluating, 49–50
computer language(s)
  programming advances due to, 37
  selection of common, 106–107
  and systems compatability, 56–57
  translator language for, 57
  use of, in minicomputers, 17
computer power
  distribution of, 111
  location of, in distributed-processing systems, 22–23
computer processing
  centralized era of, 1, 3–5
  decentralized era of, 1, 5–8, 9
  development of, 1
  distributed era of, 2, 3
  elements of, 2
computer selection
  basis of, today, 76–79
  and computer structure, 64–68
  consulting firm and, 62
  and distributed-processing systems manager, 94
  and hardware, 68–69
  past basis of, 63–64
  and top management, 61–62
computer structure, 64–68
computer system
  development of, in-house, 120
  redevelopment of, 120–121
  structure of, 119–122
Computerworld, computer journal, 35
Control Data, as computer manufacturer, 1
Convergent Technologies workstation concept, 158
conversion costs, and decentralizing computer processing, 6
core memory modules, 69
Corrupt Practices Act of 1976, 148
Corvus
  and LANs, 158

Omninet, 159
cost of computer processing
and computer selection, 79
as critical element, 2
and decentralized computer processing, 6–8, 11
as factor in centralized computer processing, 14, 15
savings in, with DDP, 51–52
and selecting beta site system, 114
and telephone communications, 133
CPU (central processing unit), 64–66
Cullinane, software company, 31
Cullinet, software package, 164

daisy chaining, 135
data base
designing, 116–117
order-entry, 109
use of term, 83–84
data base management
advent of, 36
basic function of, 58
definition of, 30–31
IMAGE package for, 58
and preparation of a data base schema, 109
TOTAL package for, 56
value of, 107–109
data collection, location of, 25
data concentrator, 136
data controller, 136–137
data encryption, 153
Data General
communications software by, 6
and development of minicomputers, 44
Eclipse, 28, 70
as minicomputer manufacturer, 7, 32, 46
as minicomputer software developer, 17
Nova, 28, 68
peripherals by, 45
Datalux, software package, 164
Datamation, computer journal, 35
Datapoint, communications software by, 7
DataPro, computer journal, 141
data processing, *see* computer processing
Data Products, as minicomputer manufacturer, 44
data segment, 71
DDP, *see* distributed-processing systems
decentralized computer processing, 1, 5
advantages of, 11
conversion cost issue in, 6
disadvantages of, 12
functional, 9, 19, 21
by geography, 9, 19, 21–22
investment issue in, 7–8
technology issue in, 6–7
DECNET, communications software, 6, 28, 84
dedicated satellite processing, as move toward distributed-processing, 27–28
dedicated telephone lines, for computer communication, 130
delete module, in on-line programming, 121
Department of Defense, and computer security, 150
destructive write, 43
Diablo, as minicomputer manufacturer, 44
Digital Equipment Corporation
DECNET communications software by, 6, 28, 84
growth of, 74
and minicomputer development, 44
as minicomputer manufacturer, 32, 46
as minicomputer software developer, 17
peripherals by, 45

disks
 and access, 40
 early days of, 36
 larger-scale, and communication advances, 158
 popularity of, 39
display module, in on-line programming, 121
"Distributed Processing" (Kaufman), 14
distributed-processing systems
 beginnings of, 1
 communications and, 23–24
 computer power location in, 22–23
 control, as issue in, 8
 cost savings in, 8, 51–52
 department, 95
 determining feasibility of, 24–26
 establishing, 53–55
 flexibility, as major advantage of, 19
 maintenance of, 103
 manager, 94–95
 nature/mode of distribution in, 19–22
 new technology as foundation of, 28
 security for, 97
 software for, choosing, 83–85
 standards for, 92–102, 103–110
Distributed Processing Systems: End of the Mainframe Era?, 1
documentation, of programs, 104
drum, as mass-storage device, 39
DS 3000, communications software, 6, 28, 84–89
dual-entry module, in on-line programming, 121
dumb terminals, 75–76

Eclipse, 28, 70
economies of scale, 45
editing and error correction, location of, 25–26
emulation, as conversion method, 50
Environment I package, as monitor, 96

file conversion, and constructing data base, 116
file creation and maintenance, location of, 26
film, as mass-storage device, 39
firmware, 70
fixed-partition multiprocessing, 42
forms utility program, 99
FORTRAN
 evaluation of, 107
 IV, advances due to, 37
 use of, in minicomputers, 17
friendly software, 81–82
fully integrated, definition of, 53
functional distribution, in computer processing, 19, 21

General Electric, as computer manufacturer, 1
geographical distribution, in computer processing, 19, 21–22

hardware
 and computer selection, 68
 decreasing cost of, 3
 integrated circuits in, 36
 microprocessor "chip" technology in, 36
 selection of, for beta site, 114
 silicon chip in, 36
 transistors in, 36, 37
 vacuum-tube logic in, 36, 37
 wire-board circuitry in, 36
hard-wired circuitry, 69, 70
Hazeltine, as minicomputer manufacturer, 44
Hewlett-Packard
 DS 3000, 28
 DS 3000 communications software by, 6, 84–89
 growth of, 74
 IMAGE data base management system of, 18, 58

as minicomputer manufacturer, 7, 32, 46
as minicomputer software developer, 17
peripherals by, 45
hierarchical communications structure, 147
historical files, 102
homogeneous, definition of, 53
Honeywell, Inc.
as computer manufacturer, 46–47
as minicomputer manufacturer, 44
Multecs, 154
host computer installation, as security risk, 148
HP 3000 Series III, 66
HP 3000 units, 164
hybrid transmission mode, for LANs, 159–160

IBM
antitrust fight of, 3–4
Autocoder, 37, 50
Basic Assembler, 37
CICS, 59, 73, 96
as computer manufacturer, 1, 62
development of CRT by, 35
development of "spooling" by, 42
8100, 28
1400, 50
1401, 11, 14
4300, 58, 164
IMS, 58
and LANs, 159
as minicomputer manufacturer, 46
Model 360, 12, 50
multiprocessing by, 42
Series I, 28
System 3, 41
3300, 58
3270 terminal, 73
370 series, 69, 164
360/M65, 68
360/OS, 42
3033, 164
TSO, 73
IMAGE, data base management system, 18, 58
indexed sequential-access method (ISAM), 40
indexed-sequential file management, 36
Information Systems in the 1980s (Weil), 33
input/output processor (IOP), 66
inquiry function, of on-line processing, 100–101
insurance, for large-scale computer installations, 16
integrated circuits, 36
intelligent terminals, 74, 75–76
interactive, definition of, 53
intercomputer (interprocessor) communications, 83–84
interface cards, use of, in connecting microcomputer systems, 159
International Data Corporation, study by, on decreasing hardware costs, 3
interrogative method, of on-line processing, 59

JCL (job control language), 81

Kaufman, Felix ("Distributed Processing"), 14
kernal, security, 154
keypunch, 37

library, network, 54–55
local area network(s) (LANs)
communication structures of, 159–160
configurations of, 160–161
cost savings of, 163
and distributed-processing systems, 161
as microcomputer-based terminal network, 74

local area networks (continued)
non-CPU advantage of, 162
and security, 153
as security risk, 148
use of larger-scale disks for, 158
local data inquiry and updating, as move toward distributed-processing, 27
long-haul communications, as security risk, 149, 153

mainframe computer
as electronic librarians, 46
end of predominance by, 17–18, 45
maintenance functions
extensiveness of, 103–104
of on-line processing, 101–102
management
and computer processing, 3–5
and computer selection, 61–62
management information systems (MIS)
in centralized computer processing, 14
and distributed-processing systems manager, 94
mass-storage devices, 37, 39
material requirements planning (MRP), 23, 117
mega-minis, cost issue of, 114
memory
modules, 64
random-access, 70
read-only, 69
real, 71–73
virtual, 71–73
microcomputer(s)
-based networks, LANs, 74, 158–161
influx of, 33
market of, 74
-to-mainframe communications, 164
-to-micro link-ups, 164
-to-minicomputer communications, 164
proliferation of, 157
use of Convergent Technologies workstation concept with, 158
for word processing, 156–157
minicomputers
arrival of, 43–48
cost savings in, 8, 51–52
data base management software for, 7
and end of mainframe era, 17–18
modularity in, 55
as real-time computers, 32
terminal capabilities of, 74–76
microprocessor "chip" technology, 36
MIT, as leader in communications development, 29
modem, use of, with daisy chaining, 135
modular coding techniques, 104
modularity, in minicomputer industry, 55
modulation/demodulation (modem) devices, 130
monitors, batch-processing, functions of, 102–103
monitors, for on-line processing
applications driver function of, 100
applications editor function of, 99
functions of, 97
security function of, 99
terminal communications function of, 99
value of, 96
"Moving Away from Mainframes" (*Business Week*), 45
MRP (material requirements planning), 23, 117
Multecs, secure distributed computer system, 154
multidrop lines, 135
multiplexing, 133–134
multipoint applications, 135
multiprocessing
fixed-partition, 42
and hardware selection, 69

need for, 41
variable-partitioning (MVP), 42

NCR Corporation, computer manufacturer, 47–48
NEC computers, in LANs, 159
network, in distributed-processing systems
building, 128–129
establishing, 53–55
hierarchical communications structure in, 147
and LANs, 161
library, 54–55, 92–93
local area (LAN), 74
manager, 143
monitoring, by use of news bulletin, 143
and new equipment, 114
planning of, 53
purpose of, 95
ring configuration of, 144–145
security system for, 150–153
software for, choosing, 83–85
star configuration of, 126, 138, 144
steering committee in, 95
typical, 21
Network Systems, as manufacturer of linking packages, 159
news bulletin, for network monitoring, 143
Nova, 28, 68

obsolescence factor, in system selection, 53
Omninet, 159
on-line system(s)
basic program prototypes of, 121
birth of, 42–43
degree of, 58
development of, 29
inquiry functions of, 100–101
interrogative method of, 59
monitor function in, 96–100
and multiprocessing, 70
as solution for accessibility and timeliness, 29–30
standards for, 96
and systems development, 57–58
text-editor method of, 59
transaction-processing method of, 59–60
update/maintenance functions of, 101–102
open ring network structure, 145
order-entry data base, 109
original equipment manufacturer (OEM), 44

packaged solutions, in systems development, 82
PASCAL, evaluation of, 107
password access, for security, 152, 153
PBX transmission mode, for LANs, 159–160
PL/I
advances due to, 37
evaluation of, 107
posting module, in batch processing, 122
POWER, 42
power lines, and computer security, 152
Prime
400, compared to mainframe, 66–68
growth of, 74
as minicomputer manufacturer, 7
as minicomputer software developer, 17
processing and reporting, location of, 26
program(s)
counter, 65
simplicity in, 105
types of, 105
programmable read-only memory (PROM), 69
programmers
low productivity of, 103–105
migratory nature of, 93

program models, for use in in-house programming, 121

Quantel, as software systems developer, 44

random-access device, 39–40
random-access memory (RAM), 70
RCA, as computer manufacturer, 1
read-only memory (ROM), 69
real memory, 71–73
real-time systems
  definition of, 29
  as solution for accessibility and timeliness, 29–30
record add, on-line procedure, 101
record delete, on-line procedure, 101
record update, on-line procedure, 101
remote field-service support, 85
remote job entry (RJE)
  in centralized computer processing, 12–13, 26
  as move toward distributed processing, 27, 43
report module, in batch processing, 122
ring LAN structure, 160–161
ring network configuration, 144–145
RPG
  IV, advances due to, 37
  use of, in minicomputers, 17

screen data base, 99, 100
security
  access codes for, 152
  control program, 99
  data base, as function of monitor, 97
  determining need for, 149–150
  for distributed computer systems, 148
  emanation protection for, 152–153
  kernel, 154
  password access for, 152–153
  policy, 150
  procedure, 151
  for softward modification, 152
  system, as function of monitor, 97
  system, implimentation of, 150–153
  and telephone lines, 149
  terminal user, 99
security reference monitor, 153–154
semiconductor(s)
  high-speed, 69
  random-access memory, 70
  as replacement for core memory, 69
sequential files, 102
Series I, IBM, 28
silicon chip, 36
single-phase processing, 41
smart terminals, 75–76
software
  choosing, 83–85
  communications, 6–7
  factory, as approach to program development, 103
  friendly, 81–82
  maintenance, 85
  modification, controls for, 152
  packaged, evaluation of, 119–120
  selection of, for beta site, 114
  systems, for minicomputers, 17–18
  vendor-supported, 82
sort module, in batch processing, 122
source data entry, as move toward distributed processing, 27
Sperry Corporation, as computer manufacturer, 46
SPL, use of, in minicomputers, 17
stack management, 71
  and memory, 73
star LAN structure, 160–161
star network configuration, 126, 138, 144

standards
for batch processing systems, 102–103
for distributed-processing systems, 92–102, 103–110
static ring network structure, 145
steering committee, for distributed-processing network, 95
string networks, 165–166
"Superman III," and computer security, 149
synchronous mode of terminal/computer communication, 75
systems development, guidelines for, 55–56
System 3, IBM, 41

Tandem Computers
growth of, 74
as minicomputer manufacturer, 46
tapping, of telephone lines, and computer security, 149
telephone service, for computer communication
as security risk, 149, 153
use of dedicated lines in, 130
use of multiplexing in, 133–134
use of voice-grade WATS lines in, 130
temporary files, 102
terminal(s)
asynchronous, 75–76
capabilities of, 73–74
communications, as function of monitor, 97, 99
dumb, 75–76
intelligent, 74, 75
limitations of, 74–75
smart, 75–76
synchronous, 75
unintelligent, 74, 75
text-editor method of on-line processing, 59
time-sharing operating systems, 7
token passing, in baseband transmission, 160
TOS software package, 59
TOTAL, data base management package, 56
transaction-processing method of on-line processing, 59–60
transaction screen, 97, 99, 100
translator language, 57
transistors, 36, 37
TSO, IBM, 73

unintelligent terminals, 74, 75–76
update functions, of on-line processing, 101–102

vacuum-tube logic, 36, 37
variable-partitioning multiprocessing (MVP), 42
Varian Associates, peripherals by, 45
Vax units, 164
video display terminal, *see* cathode-ray tube
VIEW/3000 package, as monitor, 96
virtual memory, 71–73
VisiCalc®, microcomputer, 156
voice-grade WATS lines, for computer communication, 130

Wang Laboratories
growth of, 74
and LANs, 159
and microcomputer word processors, 163
as minicomputer manufacturer, 32, 46
product compared to mainframe, 66–68
WANGNET broadband system by, 160
WANGNET broadband system, 160
"WarGames," and computer security, 149
Weil, Ulric (*Information Systems in the 1980s*), 33
wire-board circuitry, 36

word processing, microcomputers for, 156–157, 163
writable control storage, 65

Xerox, as manufacturer of linking packages, 159

Yourdon, Edward, and efficient programming, 105

Zenith computers, in LANs, 159
Zilog, as manufacturer of linking packages, 159